CW00927968

What People Are Saying About Dr. M
and Power of the Ho

[Dr. Myles Munroe's] wisdom is to the believer what a phone booth was to Superman! Step into every page and be changed!

—*Bishop T.D. Jakes*
The Potter's House of Dallas

Myles Munroe stands as a pillar of strength in the midst of so much wind-blown confusion that is ripping apart sectors of the church. His commitment to integrity and spiritual passion—to a biblical lifestyle uncluttered by dead tradition—is a joy to behold.

—*Jack W. Hayford*
Chancellor Emeritus, The King's University, Los Angeles, CA

Myles Munroe gives a fresh look at the ministry and person of the Holy Spirit. *The Purpose and Power of the Holy Spirit* is a powerful book that makes the truth simple and easy to understand.

—*Billy Joe Daugherty*
Founder and Senior Pastor, Victory Christian Center, Tulsa, OK

Every kingdom features a carefully structured administrative system. In this book, Myles Munroe focuses on the administration of God's kingdom on earth from a heavenly perspective. In doing so, he offers fresh and challenging insights into the principles of kingdom citizenship, the character and purpose of the divine administrator, and the resources our Governor provides to enable kingdom citizens to fulfill the responsibilities of citizenship.

—*Dr. Jerry Horner*
Founding Dean, School of Divinity, Regent University,
Virginia Beach, VA
Former Dean, School of Theology, Oral Roberts University, Tulsa, OK

THE
PURPOSE & POWER
OF THE
HOLY SPIRIT

GOD'S GOVERNMENT ON EARTH

DR. MYLES MUNROE

WHITAKER
HOUSE

Unless otherwise indicated, all Scripture quotations are taken from the *Holy Bible, New International Version*®, NIV®, © 1973, 1978, 1984 by the International Bible Society. Used by permission of Zondervan. All rights reserved. Scripture quotations marked (NKJV) are taken from the *New King James Version*, © 1979, 1980, 1982, 1984 by Thomas Nelson, Inc. Used by permission. All rights reserved. Scripture quotations marked (KJV) are taken from the King James Version of the Holy Bible. Scripture quotations marked (NASB) are taken from the updated *New American Standard Bible*®, NASB®, © 1960, 1962, 1963, 1968, 1971, 1972, 1973, 1975, 1977, 1995 by The Lockman Foundation. Used by permission. (www.Lockman.org). Scripture quotations marked (NCV) are taken from the *Holy Bible, New Century Version*® © 1987, 1988, 1991 by Word Publishing, a division of Thomas Nelson, Inc. Used by permission. All rights reserved.

Publisher's note: Personal pronouns for God and Jesus are lowercased in keeping with the *New International Version*, the primary Bible translation used in this book.

All emphasis in the Scripture quotations is the author's.

The Purpose and Power of the Holy Spirit:
God's Government on Earth
(formerly titled *The Most Important Person on Earth*)

Munroe Global
P.O. Box N9583
Nassau, Bahamas
www.munroeglobal.com
office@mumroeglobal.com

ISBN: 978-1-64123-135-0
eBook ISBN: 978-1-64123-137-4
Printed in the United States of America
© 2007, 2018 by Munroe Group of Companies Ltd.

Whitaker House
1030 Hunt Valley Circle
New Kensington, PA 15068
www.whitakerhouse.com

The Library of Congress has cataloged the original hardcover edition as follows:
Munroe, Myles.
  The most important person on earth : the Holy Spirit, Governor of the
Kingdom / Myles Munroe.
    p.   cm.
Summary: "Explores how the Holy Spirit is the most important Person on earth because he is the presence and power of heaven in the world, bringing true life and transforming individuals, societies, and nations"— Provided by publisher.
Includes bibliographical references and index.
ISBN-13: 978-0-88368-986-8 (trade hardcover : alk. paper)
ISBN-10: 0-88368-986-3 (trade hardcover : alk. paper) 1. Holy Spirit. I. Title.
BT121.3.M86 2006
231'.3—dc22   2006030325

No part of this book may be reproduced or transmitted in any form or by any means, electronic or mechanical—including photocopying, recording, or by any information storage and retrieval system— without permission in writing from the publisher. Please direct your inquiries to permissionseditor@whitakerhouse.com.

6 7 8 9 10 11 **ᵾᵾ** 25 24 23 22 21 20

CONTENTS

INTRODUCTION

Human beings of all ages, genders, nationalities, and ethnic groups are on a search for purpose and significance. Consider:

+ the multitude of religions in the world that seek to explain our existence.

+ the large and growing number of books on the "self-help" shelves in bookstores.

+ the enormous emphasis in Western countries on self-actualization.

+ the scientific community's continual pursuit of the origins of life.

+ the ongoing struggle of Third-World peoples to gain freedom and a sense of identity for their nations and themselves.

We seek to understand why we are here, the significance of the world we live in, and how we can fulfill our personal potential. We want to know if our individual lives have any real meaning in the vast expanse of history and time.

Why do we struggle with these questions? Why don't we already know the answers to them?

What makes us so introspective and continually longing to find meaning for ourselves and our world?

"RETURN TO MANUFACTURER"

Wouldn't it be wonderful if all human beings were born with "manufacturer's instructions" tied to their wrists, explaining who they are and how they work? (Of course, even if we did, most of us would probably skip the instructions and try to figure out life as we went along!)

I believe human beings do come with the equivalent of operating instructions that give us answers to our deepest questions about ourselves and our world. Some of this information has been placed within us; the rest has been given to us by our Creator, or "Manufacturer," in written form. The reason we're filled with such uncertainty and confusion about life is that we've lost our connection to these original instructions. We haven't stopped to recognize our internal programming or to read our life manual in order to understand our personal potential or how we work. This is why we can't see the purpose of the world itself and how it is supposed to function.

When we try but fail to solve what is broken in our lives and in our world, it is because our Manufacturer's labels have become faded, and we haven't read this crucial instruction: "Do not try to repair yourself. Return to Manufacturer."

It is the Manufacturer who…

+ has the original blueprints.

+ knows how to repair what is broken inside us.

+ can provide the replacement piece for what is missing in our lives.

When we rediscover the Manufacturer's original intent, we come to understand our purpose, our potential, and the significance of our role in this world.

KINGDOM GOVERNMENT

The mind of our Manufacturer didn't invent the fragmented life we have today, with its divisions among nations and people groups, its strife among families, its double-mindedness and double standards, its abuse and waste. He conceived of an orderly but energetic life in which every person could reach their fullest potential in conjunction with others for the greatest good of individuals and the community of human beings.

The original blueprint of the Creator was for a *kingdom government on earth* as an extension and reflection of his own greater, spiritual kingdom. This earthly government was to be a thriving colony with humanity as (1) its citizens, and (2) its local vice governors representing the home kingdom. Our mandate was to transform the colony into the nature of the kingdom.

The character of the initial colony was both peaceful and productive because of the generous nature of its Creator and Sovereign. His interests are the welfare, fruitfulness, and fulfillment of his citizens. His is a *perfect* government, a benevolent rule.

INTER-REALM CONNECTION

The key to the success of this plan was the establishment of an *inter-realm connection* and ongoing relationship between the home kingdom and the colony of earth. This connection was completely effective because it was direct—from Sovereign to individual citizens—through a super-natural communication that allowed the citizens to know the desires and plans of the King. That connection was the very Spirit of the Sovereign living within humanity—his Holy Spirit.

To understand this inter-realm connection, we have to look at the concept of *supernatural*, and we must address the various misconceptions people have when they hear the term *Holy Spirit*. I am not talking about some kind of "force," "mist," or "feeling," but a Person. I am referring to the Creator "extending himself" to us in personal interaction, a Person-to-person communication.

THE CONCEPT OF THE SUPERNATURAL

The word *supernatural* does not exist in Scripture, but it does describe a concept clearly presented there. Supernatural simply means "outside" or "above" the natural; it is spiritual rather than physical. The supernatural world is above our natural world. Paul of Tarsus, the first-century theologian, defined this concept as *invisible* or *unseen*:

> Since the creation of the world God's *invisible* qualities—his eternal power and divine nature—have been clearly seen, being understood from what has been made.

> So we fix our eyes not on what is seen, but on what is *unseen*. For what is seen is temporary, but what is *unseen is eternal.*

The supernatural realm is therefore an invisible or unseen world that is distinct from our physical one. It is what the incomparable young rabbi,

Jesus of Nazareth, was referring to when he said, "My kingdom is not of this world....But now my kingdom is from another place."

When someone "experiences" the supernatural world of the Creator-King, it refers to their encounter with the kingdom of their Sovereign. The key to their interaction with the unseen kingdom is the Holy Spirit communicating the King's mind and heart to them so they can carry it out on earth.

The nature of this relationship between the unseen world of the kingdom government and the seen world of the physical earth underscores the incalculable value of the one who makes the connection between these two realms possible—the Holy Spirit.

THE CONCEPT OF THE KINGDOM

To fully appreciate the invisible kingdom government, we must realize that the *idea* of "kingdom" didn't originate on earth with the ancient civilizations of Babylon and Egypt. It didn't come from earth at all. The concept of kingdom is rooted in the desire of the Creator to design and sustain both the unseen and seen realms in order to express, represent, and manifest his nature.

Ideas are one of the most powerful forces in existence. We see how the greatest ideas transcend generations and serve as the source of people's creative activity and the motivation for their productivity. Ideas are the starting point of all that is created. An idea becomes a full-fledged, viable concept when it is envisioned and executed. The concept of an ideal kingdom is so beautiful that only a Creator-King of a certain nature could have envisioned and established it. We need to understand the King and kingdom out of which we come.

The word *king* refers to the person or personality who influences and oversees the productive development and profitable service of everything under his care, for the fulfillment of his noble desires and the benefit of all those living in his realm. The environment, territory, and authority over which he presides are his "domains" or "realms." A king effectually relating to his domains is the essence of the concept of kingdom.

Kingdom is thus the perfect example of the divine, creative act of the Creator. The first realm of his dominion is described as heaven. Heaven is the original kingdom; it was the origin of kingdoms. No kingdom existed before it, and nothing natural can be adequately compared to it. It is the first real kingdom because the first King created it. The kingdom of heaven is the only perfect prototype of kingdoms in existence.

When our Creator-King desired to extend his perfect kingdom from the invisible realm to the visible realm, the result was the creation of the physical universe and the appointment of planet earth as the destination for a unique extension of his divine being. Paul of Tarsus attempted to communicate this divine process of creation and extension when writing to people in the city of Colossae: "By him all things were created: things in heaven and on earth, visible and invisible, whether thrones or powers or rulers or authorities; all things were created by him and for him."

The kingdom of heaven and its colony of earth exist through the will of our Creator-King. It is therefore impossible to comprehend humanity's purpose without understanding the kingdom concept and how we are meant to live it out on earth. An inter-realm connection through the Holy Spirit is what enables us to fulfill our very purpose as human beings. The kingdom government is the ultimate answer to our search for personal significance and the meaning of the world around us.

We can no longer ignore the fading instructions on our Manufacturer's label. Let us return to the initial intent of our Creator-King, so we may understand the original blueprints of both kingdom and colony.

PROLOGUE

In the beginning was the King's Word. His Word was himself and was inseparable from him. His Word was with him from the start. Everything that exists came into being through the King's Word; no other source of life exists. In his Word was life, and this life manifested the knowledge of the King and his kingdom to the darkened and confused minds of humanity. But although the light of this knowledge shines brightly, those who choose to remain in a darkened state cannot see it.

In the beginning, the King created a colony for his kingdom. The colony was raw and undeveloped, and there was no life there. The King's Governor was poised to bring order and kingdom influence to the colony through the King's Word...

PART 1

THE PROGRAM OF CELESTIAL EXPANSION

ONE

THE POWER OF INFLUENCE

NOTHING IS MORE DAMAGING TO A NEW TRUTH THAN AN OLD ERROR.
—JOHANN WOLFGANG VON GOETHE

I found myself sitting between kingdom and colony.

I was the guest of the United States ambassador to the Bahamas for an official state function at his residence. Also attending this function were both the premier of the Turks and Caicos Islands, and His Excellency, the royal governor of the Turks and Caicos Islands.

This group of islands lies off the southeastern coast of my country of the Bahamas. At the writing of this book, the Turks and Caicos is a colony of Great Britain. The colony is overseen by the royal governor, who was appointed by Queen Elizabeth II of Great Britain. He is the highest authority in that colony. The premier, however, is an elected official, approved by the Crown, who heads the local government.

The premier was the special guest of the American ambassador. The ambassador had also invited other members of the diplomatic corps, as well as distinguished governmental officials and guests from around the world. Previous to this gathering, I had already become well acquainted with the premier. At his invitation, I had visited his beautiful island territory to address governmental and civic leaders in a special national event, and we had become good friends.

During the state function at the US ambassador's residence, I also came to know the royal governor fairly well because I was seated between him and the premier for over three hours during the proceedings. While the premier is a native-born Turks and Caicos Islander, His Excellency the Governor is pure British. When he spoke, you knew immediately that he was not from the islands.

As I conversed with these two distinguished leaders, one on either side of me, I realized once again the principle of kingdoms and their impact on their colonies. It refreshed my perspective and reminded me of my personal experience as a citizen of a former colony of the kingdom of Great Britain. There I sat between the crown and the colony, the governor and the administrator, the authority and the power. The governor was sent from the kingdom to live in the colony, among the people, to represent the Queen and execute her wishes and will in the colony. His primary purpose was to maintain the kingdom's influence and presence in that territory.

THE KINGDOM LIFE

Years of research have led me to the conclusion that the practical outworking of kingdoms points us to truths and principles that transcend the mere political fortunes of individual empires. Seeing how they function actually:

- ✦ provides us with a deep understanding of our own nature as human beings,

- ✦ reveals the key to our remarkable life purpose, and

- ✦ enables us to exercise our full potential in the world.

These things have tremendous implications for the human race personally, professionally, socially, and politically; for our families, communities, nations, and the world.

I am in a somewhat unique position to discuss the nature of kingdoms and their colonies, having grown up in a land that was a British colony for nearly two hundred years, and having witnessed its peaceful transition to independence. I well remember what it meant to live under a monarch— both the mind-set of a kingdom and its functioning and procedures. Yet I also understand what it means to live in an independent nation, having eagerly followed our transition to self-government as a young person. My close acquaintance with these two ways of governing has been extremely beneficial to me as I have explored the nature of kingdom and what it means for every person on this planet.

My investigation into the concept of kingdom has convinced me that the success of your life and mine depends upon how well we understand

and live out what I will call the *kingdom life*. I am not referring to a political system or to any particular national government, but to a way of understanding and living everyday life.

AN ANTI-KINGDOM PERSPECTIVE

The concept of kingdom may seem antithetical to the contemporary mind. Empires and their colonies seem outdated in the twenty-first century, just fading remnants of the past. Many nations today have representative governments. A number of former colonies and protectorates have gained their independence. Opportunities for self-government have expanded greatly throughout the world, and we rightly celebrate the political freedoms and opportunities these changes have brought. Human history has seen enough tyrannical kingdoms and dictators to want to move on to a different form of government.

Democracy is essentially humanity's reaction to perverted kingdoms. The founders of the United States rebelled against what they considered an oppressive government, and the very genetics of contemporary Western society are anti-kingdom. Because of the strong influence of political and social ideas of independence and freedom, this perspective has permeated the world and affects many areas of our thinking, not just the governmental realm. It shows up in how we view and conduct ourselves in personal relationships, business, media, education, and even religion because our cultural experiences produce our definitions. This is why the concept of kingdom is dismissed by most people today as irrelevant and is even considered out-and-out frightening by others.

In the light of these developments, however, many people no longer understand what life in an authentic and uncorrupted kingdom entails. I believe this lack of understanding has hindered them in the way they've approached their lives. Most of us have forgotten why kingdoms historically had such a profound impact on people and nations for thousands of years, some of which is still being felt. They haven't recognized what the concept and history of kingdoms reveal that is vital to us today.

I therefore want to present to you, step-by-step, how the practical working of the kingdom life answers essential questions about our human existence, purpose, and fulfillment. We have approached our personal goals and problems, as well as our national and global crises, from many vantage points, but not often from this perspective. Democracies are valuable political institutions for us today, but I'm referring to something that transcends our contemporary politics and government—something that speaks to the basis of our very being as humans. It has significance for people of all nations, religions, and creeds. It lies at the heart of the existence of every person on earth, *whether Christian, Buddhist, Hindu, Muslim, Jew, agnostic, or atheist.*

Just as I found myself sitting between kingdom and colony, you and every other person on the planet are, in a sense, supposed to find yourselves in a relationship between kingdom and colony, and to experience that dynamic in your own lives.

KINGDOM POWER

The character of this kingdom is, again, nothing like the political kingdoms of the past and present that seek to force others under their control based on territorial power, greed, or religious doctrine. Those kingdoms enslave. But the very nature of humanity, as well as the personal and corporate progress of the world, are designed to develop and thrive from the outworking of this kingdom.

I mentioned in the preface to this book that the principal issue of humanity is power, defined as "the ability to influence and control circumstances." We all want to direct and influence our lives in a positive and fulfilling way. The nature of this kingdom speaks directly to this need.

Understanding our association with this kingdom begins with an exploration of what all human kingdoms have shared in common and how they were different from the contemporary experience of government most of us are familiar with today. Then we can move to the larger context of what these qualities reveal about our human existence and purpose.

THE NATURE OF KINGDOM GOVERNMENT

I define a kingdom as **"the governing authority and influence of a sovereign ruler who impacts his territory through his will, purpose, and intentions, which are manifested in the culture, lifestyle, and quality of his citizenry."** A king must have his dominion, or his territory. We call it his "king-dominion" or his kingdom. You cannot be a king without having territory; you have to be ruling over something. And you cannot be a king without having kingdom citizens who live and work in the kingdom.

In a true, traditional kingdom, all power is vested in the monarch. The king actually, personally *owns* the country, including the people. In contrast, a president or prime minister in a representative government doesn't own the country; he governs it on behalf of the people.

The king implements his vision for the kingdom. There is no congress or parliament to discuss which laws they're going to create. There is only the monarch, and he has immediate access to his handpicked, trusted council, who carry out his wishes. The job of these advisors is to take the will of the king, translate it into the law of the land, and make sure it is enacted throughout the kingdom.

A kingdom is therefore the governing influence of a king over his territory, impacting and influencing it with his *personal will*. In a kingdom, the king's personal interest becomes policy, and the king's personal will becomes law. Thus, the effectiveness of a kingdom and its power is its ability to influence and control the territory according to the vision of the king.

THE GOAL OF THE KINGDOM: RULING AND GAINING TERRITORY

Most kingdoms throughout history have sought to take additional land, sometimes at some distance from the home country, because the power of a king is related to the territory he owns. The more territory a king had, the greater he was respected by other kingdoms, especially if the territories had abundant natural wealth. The home country of the king was his *domain*, and the outlying territories were his *colonies*.

Once a colony was gained, the sovereign's number one goal was to exercise his personal influence over it.

THE TRANSFORMATION OF COLONIES INTO THE KINGDOM

A colony is comprised of "a group of emigrants or their descendants who settle in a distant land but remain subject to the parent country."[1] The word *colony* comes from the Latin word *colonia*, derived from *colere*, meaning "to cultivate."[2] In this sense, a colony is:

+ the presence of a distinct cultural citizenry in a foreign territory that is governed by the laws and customs of its home country.

+ established to influence the territory for the home government.

This means that a colony's purpose was essentially to:

1. be an extension of the home country in another territory.

2. establish a prototype of the original country in another territory.

3. represent the values, morals, and manners of the home country.

4. manifest the culture and lifestyle of the original nation.

When a kingdom takes a territory, therefore, its goal is to make that territory exactly like the kingdom. The purpose is not only to gain lands, but also to transform those lands so that they mirror the country in its mind-set and lifestyle, its characteristics and culture. In this way, the kingdom not only extends its power, but it also expands the influence of its very nature.

The Roman Empire had a specific way of ensuring the permanency and effectiveness of kingdom influence over its colonies. When the Romans conquered a region, they planted a group of about three hundred of their own citizens, as well as a larger number of those allied with the empire, and a number of settlers, within it to serve as a type of military outpost. These constituted a "colony of Romans citizens" (*colonia civium Romanorum*) or a "little Rome." A colony of Roman citizens was free from taxation and military duty. It had its own constitution based on the Roman constitution and was allowed to elect its own senate and other offices of state. The original inhabitants had to adhere to this new government and its constitution.[3] These "little Romes" brought the culture and values of the Roman empire throughout Europe and northern Africa.

CHARACTERIZING THE KINGDOM

A striking picture of the power and influence of kingdoms over a territory and the lifestyle of its inhabitants can be seen in the various nations of the Caribbean and West Indies. You can always tell who controlled a colony by studying its culture. The Bahamas, Jamaica, Trinidad, and Barbados are former colonies of the United Kingdom. Cuba was a colony of Spain. Haiti was a colony of France. The cultures of all these islands are distinctly characteristic of the countries that claimed them.

You can still see the kingdoms' influence in the daily lives and customs of the people. If you visited the Bahamas, you'd see the influence of Great Britain in our narrow streets, our driving on the left-hand side of the road, and our habit of drinking tea. When I was a young boy attending school, my classmates and I grew up singing "God Save the Queen." We were being taught to be a "little Britain." Similarly, if you went to Cuba, you might think you were in Spain as you observed its architecture and food. Significantly for their cultures, each of these former colonies speaks the language of the kingdom that conquered it.

Most kingdoms in the colonial period had to fight for new territory because there was a limited amount of land in the world. Under European control, the Bahamas was initially claimed by the Spaniards. The French tried to conquer it, but the Spaniards held them off. Finally, the British won out over the Spanish. If the British Empire hadn't won, I might be speaking Spanish today. So even though the Bahamas, Haiti, and Cuba are all part of a chain of islands, whoever controlled the domain controlled the language and culture of the people. If you really want to investigate the power of kingdoms, study the island of Hispaniola, home of both the Dominican Republic and Haiti. Two kingdoms grabbed the same island, and now there's a border separating the eastern part from the western part; one side speaks French, while other side speaks Spanish.

THE MOST IMPORTANT PERSON IN THE COLONY

The transformation of a colony into the culture of the kingdom didn't happen automatically. A purposeful development was involved. The king didn't usually directly extend his influence to his colony by physically going there. He administrated his will through his personal representative, called a governor or regent. He sent his representative to physically live in the colony in his place. Therefore, the royal governor was the *presence of the absent king* in the colony.

With the governor in the colony, you didn't need the physical presence of the king to experience and be changed by the king's influence. I mentioned that the British monarchs who influenced the English-speaking

Caribbean nations didn't frequently visit their colonies. Yet, in the Bahamas, we all learned to speak English, drink tea, wave the Union Jack, and sing the songs of Britain. We became part of the United Kingdom. And the royal governors were the direct instrument of that transformation.

The governor was therefore the most important person in the colony. We get a greater appreciation for why this was true when we look at his purpose.

THE GOVERNOR'S PURPOSE

The governor's purpose was sixfold:

1. *Relationship*: The governor was the guarantee that the kingdom could always have access to the colony. The interrelationship between king and colony was totally dependent on him.

2. *Communication*: Anything the king wanted the colony to know or to receive, he would send through his governor, his avenue of communication.

3. *Representation*: The governor was the chief representative of the king and his kingdom in the colony. He also represented the colony to the king.

4. *Interpretation*: The governor understood intimately the king's desires, ideas, intent, purposes, will, and plans; therefore, he was the only one who could effectively interpret these aspects for the colony.

5. *Power*: The governor was the only one empowered with the authority and ability to execute the king's desires and commands for the colony.

6. *Partnership*: The governor was effectively the king's partner in rulership.

THE GOVERNOR'S QUALIFICATIONS AND ROLES

The qualifications and roles of a governor were significant in terms of kingdom and colony:

1. *The governor was appointed by the king.*

Unlike the governors of representational governments, the royal governor was not voted in; he was appointed by the king.

2. *The governor came only from the kingdom, never the colony.*

Governors were never chosen from the indigenous peoples of the colonies. They were always appointed from the home countries. Why? A governor had to be steeped in the *original culture* of the kingdom. He had to be a person who knew the kingdom and understood the heart, mind, desires, will, and intent of the king in carrying out the kingdom's purposes in the territory.

3. *The governor represented only the king.*

Again, the difference between the governors of colonies and the governors many of us are familiar with in representative governments is like night and day. Every state in the United States has a governor who is voted in by the people and can also be voted out by them. He or she is ultimately accountable to the people of the state, not to the federal government or its leaders. In contrast, the royal governor was responsible and accountable to the king alone in his allegiance, attitude, actions, and responsibility.

4. *The governor only expressed the mind and will of the king.*

The governor was not there to promote his own personal policies or agendas. He was to take the vision and will of the king and communicate them to the people, translating them into policy and law.

5. *The governor was responsible for converting the colony into the kingdom.*

Once more, it was the governor's job to oversee and carry out the transformation of the colonies according to the character of the kingdom. The governor was "planted" in the colony to sow the seeds of the home country into the culture of the new territory. Colonization was for the purpose of *conversion*—to exchange the culture of the territory for the culture of the kingdom. Whatever was happening in the kingdom was supposed to happen in the colony, as well.

6. *In converting the colony, the governor transferred the kingdom's culture, values, nature, language, and lifestyle to the people.*

The governor made sure that every subject of the kingdom took on the kingdom culture in language, attitude, dress, food, and so forth. The colonists were even to take on the history of the kingdom as if it were their own, which in fact it now was, because they had become a part of the chronicles of the nation. The subjects were to take on the mind-set and lifestyle of the kingdom until, if you visited the territory, you would think you were in the home country itself.

7. The governor prepared the subjects for citizenship.

When a king took over a colony, the people essentially became his possessions. The inhabitants of the colony did not automatically become citizens; they were called *subjects*. For example, when the Bahamas was a colony, the people were not citizens of Great Britain. We couldn't vote, and we didn't have other rights of British citizens.

In a kingdom, citizenship was a privilege. Who became a citizen was the king's prerogative, and he personally granted it. The reason citizenship wasn't automatic is that, once a person was appointed a citizen, he had special benefits and protections in the kingdom. In the Roman Empire, citizenship was a high honor and privilege involving many rights. In the first century, Paul of Tarsus was arrested in Jerusalem by the Roman commander for allegedly disturbing the peace. He was about to be whipped when he declared to a nearby centurion that he was a Roman citizen. Immediately, the soldiers' attitude toward him changed. The following exchange dramatically reveals the power of kingdom citizenship in the Roman Empire, especially if you were *born* a citizen:

> As they stretched him out to flog him, Paul said to the centurion standing there, "Is it legal for you to flog a Roman citizen who hasn't even been found guilty?" When the centurion heard this, he went to the commander and reported it. "What are you going to do?" he asked. "This man is a Roman citizen." The commander went to Paul and asked, "Tell me, are you a Roman citizen?" "Yes I am," he answered. Then the commander said, "I had to pay a big price for my citizenship." "But I was born a citizen," Paul replied. Those who were about to question him withdrew immediately. The commander himself was alarmed when he realized that he had put Paul, a Roman citizen, in chains.

Once you are a citizen, your privileges, rights, and demands upon the throne change. The king is responsible for taking care of you. Therefore, the governor's role of preparing subjects for citizenship was a tremendous responsibility. If the governor believed a subject was ready to be a citizen or especially deserved citizenship, he recommended the subject to the king. Since the governor lived in the colony and knew the subjects firsthand, the king accepted the suggestions of the governor in this regard.

8. *The governor lived in a residence built by the government of the home country.*

A kingdom would build a residence in its colonies specifically for its royal governors to live in. This emphasized that the governor, the chief representative of the kingdom in the colony, was not just a visitor; he lived there, he was there to stay, and this was his legal residence. The British built a governor's mansion in Nassau, the capital of the Bahamas, specifically for the royal governor to live in, which today is called the Government House. Great Britain similarly built governors' houses in Jamaica, Trinidad, Barbados, and in every colony where it ruled.

9. *The governor's presence in the colony was evidence that the kingdom itself was in the colony.*

As long as the governor lived in the colony, the kingdom itself was present. The first time the Bahamas was declared a British colony was when a royal governor drove out the remaining Spanish garrisons, solidifying its ownership by the kingdom of Great Britain.

10. *The governor left if the colony declared independence.*

Either by force or recall, the royal governor would leave a colony if it declared independence and the kingdom was no longer officially governing. In the American Revolution, the royal governors of the colonies were forced to withdraw from their posts. When the Bahamas received independence, it was through negotiation with Great Britain, and the governor was recalled because he no longer had a legal right to be there.

THE VALUE OF THE GOVERNOR

In kingdom terms, then, the governor was the most powerful and important person in the colony. Because he introduced the kingdom's culture, language, and lifestyle—every unique aspect of the kingdom—to the colony, he had great value for the kingdom and its larger purposes. To summarize, the governor was valuable:

1. *As the presence of the government.* Without him, the kingdom would not exist in the colony.

2. *For representing the government.* If he wasn't there, the king would not be adequately or effectively represented.

3. *For the enablement of the colony.* He was the one with the authority and ability to supply power and resources to the colony.

4. *For protection.* As long as the kingdom was represented in a colony by the governor, the king was obligated to protect the territory from outside threats and danger.

5. *For his ability to know and communicate the mind of the king.* The governor represented the king's interests and will to the colony and made sure they were carried out.

6. *For enabling the colony's citizens and subjects to fulfill the will of the kingdom.* The colony received its instructions only through the governor and therefore was dependent on him for its effectiveness. The citizens and subjects would not be able to carry out their kingdom mandate without the governor's guidance and empowerment.

THE INFLUENCE OF ANOTHER KINGDOM

These were the main features of a kingdom-colony relationship, including the pivotal role of the governor in the process of transforming colonies into the home country. This brings us back to the kingdom I mentioned earlier in this chapter, which transcends our human governments and speaks to the basis of our very nature and existence as human beings. This kingdom has properties that are similar to, but go beyond, those of the traditional earthly kingdoms we've been looking at.

Two millennia ago, a startling young teacher described this transcendent kingdom. When Jesus of Nazareth began traveling and speaking around Palestine, the first thing he is recorded as saying is, "The time has come…. The kingdom of God is near."

This statement intrigues me and brings up several questions for us to explore in terms of kingdom:

+ What "time" was he speaking about? And why then?

+ What was the nature of the kingdom he was referring to?

He was announcing the imminent return of a kingdom and its influence on earth. Notice that he didn't proclaim the entrance of a new religion, nor did he announce the beginnings of a democratic form of government. We have to ask:

+ Why would he use this particular governmental reference at the beginning of his public life?

+ What did it signify about his message and purpose?

+ If the influence of a kingdom was entering the world, what new culture would emerge for the citizens of earth?

To understand the context of these thought-provoking statements and their implications, we need to go back to the first book of Moses, the book of Genesis, to the origins of this kingdom. For this wasn't the first time the transcendent kingdom had entered the world and impacted its inhabitants...

CHAPTER ONE STUDY QUESTIONS

QUESTION FOR REFLECTION

1. Would you rather live under a kingdom or under a republic/democracy? Why?

EXPLORING PRINCIPLES AND PURPOSES

2. What does the success of your life depend on, according to Dr. Munroe's investigation into the concept of kingdom?

3. Why is the contemporary world generally anti-kingdom?

4. You are meant to find yourself in a relationship between _____ and _____.

5. What essential questions does the transcendent "kingdom life" answer for people of all nations, religions, and creeds?

6. What principal issue of humanity does the kingdom life address? How is this issue defined?

7. What is Dr. Munroe's definition of kingdom?

8. What is the job of a king's advisors?

9. What is a sovereign's number one goal after gaining a colony?

10. What was the word *colony* derived from in the Latin?

11. List the four purposes of a colony:

   (1)

   (2)

   (3)

   (4)

12. What made the governor the most important person in a colony?

13. Match the six purposes of a governor with their significance:

   (1) *relationship*   (4) *interpretation*

   (2) *communication*   (5) *power*

   (3) *representation*   (6) *partnership*

   Clarifies the king's desires, ideas, intent, purposes, will, and plans:
   _____

   Conveys what the king wants the colony to know or receive:
   _____

   Shares rule with the king: _____

   Provides the kingdom access to the colony: _____

   Acts on behalf of the king to the colony, and on behalf of the colony to the king: _____

   Exercises authority to execute the king's desires and commands for the colony. _____

14. List several reasons the governor was of great value to the colony.

15. What statement did Jesus of Nazareth make about a kingdom that transcends human governments and speaks to the basis of our very nature and existence as human beings?

16. What properties does the transcendent kingdom have in relation to traditional earthly kingdoms?

APPLYING THE PRINCIPLES OF KINGDOM LIVING
THINKING IT OVER

+ What did you learn about the relationship between kingdoms and colonies in this chapter that you hadn't thought of before?

+ What kingdom do you think Jesus of Nazareth was referring to? What do you think is the nature of this kingdom?

ACTING ON IT

+ Do a search of the various references Jesus made to *kingdom* in the accounts of his life in the Scriptures. (See the first four books of the New Testament, also called the Gospels. A Bible concordance [topical index] or a computer Bible program is a good way to do this.) What do you learn about the transcendent kingdom from these statements?

The success of your life depends upon how well you live out the kingdom life.

TWO

THE ADAMIC ADMINISTRATION

THE PRINCIPLE AND PURPOSE OF DELEGATED AUTHORITY ARE ACCOUNTABILITY AND RESPONSIBILITY.

The first government on earth came from a kingdom outside it. The world was governed in a way similar to the colonies described in chapter one. Yet the transcendent kingdom had significant differences from the earthly kingdoms we know about:

+ The territory of earth was created by the home country rather than taken by force. It was not anyone else's possession beforehand.

+ There were initially no inhabitants on earth, which was designed with its citizens in mind; it was specifically prepared for those who would live there.

+ The original inhabitants were not of a different culture from the home country but were actually the offspring of the King himself.

However, the similarities are these:

+ The home country desired to expand the realm of its influence by bringing the nature, mind-set, and purposes of the kingdom to the colony of earth.

+ The King's Governor was present in the colony to oversee the transformation process. He was to guide the King's children—his local governors—who were to convert the colony into a replica of the kingdom.

Let's take a closer look at the creation of this colony of earth.

THE ORIGINAL GOVERNMENT

The first book of Moses begins with these words: "In the beginning God [the Creator-King] created the heavens and the earth [the physical universe]." The Creator-King is described by first-century theologian Paul of Tarsus as "the blessed and only Ruler, the King of kings and Lord of lords, who alone is immortal and who lives in unapproachable light, whom no one has seen or can see." The eternal King of an unseen kingdom conceptualized and made the entire physical universe. By creation rights, it is his property.

It would be impossible to grasp the vastness of the unseen kingdom that encompasses our universe—especially when we consider that the physical realm in which the earth exists is too immense for us to comprehend. Our universe is so enormous that we're still trying to find out where it ends. Astronomers have discovered billions (some say up to 200 billion) of galaxies in the observable universe. It is estimated that each of these galaxies has tens—or hundreds—of billions of stars. Multiply billions of galaxies by billions of stars in each galaxy and you have a staggering number of stars in the universe.[1] If these sheer numbers were not enough to astound us, consider the way the objects in the universe are held together. As NASA records,

> Almost every object in space orbits around something. The planets orbit the Sun; our Moon and the moons of other planets orbit their planets; comets orbit the Sun....Even the Sun is orbiting around the center of our galaxy....
>
> An orbit is the result of a precise balance between the forward motion of an object in space (such as a planet or moon) and the pull of gravity from the body it orbits. An object in motion will stay in motion unless something pushes or pulls on it. This is Isaac Newton's First Law of Motion. Without gravity, an Earth-orbiting satellite would go off into space along a straight line. With gravity, it is pulled back toward the Earth. There is a continuous tug-of-war between the one object's tendency to move in a straight line and the tug of gravity pulling it back.[2]

The universe exists in remarkable balance. This is why the Scripture says, in essence, that only a fool thinks, *Nobody is keeping this universe in order.* Clearly, an orderly government of vast ability and power maintains our universe.

EXPANDING THE INVISIBLE KINGDOM

One of the New Testament writers said, "The universe was formed at God's command, so that what is seen was not made out of what was visible." The King of the *invisible* world decided to create a *physical* world. He did this for the purpose of expanding his heavenly domain as an extension of himself and his government. He created the physical universe so there would be additional territory to rule and to transform into the expression of his nature and desires. Returning to our definition of *kingdom*, we can say that the invisible kingdom is the governing influence of God over the territory of earth, impacting and influencing it with his will, his purpose, and his intent. Heaven is God's kingdom or home country, and earth is his colony.

We see various types of governing influence in our everyday human experience, not just in a political context:

+ An artist extends the domain of his mind and heart by expressing himself in physical paintings or sculptures, which can have an impact on those who view them.

+ A writer expresses the vision of his inner world through the printed word, and these words can influence the thoughts and attitudes of those who read them.

+ A businessman transforms his entrepreneurial concepts into specific companies that reflect his personal philosophy and provide new products and services that change the way others live.

All these are examples of individuals enlarging their personal influence in the world.

What people create, express, or build is usually a reflection of their personalities and outlook. Therefore, as we look at the Creator-King's desire to extend the influence of the invisible kingdom to earth, it is natural for us to want to know the nature of this King and his kingdom. What influence did he want to bring to earth?

THE NATURE OF THE KING: A PERFECT GOVERNMENT

The nature of the invisible kingdom becomes especially significant when we learn that the inhabitants of earth are to have this very nature themselves. The first book of Moses records these words of the Creator-King:

> "Let us make man in our image, in our likeness, and let them rule ["have dominion"] over the fish of the sea and the birds of the air, over the livestock, over all the earth, and over all the creatures that move along the ground." So God created man in his own image, in the image of God he created him; male and female he created them.

Human beings were not made as machines or as beings with no direct relationship to the Creator. They were drawn out of his own person: "Let us make man in our *image*, in our *likeness*, and let them *rule*...over all the earth."

After creating the universe by his own divine prerogative, the Creator chose one planet amid all the planets of the universe as the practical and unique extension of his influence—earth. Then he extended rulership of earth to those made in his own image, his royal "children."

The original Hebrew word for "image," *selem*, "means 'image' in the sense of essential nature."[3] The Hebrew word for *likeness* is *demuth*, which "signifies the original after which a thing is patterned."[4] These words define and describe our design, capacity, potential, and value as human beings made to reflect the personhood of our Creator.

The nature of our Creator-King was recorded by Moses as "the compassionate and gracious God, slow to anger, abounding in love and faithfulness." The only way a kingdom can function perfectly is if it is ruled by a perfect king who will not betray his citizens through corruption or oppression. If he does, he is not a true king but a tyrant and dictator. Since a king is the owner of everyone and everything in his kingdom, the key to a true kingdom is benevolence. A perfect government does not exist for itself; it exists for its citizens.

THE NATURE OF EARTH'S CITIZENS

Being made in the image and likeness of the Creator-King means that human beings possessed his spiritual nature, characteristics, and essential specifications. We were designed to be like, act like, and function like the Ruler of the invisible kingdom.

After the Creator gave us his own nature, he (1) gave us physical bodies so we could function in the physical world he had created and prepared specifically for us, and (2) breathed his very Spirit *into* us, animating and empowering us to fulfill our calling on earth. Moses recorded, "The LORD God formed the man from the dust of the ground and breathed into his nostrils the breath of life, and the man became a living being."

The Creator-King formed man, Adam, from the dust of the earth, which means that this human "product" was present in the world but wasn't yet alive. His body and brain were ready, but they were dormant. We couldn't say that Adam was "dead" because there was no death at that time. He was what we could call an "un-living being." It was when the Creator breathed into him the breath of life that Adam became a living being.

That breath of the Spirit ignited life in Adam in three distinct ways: (1) in the invisible spirit of man, which, being made in the image of God, is eternal; (2) in the soul of man—meaning the total human consciousness of his mind, will, and emotions; and (3) in his physical body, which became a living vessel housing the spirit and soul. Man's soul and body gave him an awareness of his earthly environment, while the Spirit of God, dwelling within man's spirit, gave him a consciousness of his Creator-King and the ability to communicate directly with the heavenly government.

So the Spirit gave life to all aspects of Adam as a human being. The same was true in the creation of Eve, the first woman. When God imparted his Spirit to human beings, humanity experienced the reception of the Spirit of God for the first time. The Creator's Spirit was our heavenly "Governor" on earth, who proceeded from the King and dwelled with us in the colony of earth, enabling us to receive, know, and carry out his will, much as the royal governors guided and led the people of the later national colonies.

The statement, "Let us make man in our own image," does not refer to *looking* alike, but *being* alike. The intent of the Creator-King was to express his nature through humanity. That nature was to be communicated through man's spirit and manifested through his soul—mind, will, and emotions—eventually finding expression through his physical body. In this way, human beings were created by God to live from the "inside out."

Human beings were created to express the *nature* of God—in other words, what he is like naturally. (We might say "supernaturally-naturally," since the Creator-King is a purely spiritual Being.) A human being can relate to and reflect the nature of the Creator only if he possesses his essential image and has his Spirit living within him.

Paul wrote, "The God who made the world and everything in it is the Lord of heaven and earth and does not live in temples built by hands," and "Do you not know that your body is a temple of the Holy Spirit, who is in you, whom you have received from God?" The Creator-King does not live in any type of building, whether church, temple, shrine, or mosque. His only true residence on earth is within his human creation. When his Spirit fills our bodies, we are his dwelling place. In this way, through the creation of humanity, the King built his own royal residence to settle in and from which to govern the colony of earth.

ROYAL CHILDREN AND FULL CITIZENS

Adam and Eve were the offspring or children of the Creator-King. Humanity is therefore really a royal family whose Father is the King of a vast and eternal kingdom. Human beings were not subjects but had full status as *citizens* of the kingdom, having been given free access to everything on earth.

> Then God blessed them, and God said to them, "Be fruitful and multiply; fill the earth and subdue it; have dominion over the fish of the sea, over the birds of the air, and over every living thing that moves on the earth."

The only exception to their complete access to the earth was a restriction on one part of their garden home, which was under the jurisdiction of the King alone. He told them, "You are free to eat from any tree in the garden; but you must not eat from the tree of the knowledge of good and evil, for when you eat of it you will surely die." We will talk more about this restriction in the next chapter.

ASSIGNMENT AS VICE GOVERNORS

When the King gave Adam and Eve dominion over the earth, he was delegating authority to humanity. They were made local rulers in the territory of earth under the heavenly Governor. Humanity was like a "little Rome," established on earth for the purposes of the kingdom of heaven and given the assignment of making the earth like the home country. As such, they were like the *patroni* of the Roman colonies who founded and guided the colony on behalf of the kingdom.[5] But while the Roman *patroni* were limited to about three members, each member of humanity to be born on earth was given the mandate of dominion. The earth was to be colonized by all members of the human race. I call this assignment the "Adamic Administration."

To have *dominion* means to govern, to rule, to control, to manage, to lead, to affect, and to impact. Human beings are essentially spiritual beings who live in physical bodies to carry out their governing responsibilities in the material world of the colony of earth. When the Creator-King said, "Let them have dominion," he was saying, "Let them have 'kingdom' over the earth. Let them influence the earth on behalf of my country of heaven." Humanity's job was to execute heaven's policies, legislation, and oversight on earth—to cultivate the life of the heavenly kingdom, manage the earth's natural resources, rule over the animals, govern wisely and justly, and keep everything in order. All these things have to do with the administration of the territory.

THE ROLE OF THE HEAVENLY GOVERNOR

It is important to note that since human beings were made in the image of the Creator-King and given the assignment of administering the earth, the key to their effective rulership was a benevolent governing that had the best interests of the kingdom and its citizens at heart. Only a perfect colonial government could work in a perfect kingdom.

I emphasized earlier that, in a colony, in order for delegated authority to function, it had to have an open channel of communication to the king, as well as the power to perform its responsibilities in accordance with the king's wishes. This is why the Governor—the very Spirit of the King himself—was given to humanity.

The Governor came from the King and was the only one who could suitably transform the colony into the home country. He knew the King's heart, mind, desires, will, and intent, and he was committed to carrying out the King's purposes in the territory. Paul wrote, "For who among men knows the thoughts of a man except the man's spirit within him? In the same way no one knows the thoughts of God except the Spirit of God." In addition, human beings were made in the image and likeness of the King, *with his own personal presence living within them*, so they would be able to transform the colony of earth into an extension of the invisible kingdom. Who could better implement the transformation process than those who had the very nature of the King and were guided by the very Spirit of the King? In this way, the earth would be intimately related to the home country in nature and purpose.

We see therefore that *the Creator-King's intent was to rule the seen world from the unseen world*. He desired to rule the visible world through the spirit of man. And the Holy Spirit, as Governor of the human spirit, was humanity's bridge to the home kingdom; he was the direct channel of communication between the spirit of man and the government of heaven.

It was the presence of the Holy Spirit within human beings that gave them the *authority* and *ability* to have dominion over their environment. I mentioned earlier that the primary issue of humanity is one of power, the ability to influence and control life's circumstances. We desire this ability because we were designed to fulfill our original assignment as vice governors on earth. One of the psalmists wrote, "The highest heavens belong to the LORD, but the earth he has given to man."

RULERSHIP OVER A NEW TERRITORY

Let's look at humanity's assignment from one other perspective. A prince or princess who is the king's heir doesn't succeed to the throne if the king is still alive. The only way this might occur (apart from a king abdicating his throne) is for the king's heir to go to another territory to rule. This has happened in history, although rarely. Therefore, while the heir is in the same territory as the king-father, he or she remains a prince or princess. Yet if the heir lives in a foreign country or territory, he or she can rule as sovereign, while the king-father still rules the home country. So, if a king wanted his children to have the same power, authority, glory, and rulership that he possessed, he had to send them to a different territory (or territories) to rule.

The King of the invisible realm of heaven is eternal. He cannot die. No one will ever succeed him on his heavenly throne. Yet because he delighted in humanity, his children whom he had made in his own image, he wanted them to rule a territory of their own in his name.

This was not a last-minute idea. He prepared the earthly colony before he created the first man and woman. He designed the perfect physical environment for his children to rule in. The first book of Moses recounts the creation of the earth, sea, and animals—which human beings were to rule over as vice governors—prior to the creation of humanity. Then, we read, "The LORD God took the man and put him in the Garden of Eden to work it and take care of it." The natural world, as distinct from the encompassing invisible realm, was an entirely new realm over which humanity could legally have dominion.

The message of the creation of humanity is therefore very practical. It is not about "religion" as we tend to think of it; it is not about rituals. It describes the government of an eternal King and kingdom and the King's royal children whom he made his local governors on earth through the authority and power of his own Spirit. It is about the rule of a King over his territory and the transformation of that territory into the manifestation of his kingdom.

CHAPTER TWO STUDY QUESTIONS

QUESTION FOR REFLECTION

1. Do human beings have a purpose on earth? If so, what is it?

EXPLORING PRINCIPLES AND PURPOSES

2. Where did the first government on earth come from?

3. In what ways is the transcendent kingdom different from a traditional earthly kingdom?

4. In what ways is the transcendent kingdom similar to a traditional kingdom?

5. To whom does the universe belong, and why?

6. What is the definition of the invisible, transcendent kingdom, based on Dr. Munroe's definition of kingdom from chapter one?

7. What did the Creator-King extend to human beings after creating them in his own image and likeness?

8. What do the words *image* (essential nature) and *likeness* (the original after which a thing is patterned) tell us about who we are as human beings?

9. What is the only way a kingdom can function perfectly?

10. What did man's spirit—through the Spirit of God dwelling within him—give him an awareness of?

11. What did the Creator's Spirit, the Governor, enable humanity to do?

12. What was the assignment of the Adamic Administration?

13. Define what it means to have dominion.

14. Describe humanity's basic job description on earth.

15. What was the key to human beings' effective rulership of earth?

16. What two things did the presence of the Holy Spirit within human beings provide them? What primary issue of humanity did these two things address?

APPLYING THE PRINCIPLES OF KINGDOM LIVING

THINKING IT OVER

+ Has your thinking about the nature of God and humanity changed after reading this chapter? If so, in what way?

+ To what extent are you living out humanity's purpose of transforming the earth into a replica of the heavenly kingdom?

+ How much influence do you allow the Spirit of God—the Governor—to have in your life?

ACTING ON IT

+ Which aspects of the nature of the kingdom would you like to develop in your life?

+ List two ways in which your daily activities could better fulfill humanity's purpose of cultivating the earth according to the nature of the kingdom.

PRAYING ABOUT IT

+ Dr. Munroe said human beings are designed to live from the "inside out" rather than the "outside in." We are meant to be led by the Spirit of God, who lives in our spirits. This leading is to be manifested through our souls—mind, will, and emotions—and eventually find expression through our physical bodies. Ask God to help you live your life according to His Spirit so you may fulfill your purpose on earth.

We were designed to be like and function like the Ruler
of the invisible kingdom.

THREE

DECLARATION OF INDEPENDENCE

THE GREATEST THREAT TO KINGDOM PRIVILEGES AND BENEFITS IS AN INDEPENDENT SPIRIT.

The territory of earth had been created and the colony established. The King's children were provided with a rich home and given authority to rule and prosper on earth on behalf of the King. However, something happened to disrupt the home country's plan of expanding the realm of its heavenly kingdom on earth. A rebellion that started in the home country spread to the colony.

A BREACH OF TRUST

THE PLOT: OVERTHROW

The rebellion had been instigated by one of the King's top generals, named Lucifer. He had attempted a coup of the heavenly kingdom and been banished from the presence of the King, along with his followers. This disgraced former aide was bent on revenge and still craved the power to rule a kingdom. He thought that if he could gain control over the King's own children, he could insult the King, thwart the purposes of the heavenly kingdom, and usurp the colony.

THE PLAN: DETACHMENT

Lucifer's plan was to sever the relationship between the King's children and their Father and separate the citizens of the colony from their true government. So he went to the colony in disguise, where the King's children had just begun to rule, and infiltrated their government using craftiness and deceit.

THE STRATEGY: AN INDEPENDENT SPIRIT

His strategy to accomplish this broken relationship was to promote a spirit of rebellion and independence. Subtly questioning the integrity and goodwill of the King, he seduced the King's children to disregard their Father's authority over the colony and encouraged them in an act of insurrection. The following is an account of this incident from the first book of Moses:

> Now the serpent…said to the woman, "Did God really say, 'You must not eat from any tree in the garden'?" The woman said to the serpent, "We may eat fruit from the trees in the garden, but God did say, 'You must not eat fruit from the tree that is in the middle of the garden, and you must not touch it, or you will die.'" "You will not surely die," the serpent said to the woman. "For God knows that when you eat of it your eyes will be opened, and you will be like God, knowing good and evil." When the woman saw that the fruit of the tree was good for food and pleasing to the eye, and also desirable for gaining wisdom, she took some and ate it. She also gave some to her husband, who was with her, and he ate it. Then the eyes of both of them were opened, and they realized they were naked.

The children of the King went against their Father's explicit instructions, which he had instituted for their protection. The renegade general had planted doubts about the motivation of the King, and distrust grew in their hearts. They immediately turned their backs on all their Father had given them and instead believed the lie placed before them. The children's response was contrary to the nature and desires of the King. It was also a corruption of their own nature, which had been made in his likeness. What seemed to be a harmless act to their benefit was actually a disaster; it represented a serious breach of faith and departure from the heart and will of the King. If they could not be trusted with even the simplest aspect of their assignment in the colony, how could they transform the earth into the culture of the kingdom of heaven? Especially now that their minds and hearts were shown to be aligned with the King's bitter enemy?

THE RESULT: TREASON

The King's own children had declared, "I don't want to be under the kingdom's jurisdiction anymore; I don't want to be under the King of Kings; I don't want to be subjected to heaven's government." Yet the earth is heaven's property. When Adam and Eve rebelled and declared independence, they violated the legal contract the government of heaven had established with human beings. Many people think of "sin" as things a person does. Yet it is both deeper and more specific than that. Sin is rebellion against the essential nature and authority of the heavenly government.

By their rebellion, the children not only took something that wasn't theirs, but they also handed it over to someone who didn't deserve it and would never be qualified for it. Lucifer, the unfaithful former general of heaven, would never transform the world into the heavenly kingdom. He would transform it into something completely opposite, a kingdom of darkness.

RENOUNCED ALLEGIANCE AND EXPATRIATION

How did the King react to his children's breach? Although he knew what they had done, he gave them a chance to admit their fault. Instead, they blamed each other, as well as the one who had enticed them to revolt. Like many rebellious children exposed for disobedience, they seemed sorry only to have been caught. The King had no choice but to remove them from the garden; they were banished from the special home they had been provided because they no longer had the nature necessary to live there, and were no longer able to care for it properly.

The first book of Moses says, "After [the Creator-King] drove the man out, he placed on the east side of the Garden of Eden cherubim and a flaming sword flashing back and forth to guard the way to the tree of life." The word *drove* used here means "to drive out from a possession; especially to expatriate or divorce." It is significant that we find the concept of *expatriate* here, which means "to renounce allegiance to one's native country." Adam and Eve virtually cut themselves off from their own King-Father and home country. Having to drive them out of the garden was as painful to their Father as experiencing a wrenching divorce after the betrayal of a loved one.

Adam and Eve had committed high treason. The King had given them authority under delegated power, but they had abused that authority to cut the territory off from the government of heaven.

THE RECALL OF THE GOVERNOR

Although they were removed from the magnificent garden, their former rule, and their previous kingdom lifestyle, their rejection of the King and his nature led to something far worse. The King had previously alerted them, "You are free to eat from any tree in the garden; but you must not eat from the tree of the knowledge of good and evil, for *when you eat of it you will surely die.*" This was the only area on earth over which the King claimed jurisdiction because he knew its misuse would lead to death.

The death the King referred to was not an immediate, bodily death. Adam and Eve did not physically die right away, but they lost their *essential source of life* as human beings—the King's Spirit. Remember that the Spirit of the King gave life to their spirits, souls, and bodies. When they rejected the King, they also rejected and lost his Spirit. The Governor alone was their dynamic connection between the seen and the unseen realms. Therefore, their spirits and souls were cut off from the home country, and their physical bodies began to die a slow death. They were still physically alive for a time, but spiritually and soulically, they were dead to the King and his kingdom.

We saw earlier that whenever a colony became independent from the mother country, the governor was either forced out or withdrawn by the kingdom. Likewise, when Adam and Eve declared independence, the Governor had to be recalled to the heavenly kingdom. I saw a striking illustration of this circumstance the night that governing power in the Bahamas was transferred from Great Britain to the new independent government. The Bahamian people had said, "We no longer want to be connected with Britain, as far as direct governmental control is concerned," and we won our freedom.

Thousands of emotionally charged Bahamians gathered at Clifford Park a few hours before midnight on the evening before independence. The official change in government was scheduled for 12:00 a.m. on July 10, 1973. Prince Charles, as the representative of the crown, was present, as well as our premier, whose title would soon change to prime minister. There were various ceremonies, and the musical group that I had founded was invited to sing as representatives of the youth of the nation.

At 11:50 p.m., the Union Jack was still flying on the flagpole in the middle of the park. The symbol of the kingdom of Great Britain signified that we were still under England's rule. At 11:59, one of our law enforcement officers stood at that pole and began to lower the flag. Another officer was next to him, pulling up the new flag of the independent Bahamas. We were witnessing a change of kingdoms firsthand. The lower the British flag got, the closer we came to no longer having a royal governor. The higher the new flag got, the closer our premier came to becoming prime minister. When the British flag reached the bottom and the Bahamian flag reached the top, it was over. Early the next morning, the royal governor left the governor's house, got on a plane, and departed from the Bahamas. The queen had recalled him. He no longer had the authority or legal right to be there.

While I've described a joyful period in the national life of Bahamians, it was not a jubilant time for the citizens of earth when they rejected the heavenly government. They had not thrown off foreign rule from their lives. They had rejected their own homeland and their beloved King-Father, who desired to give them the riches of his kingdom. As Adam raised the "human independence flag," the flag of the heavenly kingdom was simultaneously being lowered until humanity was severed from the King and his kingdom.

I mentioned that the governor of the Bahamas had to vacate the governor's house when he was recalled to the home country. On the colony of earth, the *human beings themselves were the house the heavenly Governor had lived in*. So when humanity declared independence from the King-Father, this house became a hostile and unclean environment, and the Governor could no longer dwell there. As stated previously, he was recalled to the home country.

EXISTENCE WITHOUT THE GOVERNOR

What was life like for Adam and Eve after they turned their backs on the kingdom and lost the presence of the Governor? Their act of rebellion is often referred to as "the fall" because of the extreme change in the quality of human existence they experienced. It was like a prince falling from a luxurious royal coach into a muddy ditch and then having to live there. Independence, in a human political sense, is a positive concept to us. The American Revolution, in which America declared independence from Great Britain in 1776, is celebrated with fireworks and family gatherings. Yet humanity's independence from heaven's kingdom is nothing to celebrate. It's something to mourn because it's the worst thing that ever happened to human beings, whereas the kingdom was the best thing we could have been given.

We can begin to comprehend the value of the Governor on earth by looking at what existence without him is like.

LOSS OF THE KINGDOM

The loss of the Governor meant the loss of the environment of the kingdom on earth. Since the Governor was the evidence of the presence of the kingdom, his absence inevitably meant the absence of the kingdom presence. Earth's environment changed to the antithesis of the heavenly kingdom.

CUT OFF FROM TRUE LIFE

Although human beings were designed to live from the *inside out*, this situation was now reversed. Because they had lost the Holy Spirit, who had been their connection with their Father, they now had to live from the *outside in*. They became totally dependent on their five physical senses. The physical world—which could give them only a limited perspective on life's realities—imposed itself on their inner world. I believe this is why one of the first words we read about Adam and Eve after their rebellion is the word "realized" or "knew." Suddenly, they *realized* they were naked. Does this imply they didn't know this before? I don't think so. I believe it implies this: nakedness is an external consciousness rather than something that is spiritually discerned. The body and its senses, rather than the spirit, took over humanity's focus in life. Human beings no longer had a *spiritual* perspective at their essence but a *sensual* one.

A perspective based *only* on the senses inevitably leads to confusion. Humanity began to depend on the soul—the mind, will, and emotions informed by the senses—to interpret life. From then on, what we saw, heard, touched, tasted, and smelled became the dominant components in our human experience. Consequently, we began to interpret our Creator-King mainly from our physical senses, as well. For example, the field of science attempts to understand the unseen world only from the seen world. This approach is dangerous because human beings were never intended to interpret the physical world from itself but from the spiritual reality of the kingdom.

I am not saying that science is "bad." Neither am I saying that the intellect is evil, but only that it has been moved out of its proper position. The intellect is a wonderful gift created by God. It must be in its right position, however, for it to effectively execute its purpose and fulfill its potential. The things that are seen were made from things that are not seen, and the only way to truly understand something is to relate to how it was made and who made it. The Spirit of the Creator is the only avenue we have for fully understanding ourselves and the physical world since he is the Source, Author, and Manufacturer of creation.

We must grasp the deep significance of this truth: Having the Spirit of the King is essential not only for our relationship with the invisible King, but also for understanding our own humanity. Only through the Governor can we know why we are really here and how to interpret the world in which we live; in other words, how to truly *see* our environment. *The Governor is the key to our being fully human.* We can't express the King's nature unless we are in relationship with him, and the Governor provided that relationship.

Only the Governor knows the mind of the King. We can't really be what we were born to be as human beings unless we have a vital connection to his original intent. The Governor is our reference to ourselves; he is the key to our self-understanding. To be true and complete human beings, we must somehow become reconnected to and re-indwelled by the Holy Spirit.

LOSS OF AUTHORITY AND POWER

We not only lost communication with the home country through the loss of the Governor, but we also lost the power and authority he provided. Remember that power is the ability to control and influence circumstances. One of the first things the King said to Adam after his rebellion was, in effect, "From now on, you will have to fight the earth in order to get food." Beforehand, he had said, "Rule over...all the earth." Now the King had to sadly inform him,

> Cursed is the ground because of you; through painful toil you will eat of it all the days of your life. It will produce thorns and thistles for you, and you will eat the plants of the field. By the sweat of your brow you will eat your food until you return to the ground, since from it you were taken; for dust you are and to dust you will return.

The King wasn't only speaking of literal thorns. He was saying, "It's going to be hard for you to provide for yourself. You're going to have to sweat for it." Before that, Adam's work was not exhausting. He had authority and dominion over the natural world. It worked for him, rather than the other way around.

RAMIFICATIONS OF SELF-GOVERNMENT

The Governor had been humanity's connection with the home country, enabling human beings to fulfill their authority and dominion on earth. When he left, the earth basically became an independent nation. A colony without a governor results in self-government. Again, to our contemporary minds, *independence* and *self-determination* are positive words. We celebrate freedom and self-government. But again, this was not the triumph of freedom over tyranny. This was not removing the shackles of foreign occupation. It was like rejecting your beloved family, your home country, and your billion-dollar inheritance all at once. To paraphrase the wise King Solomon, "Some paths in life *seem* right, but they lead to death."

There's nothing more dangerous and threatening to a kingdom than a spirit of independence. For human kingdoms, this translates into a loss of power and wealth and probably some pride. For the heavenly kingdom, however, it meant the spiritual death of beloved children who were meant to carry on the family name and legacy. For the children, it meant the introduction of fear, a survival mind-set, and the knowledge of the inevitability of death.

DECLARATION OF INDEPENDENCE 51

When you are an independent person, you have to survive by your own wits. Likewise, when a country becomes an independent nation, it has to totally pay its own way. When the royal governor left the Bahamas on the morning of July 10, we were totally on our own—in our political and economic life, caring for our infrastructure, and all aspects of governance. Likewise, humanity was left to fend for itself. Yet, as noted earlier, human beings weren't designed to function using only their senses. They weren't supposed to live like orphans left to survive in a hostile world on what they could scrape by on, or like convicts left to scratch out an existence on a remote, punitive island. Human beings were designed to thrive and prosper and use the heights of their creativity through the guidance and power of the Holy Spirit. The recall of the Governor was a devastating loss to the inhabitants of earth.

A REBELLIOUS STATE

Humanity's declaration of independence and subsequent loss of the Governor left human beings in a state of rebellion. The government of earth, as exercised in the life of every human being, became essentially one of rebellion that did not have the purposes of the kingdom at heart. Every person has been born into this state since the initial rebellion. Theologian Paul of Tarsus put it this way: "For all have sinned and fall short of the glory of God." We all fall short of the essential nature of God and everything that makes him praiseworthy. He is the perfect King; his kingdom is the perfect government. Yet we have distorted the image of that perfection within us. And all our efforts to execute government on earth in personal and corporate ways have fallen deeply short as well.

A CULTURE OF DARKNESS AND DEATH

When a country becomes independent after being a colony, it usually elects or appoints its own governor. This governor does not teach the people about the culture of the former home country, but only their own. Similarly, when the heavenly government recalled the Governor, human beings stopped learning the culture of heaven and created their own culture, which they passed along to their children. We stopped living heaven's values and began to have our own independent ideas about life.

We must ask ourselves: How well are we doing? What has the nature of our culture become? One of the first things that took place after earth lost the Governor was that a man was murdered by his older brother. What a way to start a new culture! Instead of the kingdom of heaven defining and transforming earth, a kingdom and culture of darkness came upon it and began to spread. Adultery, incest, abuse, and domestic violence are all parts of this culture of darkness; it destroys young and old, strong and weak. We are still experiencing crime upon crime, brother killing brother. Wherever the Governor of the King does not rule, you will find murder and other instances of man's inhumanity to man. The abuse and destruction afflict families, communities, businesses, and government—the whole realm of human existence.

All this transpired because human beings listened to the treacherous lies of a rebellious former aide to our King-Father, who wanted to usurp the colony for himself. Jesus of Nazareth described Lucifer as the "father of lies" and a "murderer." He also said, "The thief comes only to steal and kill and destroy."

When this disgraced former general took authority over the territory of earth, the natural result was devastation and death. His intent as the illegal governor on earth was not to bring freedom. It was to steal people's lives so he could ultimately destroy them. He is a foreign ruler who has taken over the colony of earth and desires to destroy the original culture of the inhabitants. He rules over a destructive kingdom of darkness in which human beings have become either his willing or unwilling accomplices.

What have we done to this planet? From the time of humanity's rejection of the King and the loss of the Governor, human beings have been attempting to dominate the King's colony without the mind and heart of the King. Trying to run the planet without the King's nature has led to a breakdown in human authority and power to address vital issues. It is the source of the world's poverty, genocide, terrorism, political corruption, drug addiction, broken homes, and every kind of evil that can be named. We have created a state of rebellion and confusion. This world is a disaster without the Governor.

THE PROMISE OF THE KING

The colony of earth crumbled under the absence of the Governor. Without his presence, the human race lost its dignity and sense of responsibility; it became confused and chaotic. The people experienced a living death. Even though many people still struggle to do good, this is the essence of the culture of earth today. As the descendants of Adam and Eve, we are unable to rule on behalf of the heavenly kingdom because we abdicated our rule to Lucifer's culture of darkness.

Yet, remarkably, immediately following humanity's rebellion and the loss of the Governor, the King promised the *return* of the Governor and the restoration of earth as a territory loyal to the kingdom of heaven. The most important promise the government of heaven ever made to humanity was the return of the Governor because he is what every human being needs for true life. He is what the entire world needs; without him, the territory would forever remain in a state of chaos and death.

Even in the immediate aftermath of the rebellion, the King gave an indication of how he would restore the Governor. He told Lucifer, "I will put enmity between you and the woman, and between your offspring and hers; he will crush your head, and you will strike his heel." The King's plan was to send an Offspring, to be born in the colony, who would restore kingdom influence to the colony. He would crush the power of the realm of darkness, take back the kingdom authority that had been stolen, and restore power and authority to those to whom it was first given—humanity. We would be reinstated as local rulers on behalf of the heavenly kingdom once again. This would happen because the King would reappoint the Governor to the colony of earth.

SEEKING THE GOVERNOR

I believe that the bottom line in every person's search for power and meaning in life is this: they are actually seeking the return of the Governor, though they may not realize it. Many people feel they are missing something in their lives yet aren't sure what it is. They try to fill the emptiness with a variety of things: money, relationships, parties, drugs, sex, alcohol, work, sports, or vacations. In fact, I believe that every person, whether they are Christian, atheist, Hindu, Buddhist, Muslim, Shintoist, Scientologist, animist, or even Satanist ultimately desires the same thing. They want to fill what is missing in their life, and only the presence of the Governor in their life can accomplish this. A human being without the Governor is dysfunctional because they're never complete; their very purpose requires the presence of the Holy Spirit.

Therefore, if a message were sent from the kingdom of heaven to earth regarding the fulfillment of the King's promise—the restoration of the Governor—that message would not be a religion. Neither would it be a self-help method by which human beings could use their own abilities to solve their problems. It would be a message about the kingdom and the return of the King's Spirit.

CHAPTER THREE STUDY QUESTIONS

QUESTIONS FOR REFLECTION

1. Have you ever believed a lie? What was it? What impact did it have on your life?

2. In what ways is independence a positive concept? In what ways might it be a negative one?

EXPLORING PRINCIPLES AND PURPOSES

3. What happened to disrupt the heavenly kingdom's plan of expanding its realm on earth?

4. Who instigated this disruption in the plan, and what was his motivation for doing so?

5. What was the nature of Lucifer's plan for disrupting the colony, and what was his strategy for accomplishing it?

6. In what two ways were the disbelief and rebellion of the King's children toward the King unnatural?

   (1)

   (2)

7. What did the children's rebellion ultimately amount to, and why?

8. According to the nature of the kingdom, what is the definition of sin?

9. What was the worst result of the children's rejection of the King and his nature?

10. How did this loss affect the spirits, souls, and bodies of human beings?

11. Governors in traditional human kingdoms are forced out or are called to withdraw if a colony becomes independent from the mother country. Likewise, when humanity declared independence, the Governor was _____ to the heavenly kingdom.

12. How did the environment of earth change with the loss of the Governor?

13. What did human beings become dependent on after they lost the Spirit?

14. Why is it dangerous to interpret the physical world only from the physical world itself?

15. List several reasons why the Governor is the key to our being fully human.

16. For humanity, what were the harsh realities of self-government?

17. Describe the culture human beings created as a substitute for the culture of heaven.

18. Immediately following humanity's rebellion and the loss of the Governor, the King... [choose one]

    (a) believed humanity was not worth saving

    (b) told humanity to figure out its own problems

    (c) said Lucifer and humanity deserved one another

    (d) promised the return of the Governor and earth's restoration

19. What is the bottom line in every person's search for power and meaning in life?

20. What was the King's plan to restore the Governor to earth?

APPLYING THE PRINCIPLES OF KINGDOM LIVING
THINKING IT OVER

+ Have you had a sense something is missing in your life, though you haven't known what it is? What have you used to try to fill the emptiness (for example, money, relationships, work, parties, sports)? How would the presence of the Governor in your life remove the emptiness you have experienced?

+ In what ways are you interpreting life solely through your physical senses rather than by the nature and Spirit of the Creator-King?

+ Are there any areas in your life where you have believed the lie from Lucifer that being independent from the Creator-King is a good thing? How would a full reconnection with the Creator-King change your life for the better?

ACTING ON IT

+ Dr. Munroe wrote that "sin is rebellion against the essential nature and authority of the heavenly government." Think about a sin you are currently struggling with and describe how it is in opposition to the nature and authority of the King.

+ List several things you know God expects of you, based on Scripture, but which you have felt were restrictive. Then write how the apparent restrictions are for your protection.

PRAYING ABOUT IT

+ Honestly admit to the Creator-King if you have been living a life (even parts of it) independent from him. Recognize this not only hurts you but grieves his heart, since he only wants the best for you. Then ask him to begin to restore your connection with him and to develop his nature in you.

*The greatest threat to kingdom privileges and benefits
is an independent spirit.*

FOUR

THE PROMISE OF THE GOVERNOR'S RETURN

WHEN THE END BECOMES THE MEANS, AND THE MINOR BECOMES THE MAJOR, THEN INJUSTICE IS INEVITABLE.

Before looking more closely at the King's plan to restore the Governor, let's review some major points regarding the kingdom of heaven and its plan for the colonization of earth:

+ The King of the eternal and invisible kingdom desired to extend his own nature and influence to the physical realm of earth, which he had created. The kingdom of heaven is his governing influence over the world, impacting and influencing it with his will, his purpose, and his intent. Heaven is God's kingdom or home country, and earth is his colony.

+ Human beings were created in the image of the King and were given the Spirit of the King to live within them. The King's Spirit gave life to their spirits, souls, and bodies.

+ Human beings were designed to function like their Creator-King. The presence of the Spirit of the King within human beings guaranteed that they would have his character and nature. It also assured that they would be able to rule on earth as he would rule in the heavenly kingdom, having his very nature of love, mercy, kindness, and forgiveness.

+ The King did not desire to rule the earth directly, but to cultivate his colony through his children, who also functioned as his local governors. They were to exercise dominion over the earth under the direction of the chief Governor, the Spirit of the King.

+ Adam and Eve's declaration of independence cut humanity off from the King and caused the Governor to be recalled by the kingdom of heaven.

- The departure of the Governor meant the departure of the heavenly government and its direct influence over the colony of earth.

- After humanity rebelled against the authority of the heavenly government, the King immediately promised to restore the Governor to his children.

- The most important promise the Creator-King ever made to human beings was the promise that the Governor would return to live within them, because he is the key to life.

- The restoration of the King's Spirit to humanity is central to the restoration of his kingdom on earth.

All the above leads us to this conclusion: **The principal purpose of the redemptive program of the Creator-King, in his dealings with humanity throughout human history, was the restoration of the Governor to the colony of earth.**

In light of this, let's consider the theme of the sacred literature of the Old, or First, Testament, also known as the Jewish canon of Scripture. Some say its theme is the creation of a monotheistic religion. Others say it's the story of the rise and fall of the ancient Hebrew nation. Still others see it as the record of various traditions and rituals. If we look at it in any of these terms, however, we miss its crucial essence.

THE THEME AND SIGNIFICANCE OF THE SCRIPTURES

What is the significance of the Scriptures? Why do we have the accounts of Noah, the patriarchs Abraham, Isaac and Jacob, and the story of the nation of Israel? What was the purpose of all the blood sacrifices? Why is there a record of priests, prophets, and the lineage of kings?

While its events revolve around the people and nation of Israel, the theme of the Old Testament is universal: it is the restoration of the key to *humanity's* existence, the reestablishment of true life for *every human being* on the planet. The record of the people and events depict the unfolding of the King's plan to restore his Spirit within human beings so they can be and do what they were originally intended to, so they can fulfill their remarkable purpose and potential once again.

The first two chapters of Genesis explain the heavenly government's plan for expanding the kingdom to earth. The third chapter describes the interruption of this plan and the immediate promise of restoration. From the third chapter all the way through the last book of the Old Testament, the King's plan for the return of his Governor to earth is revealed. All the situations, people, and programs we read about serve these ends:

1. They are a continual reminder of the promise of the Governor's restoration.

2. They depict the King's intervention in the lives of specific families on earth to preserve a lineage for the Offspring who would restore the Governor.

3. They depict a prototype of the restoration of the kingdom of heaven on earth.

4. They expose the fact that only the Governor himself can reconnect the earthly colony to its heavenly government.

5. They foretell the coming of the Offspring who will personally reconcile the children-citizens to the King and authorize the return of the Governor.

In other words, after humanity's rebellion, the King's intent was essentially this: "My purpose in creating the world was disrupted, and I'm going to correct it. My Spirit can no longer live in the earthly residence I created. I will therefore restore my Spirit to humanity so my kingdom can function on earth again."

Everything depicted in the Old Testament about the intervention of God in the lives of human beings was ultimately a means to this end. God was revealing to humanity, in effect, "Here's the program: Your rebellion has put you in a hopeless situation. I am therefore going to come to the earth personally, and I will provide a way of restoring purity of heart and wholeness to you, so that the Governor can come to live in you again. Second, I will reappoint the Governor to the colony of earth to live within you once more and carry out my desire to transform the earth into a reflection of my kingdom."

HUMANITY'S NEED FOR HOLINESS

The Old Testament emphasizes the fact that when Adam and Eve lost the Holy Spirit, humanity became *unholy*. I think this word has so many religious images connected with it that we don't really know what it means anymore. We find its essence by looking at what the Creator-King told the nation of Israel: "You will be for me a kingdom of priests and a holy nation." In this instance, he is using the word *holy* in relation to a *nation*. He's obviously not talking about wearing a cross or a liturgical robe or entering a religious order.

So what does the concept mean? There are two related connotations of the word that I want to emphasize here: one of them is "pure," and the other is "devoted" or "dedicated."[1]

These words signify, first of all, something that is *set apart* specifically and purely for a certain use. In this sense, holiness can be applied to many things. For example, I could set apart my favorite cup and say, "This may only be used by me for drinking hot tea, nothing else." I've sanctified it by setting it apart and dedicating it for a specific purpose. Thus, the word *pure* in this context means something beyond just "clean." It has to do with being *pure in use*.

In relation to human beings, the King said his people needed to be "holy unto me." How can you be holy unto a person? Holiness, in this connection, means, "I am devoted only to you. Not only am I dedicated to you, but my loyalty to you is not tainted by any other loyalties. I have no ulterior motives."

Next, let's look at what it means for the Creator-King to describe himself as a "holy" God. Does it mean he's devoted to himself alone? No, it means that he is *true* to himself. He is faithful and consistent in who he is, what he desires, what he says, and what he does. I associate the word *holy* with *integrity*. The King is fully "integrated" or unified. His nature is so pure that he can never have an ulterior or deceitful motive. This is why the King cannot lie. This is also why the King-Father can never disagree with the King-Son, who is the Offspring who came to restore the Governor; and this is why neither of them can disagree with the Governor. The three persons of the Creator-King are one or *integrated*.

Having personal holiness therefore means "to be one with yourself." When Jesus of Nazareth told his disciples, "Be perfect [holy], just as your [King-Father] is perfect," he was saying, "Be one with yourself, as your King-Father is one with himself." Here is the practical application: If you say that you will do something, you do it. If you promise something, you fulfill it. If you are truly holy, you can never say something and then do something contrary to it. Your public behavior is the same as your private behavior. Nothing the King does is ever in conflict with his nature so that he has to hide it. You don't have to hide anything unless you are saying or doing something that is contrary to what you say you are. Adam and Eve had been totally integrated before they disobeyed the King and then lied about it, destroying the trust he had placed in them.

The central issue of the Old Testament is that, when Adam and Eve rebelled, the Holy Spirit had to leave humanity because human beings were no longer pure in motive or integrated in themselves, and consequently were no longer set apart for God or in agreement with him. The Governor is a pure Spirit and could not live in intimate relationship with humanity in that environment.

STAGES OF THE KING'S PLAN

When human beings cut themselves off from the Governor, the King was faced with a supreme challenge. Human beings needed to live in his presence, and to have his presence within them. However, their current state would not permit this. If he wanted to restore the Governor to his children and continue his purpose of having the earth reflect his kingdom, something had to happen to change their state of being.

The King's plan to fully restore the Governor unfolded in stages:

1. He implemented a program that allowed the Governor to come *upon* people, although not *within* them, so as not to violate his integrity. *His Spirit could come upon any person who chose to submit to the influence of the heavenly government.* Since the Governor had been recalled and was therefore "illegal" on earth, he would come and rule in someone's life when that person yielded to his prompting and direction. This wasn't the same influence over the entire

world that was in place before the rebellion; it was what we might call "selective rulership" or "rulership by submission."

2. The sacrificial system, which the Hebrew people practiced, and which we will talk more about shortly, allowed the Governor to work on earth through a special nation of people who were meant to be a prototype of the return of the kingdom to the whole world.

3. The King himself would come to earth to restore integrity to humanity, and thus provide a way for the Governor to again live *within* human beings on a permanent basis.

Understanding the Creator-King's program to restore humanity puts the entire Old Testament in the proper light. It is not a group of stories strung together or a handbook of rituals. It is about the King initiating his restoration program.

In Genesis, when the King said that the Offspring would come and "crush the head" of the serpent, this was actually the first promise that he himself was coming to earth—incarnated as a human being—and would defeat humanity's deceiver, reconcile his people to himself, and restore the Governor. The prophet Isaiah wrote, "For to *us* a child is born, to *us* a son is given, and the government will be on his shoulders. And he will be called Wonderful Counselor, Mighty God, Everlasting Father, Prince of Peace."

In this sense, Christmas really began in the third chapter of Genesis. The King-Father was preparing the earth to receive the King-Son. And the old sacrificial system would be replaced by a permanent sacrifice made by the King-Son himself. The New Testament writer to the Hebrews, quoting Psalm 40, wrote, "Sacrifice and offering you did not desire, but a body you prepared for me." From Genesis 4 onward, therefore, the King-Father was working to set apart and preserve a lineage dedicated to his Son's eventual coming to earth. Let's take a fresh look at the Old Testament from this perspective.

INFLUENCE OVER EARTH'S ENVIRONMENT

The Governor's presence on earth through the submission of individuals to the heavenly government was always accompanied by the manifestation of kingdom influence over the earth's environment. In other words, when the King made himself known to people, and they responded by yielding to him and his redemptive purposes, miraculous things would happen on earth. Yet what we call "miracles" were not extraordinary from the point of view of the kingdom of heaven. They were *natural* outcomes of the influence of the heavenly government in the lives of those yielded to the King.

NOAH AND THE FLOOD

After the rebellion of Adam and Eve, the culture of the world became so evil that it had to be virtually destroyed in order to preserve a lineage for the coming Offspring. This is why the Creator-King came to a man named Noah and instructed him to build an ark to save himself and his family from the flood that would destroy the rest of the earth's inhabitants. His message was essentially this: "Noah, the people of the world have become totally wicked, and I need to preserve a pure lineage. Therefore, I'm going to start over again with you and your family because you have a heart that is obedient toward me."

Notice that the King's words to Noah after the flood were almost exactly the same as the ones he had first spoken to Adam: "Then God blessed Noah and his sons, saying to them, 'Be fruitful and increase in number and fill the earth.'" The King was continuing the same program with Noah's family that he had begun with Adam and Eve; he did not change his original purpose for humanity on earth because of the rebellion. Instead, he was working out his plan to restore it. Noah was not the actual source of the restoration but was part of the pure (set apart) lineage that needed to be preserved for the coming of the Offspring. The worldwide deluge and the survival of Noah and his family on the ark were the result of the kingdom manifesting its influence through the faith Noah placed in the King and his ultimate purposes for humanity.

ABRAHAM

Ten generations later, Noah had a descendant named Abraham, and the King's plan of preparing a lineage and a body for himself started to take more specific shape. He told Abraham that even though he and his wife were old, they would have a child. This child would be the beginning of a great nation, which in turn would be a prototype of what the kingdom of heaven on earth was supposed to look like. Moreover, one of his descendants would be the promised Offspring.

Sarah's ability to conceive and bear a son in her old age was a result of Abraham and Sarah's willingness to cooperate with the purposes of the heavenly government. Although they did not fully understand the plan, their relationship with the Creator-King brought about the next stage in his redemptive purposes for earth.

Both Noah and Abraham believed and obeyed the King's instructions. Belief and obedience were the means of their holiness or righteousness before him. *Righteousness* refers to "right standing" or "right alignment" with evident authority, and Noah and Abraham lined themselves up with the government of heaven.

THE TRIBES OF ISRAEL

Abraham had his miracle child, Isaac. Isaac had twin sons, Esau and Jacob, and Jacob was chosen as the one to carry on the lineage. Jacob's name was later changed to Israel, which means "Prince with God." He was the heir of the promise of the coming Offspring. Jacob had twelve sons, and each son's family grew and became a large tribe; this was the origin of the twelve tribes of Israel. The Creator-King chose Jacob's son Judah as the one through whom the special lineage would be carried on, even though all the tribes were destined to play a part in the unfolding drama.

THE ISRAELITES: A KINGDOM OF PRIESTS AND A HOLY NATION

Eventually, the twelve tribes moved to Egypt because of a famine in their homeland. They were preserved through the heavenly government's intervention in the life of another son of Jacob, named Joseph, who became the Egyptian pharaoh's second-in-command. But the tribes eventually become slaves of Egypt under a different pharaoh. After several hundred years, the Creator-King called a man named Moses, of the tribe of Levi, to free the Israelites as part of his plan to preserve a lineage for the birth of the Offspring.

All the events we read about in the life of Moses show the manifestation of kingdom influence on earth through Moses' submission to the purposes of the kingdom government. For example, Moses' ability to bring the plagues of locusts and flies was an example of a human being exercising dominion over "all the creatures that move along the ground" through the power of the King's Spirit. The same is true for the miracle of the parting of the Red Sea that allowed the Israelites to cross over on foot and escape the pursuing Egyptians. Moses was the heavenly government's instrument to bring about many manifestations of kingdom influence on earth during his lifetime.

I want to reemphasize that Abraham, Isaac, Jacob, Moses, and the Israelite nation were not preserved in order to create a religion. The nation of Israel was an instrument in the hand of the King's unfolding purposes to reconcile the whole world to himself and to restore the Governor—it was not an end in itself. The Israelites were called and set apart as a special nation so they could rediscover the King and his ways for the purpose of becoming a nation with a holy (dedicated) purpose. As we will shortly see, they were to be "a kingdom of priests and a holy nation" to help fulfill the King's plan of restoration for the world.

The Hebrew word for "kingdom" in this context is *mamlakah,* which means "dominion" or "rule."[2] Here we return to the theme of earthly dominion. *Kingdom* indicates governing responsibility, while the role of the priest was to help people become realigned with the heavenly government. In essence, priestly work involves lining up with true authority, and kingdom work has to do with executing rulership under that authority. The Creator-King wanted a *kingdom* or nation of priests on earth. He wanted the entire nation of Israel to be properly aligned with him, all the time, the way Adam and Eve had been when they still had the Spirit of the Creator living within them. Every human being was meant to be a priest—personally aligned with the Creator-King—and a ruler—having dominion over the earth.

God had told the Israelites when they came out of Egypt that, if they continued to believe and obey him, he would make them the greatest nation in the world. He gave them instructions for living, called the law. This was a comprehensive picture of how they were supposed to think and act as a kingdom of priests and rulers living in integrity. If they did so, he would provide for them and protect them; they would have everything they needed, and they would never be defeated by their enemies. The nation as a whole was to be a prototype of what the King would do for all who were submitted to his Governor and were ruling their homes, communities, and nations under his guidance.

Sadly, the nation of Israel didn't live up to its high purpose. The people rejected the laws of the King, just as Adam and Eve had. They were no longer in alignment with him. Consequently, they failed to be an example to other nations of the kingdom of heaven on earth. Although there were times when the people returned to their King, they rejected him over and over again throughout their history as a nation. Whenever this happened, the King allowed other nations, which didn't acknowledge him, to overrun them so they would see their need and return to him. Throughout the Old Testament, we read how the nation was often overtaken by other peoples, such as the Canaanites, Moabites, and Hittites.

THE MEANING OF THE LAW

When the Israelite people first came out of Egyptian slavery, they had forgotten much about the King and his ways. They had lost a clear conception of his nature and will. They didn't know about Abraham's personal relationship with the King, but had only a vague idea that Abraham was their forefather. This is when God instructed Moses to tell them who they were and what their true purpose was as a nation of kings and priests:

> This is what you are to say to the house of Jacob and what you are to tell the people of Israel: "You yourselves have seen what I did to Egypt, and how I carried you on eagles' wings and brought you to myself. Now if you obey me fully and keep my covenant, then out of all nations you will be my treasured possession. Although the whole earth is mine, you will be for me a kingdom of priests and a holy nation." These are the words you are to speak to the Israelites.

With these words, the King established his relationship to the Israelites, and their relationship to him. Then he instructed Moses to tell the whole nation to meet him at the mountain where they were encamped. He wanted to give them his laws directly. He didn't want to give them to just one person who would pass them along to the people; he wanted the whole nation to hear them because all of them were to be rulers and priests. When they came to the mountain, and the King descended to talk to them, they were afraid of the display of his power and greatness. Moses told them not to be afraid but to reverence the King. But instead, the people wanted Moses to serve as their mediator.

Again, the King gave the law so the people would know what it meant to live according to his nature. Yet his ultimate desire was not to have his laws recorded merely on stone or even paper. He wanted them to exist in the spirit of their minds. He revealed his ultimate plan with these words, which he gave to his prophet Jeremiah: "This is the covenant I will make with the house of Israel after that time....I will put my law in their minds and write it on their hearts. I will be their God, and they will be my people." This is a direct reference to the eventual return of the Governor to live within humanity.

For now, however, Moses received the written code, the laws and principles of the kingdom, or the "kingdom standards," to give to the people. Their King wanted them to understand how his Spirit thought and how his kingdom worked so they could stay in alignment with him. If the nation obeyed the King's laws, they would attract his Spirit because they would be living in holiness and be in harmony with his nature.

When Moses came down from the mountain after meeting with the King, the people agreed to obey the law. As we saw, however, this didn't last long. Joshua, Moses' second-in-command, eventually took the people into the land the King had promised them. What we consider amazing miracles at this time, such as the parting of the waters of the river Jordan, the collapse of the walls of the city of Jericho, and the sun standing still and not setting for about a full day during a battle, were merely evidence of kingdom influence over the physical universe. Yet even with all these demonstrations of the presence of the kingdom of heaven among them, the people turned away from the will of the King. They began to intermarry with citizens outside the prototype kingdom and took on the traits of nations that did not acknowledge the King. They gradually became alienated from him and unaligned with his kingdom purposes.

THE PRIESTHOOD AND SACRIFICES

This is where the priesthood comes in. I don't believe God's real desire was to have a specific group of people called priests. Remember that he wanted a *kingdom*, or nation, of priests. But in order for the Israelites to remain his prototype nation, he provided a way for them to be restored when they rebelled against him and violated his kingdom standards.

Since they had forsaken their calling to be a nation of priests, the King appointed Aaron, Moses' brother, and Aaron's sons, who were of the tribe of Levi, to be the nation's priests. Their descendants would succeed them as priests. He also told Moses to set aside certain other men of the tribe of Levi to assist the priests in their duties. The priests were to keep themselves aligned with the King. They performed rituals of sacrifice prescribed by the King, which served to atone for (cover over) the people's rebellion and position the nation of Israel in alignment with the heavenly government again. In this way, the Governor could reveal the will of the King to the people, and his kingdom culture could come on earth through them. The result was that they would bring all other nations back to the King through their example. Therefore, all the sacrifices, the rituals involving the blood, the incense that was burned, the various components of the tabernacle, and later the temple—all these things were for the purpose of realigning the people with God so they could be what they were originally called to be.

The rituals that the priests performed involved the sacrifice of animals because the culture of rebellion, murder, and death that human beings had created needed to be paid for. So did individuals' infractions of the King's law. The first-century writer of the book of Hebrews wrote, "The law requires that nearly everything be cleansed with blood, and without the shedding of blood there is no forgiveness." In the system of sacrifices, therefore, the blood atoned for the violations against the kingdom law that the people had committed.

When we read about all the intricacies of priestly dress and practice, the systems of worship, and the specific details of the animal sacrifices, we tend to get caught up in the particulars and miss their overall meaning. The ultimate goal of the King's program was not the priests, the robes, the incense, the showbread, the goblets, and the inner and outer courts. Some people almost seem to consider these things as mystical religious icons. Instead, they were a means to an end. They were God's provision (his temporary program) for realigning the people with him so that his Spirit, the absent Governor, could come back to them and intervene on the earth.

The ultimate goal of the entire Old Testament ritualistic program was designed, motivated, and developed for this purpose: when the high priest went in to the innermost chamber of the tabernacle (later, the temple), the sacrifices would be accepted on behalf of the people, and the Spirit of God would be able to come and dwell between the cherubim on the mercy seat (or atonement cover) there because the requirements for holiness had been fulfilled.

Everything that came into the presence of the Spirit had to be holy because he is a *holy* Spirit. The sacrificial blood would cleanse both the people and the high priest who would stand in the immediate presence of the Governor in the inner room of the tabernacle, called the "Holy of Holies." As a result of these sacrifices, a most beautiful thing occurred. The Spirit came back. The Governor was on earth! All the temporary sacrifices brought the Governor into the people's *presence*, but not into *them*. He could not enter into human beings at that time because the permanent sacrifice had not yet been made.

The animal sacrifices had to be offered again and again because the people were continually rebelling against the authority of heaven, and the sacrifices were a temporary method of atonement that allowed the heavenly government to intervene in their lives, even though it couldn't change their rebellious *nature*.

Whenever the people of Israel were aligned with the King and his Spirit was with them, they won every battle, had no sickness among them, and experienced peace. Why? They were living as true human beings again. They were living as they were intended to live—above their environment and circumstances.

Great lengths had to be taken by the priests just to ensure the Governor's presence in the inner chamber of the tabernacle or temple so the people could be at peace, prosper, and fulfill their role as the prototype nation. When the people disobeyed God, the Holy Spirit left them, and their lives became chaotic again. When they received forgiveness through the sacrifices and again obeyed God, the Holy Spirit would return, and they would have success.

The sacrificial system served its purpose, even though it was inadequate to fully solve humanity's dilemma of separation from the heavenly kingdom. It actually emphasized the incompleteness of the temporary cleansing to keep the people aligned with God. They were "sprinkled" with the blood because the blood of animals cannot permanently cleanse a person from the inside out. The intent of the hearts of men and women are basically and continually evil. The unholy (nonintegrated, non-set apart) state of the human heart and its potential for evil are always under the surface and always emerge in one way or another.

Yet this program was the Creator-King's temporary provision for working with human beings, whom he couldn't yet dwell within—because of their unholiness—but still needed to influence. He created his own environment of holiness through the sacrificial system in order to work among his people without violating his purity and integrity. The prophets, priests, and kings of the nation of Israel would receive the Spirit of the King *upon* them for specific instances when they would speak or act on earth on behalf of the King.

Many people like to study and teach all the intricacies of the Old Testament rituals; some even make quite a bit of money off books and products expounding on such things as the "ten keys to the tabernacle." I've found that many people are (at best) missing the main purpose of these things, and other people are (at worst) exploiting people by overemphasizing them. They were not ends in themselves. We must always remember that their whole purpose was to be a means of bringing the governing influence of heaven back to earth for the benefit of humanity.

THE KINGS

Because the Israelites wanted to be just like the other nations around them, having the same standards and lifestyle, they had asked for their own earthly king. The King had told them, in effect, "No, you really don't want an earthly king. A king will just oppress you with taxation and forced labor. I am your King, who provides everything for you and gives you what is good." He was trying to tell them, "You are *not* like other nations. You

are supposed to be an example to them. You're supposed to be the prototype for my kingdom."

Human kings were not the King's ultimate plan for his people. He
wanted a whole *nation* of kingdom rulers who would be directed by him.
This idea reflects his ultimate goal of having every citizen on earth be a local
governor, exercising authority under the chief Governor. Yet the Israelites
insisted on having a king, so he gave them what they wanted.

The people's desire for a king indicated a lack of alignment with the
King and a complete misunderstanding of their calling. After they told the
prophet Samuel they wanted a king, "the LORD told [Samuel]: 'Listen to all
that the people are saying to you; it is not you they have rejected, but they
have rejected me as their king.'" They were rejecting their heavenly King
once more.

Yet the King used the institution of kings to further his redemptive
purposes. The second king over Israel, David, was a man who desired what
the heavenly government desires. Kingdom influence was manifested in his
life in many ways. His amazing slaying of the giant Goliath when he was
still a youth was an example of a human being exercising kingdom dominion over a pawn of the kingdom of darkness. When David said to Goliath,
"You come against me with sword and spear and javelin, but I come against
you in the name of the LORD Almighty," he was saying, "I come to you
under the authority of the government of heaven."

Ultimately, the King used the line of Israelite kings to preserve the
lineage for his Son's coming to earth. The Offspring would be a descendant
of David.

THE PROPHETS

However, most of the nation's kings, who were supposed to represent
the King's justice on earth, became corrupt. The priesthood also become
corrupt. The very ones who were supposed to align the nation to the King
had become unaligned themselves. So the King raised up people from
within the Israelite nation, at various times, who could speak to both
priests and kings on behalf of the heavenly kingdom.

A distinct pattern is emerging: The nation of Israel was raised up as a prototype to address the need of a rebellious people called *humanity*. The priesthood came about when those who were meant to be a "kingdom of priests and a holy nation" failed to fulfill their corporate calling. The institution of kings was established when the people rejected the Creator-King as their ruler. The King therefore raised up individual voices—the prophets—who called upon the kings, priests, and people to change their ways and come back into alignment with him.

The prophets would begin their assignments by saying something like, "The word of the Lord came to me." Where does the word of the Lord come from? It comes from his Spirit. The Spirit would come upon the prophet, and the prophet would tell the king and the priests to correct themselves so they could correct the nation.

In other words, the prophet's job was to bring the earthly king back to the Creator-King so the king could execute the heavenly government's justice and help bring the nation back to the law and ways of the Creator-King. He was also to bring the priests back in alignment so they could help bring the people and nation back in alignment. In this way, the nation could return to being the prototype of the kingdom of heaven. The nation could then correct the *nations* of the world, for the ultimate purpose of redeeming the whole earth.

The prophets manifested the influence of the kingdom on earth in many ways. For example, because the prophet Elijah was submitted to the King, the heavenly government used him to bring back to life the son of a woman who was also submitted to the kingdom. We should not really be surprised at this particular administration of the kingdom, since the King's Spirit originally gave life to humanity and can also restore that life. The heavenly government was manifested in the life of the prophet Daniel when he received special communication through the Governor regarding the future of the Israelite people and when he escaped harm after being thrown into a den of ravenous lions. His "miracle" of preservation was, again, an example of the dominion of the kingdom of heaven over the earth.

However, how did the leaders and people usually react to the prophets? They would ignore, criticize, threaten, or kill them! Eventually, the people were so disobedient as a nation that they were perpetually unaligned; the result was that the Spirit left the temple prior to the people's captivity in Babylon. The Israelites had only the trappings of their old way of life. The prototype nation was essentially gone, setting up the next phase of the plan for the complete restoration of the kingdom on earth.

The King spoke through his prophets, saying, "I'm not going to keep sending word to you through other people. I'm going to come there myself to bring you back to me!"

GOVERNMENTAL MESSAGES ABOUT THE COMING KING WHO WOULD RESTORE THE GOVERNOR

The entire Old Testament is therefore about the repetition of the promise of the Governor's return, and the evidence of heavenly kingdom influence selectively manifested through the prototype nation and individuals who were submitted to the kingdom. Over the centuries, specific prophets, as well as other leaders such as Moses and David, spoke messages from the King announcing that he himself would reestablish his kingdom in the colony of earth, paving the way for the restoration of the Governor to humanity. For example, the prophet Isaiah said,

> For to us a child is born, to us a son is given, and the government will be on his shoulders. And he will be called Wonderful Counselor, Mighty God, Everlasting Father, Prince of Peace. Of the increase of his government and peace there will be no end. He will reign on David's throne and over his kingdom, establishing and upholding it with justice and righteousness from that time on and forever.

The King of the eternal, invisible kingdom was going to reclaim his property. When the colony was regained, he would set up his government on earth again and recommission his Spirit as Governor once more. Jesus told a parable about himself that describes the King's desire to implement his plan of extending his influence on earth, and of the resistance of most the earth's inhabitants to him until he himself came to rectify the situation:

> There was a landowner who planted a vineyard. He put a wall around it, dug a winepress in it and built a watchtower. Then he rented the vineyard to some farmers and went away on a journey.

When the harvest time approached, he sent his servants to the tenants to collect his fruit. The tenants seized his servants; they beat one, killed another, and stoned a third. Then he sent other servants to them, more than the first time, and the tenants treated them the same way. Last of all, he sent his son to them. "They will respect my son," he said. But when the tenants saw the son, they said to each other, "This is the heir. Come, let's kill him and take his inheritance." So they took him and threw him out of the vineyard and killed him. Therefore, when the owner of the vineyard comes, what will he do to those tenants?... The kingdom of God will be...given to a people who will produce its fruit.

THE MANDATE OF THE COMING KING

The last book of the Old Testament ends with the prophet Malachi giving this message from the heavenly government about the coming King of heaven: "He will turn the hearts of the fathers to their children, and the hearts of the children to their fathers." This was the mandate of the Offspring, whom the prophets referred to as the "Messiah," to reconcile the children of Adam and Eve to their Creator-King. When this was accomplished, the Governor could be restored to his earthly residence within them.

THE GOVERNOR'S RETURN IS FOR ALL HUMANITY

The prophet Joel gave one of the major messages from the heavenly kingdom regarding the Governor's return:

Afterward, I will pour out my Spirit on all people. Your sons and daughters will prophesy, your old men will dream dreams, your young men will see visions. Even on my servants, both men and women, I will pour out my Spirit in those days.

Joel was saying, in effect, "I see a day coming when we aren't going to have to read or study the law in order to know how to obey the King because his Spirit will come upon young and old, and they will obey the King as naturally as they formerly disobeyed him." No longer would there be a need for "selective rulership," with only certain individuals being influenced by the Governor. All of humanity had lost the Spirit, and Joel was saying the

Spirit would be poured out on "all people"—male, female, Israelite and non-Israelite, free and slave. Earthly prejudices related to gender, race, or social status would disappear in the face of the Governor's return.

The Holy Spirit is not just meant for people of a certain "religion" or nationality. The whole world lost the presence of the Governor within them, and the King wants everyone in the world to receive him into their lives again through the provision of the Offspring. The Governor is the key to life for *all* of humanity.

THE ERA OF THE KING'S COMING

The idea of the Spirit's coming upon the *people* probably seemed incredible to the Israelites when they heard Joel's message. In their experience, the Holy Spirit would only come upon the priests, the prophets, and some of the kings. Or, he would dwell between the cherubim on the mercy seat in the Holy of Holies in the temple. Joel referred to the time of the Spirit's coming as "the day of the Lord." The word "day" in this context means "era" or "age." Therefore, the day of the Lord would be the era or the time when the King came to earth.

The word "Lord" here is the Hebrew word for "self-Existent or Eternal" one.[3] The message of these prophets was, "Animal sacrifices and other rituals can't restore humanity to its relationship with the King, so the King himself is coming." When he came to earth, his Spirit would also return. The Governor would come upon young and old men, and young and old women. More than that, he would once more be able to dwell *within* humanity.

The prophet Malachi was the last prophet to promise the King's return before the King himself came. The heavenly government gave him this message:

> "See, I will send my messenger, who will prepare the way before me.
> Then suddenly the Lord you are seeking will come to his temple;
> the messenger of the covenant, whom you desire, will come," says
> the Lord Almighty.

The first messenger mentioned would *prepare* the way. The second messenger, "the messenger of the covenant," was the one who would "turn the hearts of the fathers to their children, and the hearts of the children to their fathers." This messenger was referred to as "the Lord you are seeking." What was his covenant message? It was the restoration of the Spirit to humanity, which had been promised since the initial rebellion.

ANNOUNCING THE ARRIVAL OF THE KING

When we turn the page of the Scriptures from Malachi in the Old Testament to Matthew in the New Testament, we encounter the messenger who prepared the way for the King's coming:

> In those days John the Baptist came, preaching in the Desert of Judea and saying, "Repent, for the kingdom of heaven is near." This is he who was spoken of through the prophet Isaiah: "A voice of one calling in the desert, 'Prepare the way for the Lord, make straight paths for him.'"

"The kingdom of heaven is near." In other words, the King's government was imminent because the King had come to earth. What was the theme of this message? *The Governor.* John said, "I baptize you with water for repentance. But after me will come one who is more powerful than I, whose sandals I am not fit to carry. He will baptize you with the Holy Spirit and with fire."

The King would *baptize* them with his Spirit, thus *aligning them with the kingdom.* The Spirit's coming would no longer be a temporary appearance but a permanent one. The Governor would be like a consuming fire, burning out every false mind-set and philosophy that alienated the citizens from the heavenly kingdom. He would correct all their confusion and satisfy all their hunger to know and fulfill their purpose in life. At last, they would be permanently reconnected to the King and his kingdom. The earth would be a colony of holiness and power again because its inhabitants would finally have the Spirit of holiness and power living within them once more.

CHAPTER FOUR STUDY QUESTIONS

QUESTIONS FOR REFLECTION

1. Are the Old Testament and New Testament connected? In what way(s)?

2. Do you generally cooperate with the way God is working in your life, or do you resist it? Why?

EXPLORING PRINCIPLES AND PURPOSES

3. What is the principal purpose of the redemptive program of the King in his dealings with humanity throughout human history?

4. What implications would the restoration of the Spirit have regarding the purpose for which human beings were created? (p. 73)

5. All the situations, people, and programs in the Old Testament serve what five ends?

   (1)

   (2)

   (3)

   (4)

   (5)

6. Why was the King's Spirit unable to return to the King's children?

7. Briefly describe the three stages of the King's plan to fully restore the Governor to earth.

    (1)

    (2)

    (3)

8. What is the identity of the Offspring who would come to earth, defeat Lucifer, reconcile the King's children to their Father, and restore the Governor?

9. Even before the coming of the Offspring, what always accompanied the Governor's presence on earth through the submission of individuals to the heavenly government?

10. What is the definition of a miracle, from the point of view of the heavenly kingdom?

11. What major purposes of the King's plan would occur through the birth of Abraham and Sarah's son, Isaac?

    (1)
    (2)

12. What does the word *righteousness* refer to?

13. What was the special calling of the Israelites in the King's plan?

14. Describe the respective functions of "kingdom" and "priests."

15. The Israelite people became perpetually unaligned with the King and were taken captive by Babylon, essentially ending the prototype nation. What was the next step in the King's plan to redeem humanity and fully restore the Governor to earth?

16. How did the King communicate this extraordinary plan to the inhabitants of earth?

17. The prophet Joel's message from the heavenly kingdom indicated... [choose one]

    (a) the King wants all people of the earth to receive the Governor.

    (b) the Governor will return to dwell in young and old, male and female.

    (c) the Governor will enable people to obey the King naturally.

    (d) all of the above

18. Why did Joel refer to the time of the Spirit's coming as "the day of the LORD" (Joel 2:11)?

19. In the New Testament, what did John the Baptist mean when he said, "The kingdom of heaven is near" (Matthew 3:2)?

20. John the Baptist said that when the King came to earth, he would "baptize [people] with the Holy Spirit and with fire" (Matthew 3:11). What would the King accomplish by this?

APPLYING THE PRINCIPLES OF KINGDOM LIVING

THINKING IT OVER

+ Has your perspective on the Old Testament changed through reading chapter four and doing this study? If so, in what ways?

+ The King said through the prophet Jeremiah, "I will put my law in their minds and write it on their hearts. I will be their God, and they will be my people" (Jeremiah 31:33). Are you still trying to serve God in your own strength through rules and regulations that are not really a part of your nature? Or are you living by the nature of the King planted within your heart, through the power of his Spirit?

ACTING ON IT

+ Dr. Munroe defined personal holiness as being "one with yourself." If you are truly holy, you don't say something and then do something contrary to it. Your public behavior is the same as your private behavior. Think about your own life and list areas in which you need to become consistent in what you think, say, and do.

+ In the "Questions for Reflection" section at the beginning of this study, you were asked whether you felt you were cooperating with the way God is working in your life, or resisting it. Write down any ways in which you are resisting his work in your life and make a conscious decision to yield to his purposes.

PRAYING ABOUT IT

+ Review the list you wrote concerning areas of personal holiness you need to work on. Ask God to help you become more consistent in these areas through the guidance and power of His Spirit.

+ We learned through this study that God's purposes for humanity have not changed. He still desires that every human being function as a priest—continually aligned with him—and as a ruler—exercising dominion on the earth in his behalf through his Spirit. Ask God to enable you to fulfill these purposes in your life.

"I will pour out my Spirit on all people."
—Joel 2:28

PART 2

THE RETURN OF THE GOVERNOR

FIVE

THE REBIRTH OF A KINGDOM

THE GREATEST MOTIVATION OF THE HUMAN SPIRIT IS TO CONTROL ITS ENVIRONMENT.

The King's goal was to cause his children to be integrated, set apart, and devoted to him—so that his Spirit could live within them once more. This would be the work of the Offspring, the one called the Messiah by the prophets. The Offspring was first mentioned in Genesis 3 and was revealed by the prophets Isaiah, Malachi, and others to be the King of heaven himself. While the First, or Old, Testament emphasizes the promise of the coming King, the New Testament reveals the rebirth of the kingdom on earth through his arrival.

The rebirth of the kingdom signified the recolonization of earth. Recolonization is unheard of in human history, or is at least very rare. Once a people declare independence, they don't go back to the home country. The plan that the King was unfolding was therefore unprecedented.

THE BIRTH OF THE KING ON EARTH

The King, of course, needed to remain in the heavenly kingdom as its ruler and sustainer. At the same time, he had to come to earth to provide for the return of the Governor. The Spirit of the King was directly involved in his coming to earth. Luke the physician, the writer of the gospel bearing his name, wrote,

> God sent the angel Gabriel to Nazareth, a town in Galilee, to a virgin pledged to be married to a man named Joseph, a descendent of David. The virgin's name was Mary. The angel went to her and said, "Greetings, you who are highly favored! The Lord is with you." Mary was greatly troubled at his words and wondered what

kind of greeting this might be. But the angel said to her, "Do not be afraid, Mary, you have found favor with God."

The angel's statement, "You have found favor with God," shows us that Mary was yielded to the heavenly government and the purposes of the King, and this is why she was chosen for this crucial assignment in the intervention of the heavenly kingdom on earth. The angel continued,

> You will be with child and give birth to a son, and you are to give him the name Jesus. He will be great and will be called the Son of the Most High. The Lord God will give him the throne of his father David, and he will reign over the house of Jacob forever; his kingdom will never end. "How will this be," Mary asked the angel, "since I am a virgin?" The angel answered, "*The Holy Spirit will come upon you, and the power of the Most High will overshadow you.* So *the holy one to be born will be called the Son of God....* For nothing is impossible with God." "I am the Lord's servant," Mary answered. "May it be to me as you have said."

Again, we see evidence of Mary's submission to the heavenly government: "I am the Lord's servant.... May it be to me as you have said."

In this passage is a fact of vital significance: the Spirit conceived God the Son, or the King-Son, whose earthly name was Jesus, in the womb of Mary. Mary was what we might call a surrogate mother for the eternal and invisible God's entrance into the physical world as a human being. Also, the King-Son was filled with the Spirit when he was conceived. This means that the Governor returned to earth at this time within the person of Jesus. The Governor was resident in the body of Jesus until the rest of humanity could be prepared to receive him as well, through Jesus's provision. At that time, the King-Son would reappoint the Governor to the earth in order to restore kingdom influence throughout the world and to give back kingdom citizenship to humanity.

The King-Son was both fully divine (as God the Son) and fully human (as the man Jesus). Yet he was not infected by the rebellious nature of humanity. The womb of a woman is designed in such a way that the blood of a mother and her unborn child never mix. Jesus's blood was pure; his life was pure. As we read in the third book of Moses, "The life of every creature is its blood." Like Adam before the rebellion, Jesus and everything about him was set apart and devoted to the King-Father.

THE GOVERNOR GAVE THE KING SO THE KING COULD GIVE THE GOVERNOR

The King-Son had to be born of the Spirit and filled with the Spirit, so that he could deliver the Governor to the people of earth in fulfillment of the promise. John the Baptist announced to the world the arrival of the King-Son who would restore the Spirit, and he said about Jesus, "The one who *comes from heaven* is above all.... For the one whom God has sent speaks the words of God, for *God gives the Spirit without limit* [to him]," and "He will baptize you with the Holy Spirit and with fire." Jesus told his disciples,

> If you love me, you will obey what I command. And I will ask the Father, and he will give you another Counselor to be with you forever—the Spirit of truth. The world cannot accept him, because it neither sees him nor knows him. But you know him, for he lives with you and will be in you. I will not leave you as orphans; I will come to you. Before long, the world will not see me anymore, but you will see me. Because I live, you also will live. On that day you will realize that I am in my Father, and you are in me, and I am in you.

Therefore, *the Governor gave the King-Son to the earth so the King-Son could send the Governor to the earth after he returned to the heavenly kingdom.* They worked in harmony to achieve this ultimate purpose.

THE KING-SON WAS COMPLETELY FILLED WITH THE GOVERNOR

The King-Son not only was filled with the Spirit at his conception, but he also continued to be filled with the Spirit throughout his entire lifetime. As John the Baptist said, "God gives the Spirit without limit [to him]." This was the first time a human being was filled with the Holy Spirit since before the rebellion of Adam and Eve. The Holy Spirit within Jesus was limitless in presence and power.

In preparation for the King's appearance on earth, John had been baptizing people who desired to be realigned with the kingdom. Then, just before Jesus began his public ministry, he also went to John for baptism.

The next day John saw Jesus coming toward him and said, "Look, the Lamb of God, who takes away the sin of the world! This is the one I meant when I said, 'A man who comes after me has surpassed me because he was before me.' I myself did not know him, but the reason I came baptizing with water was that he might be revealed to Israel." Then John gave this testimony: "*I saw the Spirit come down from heaven as a dove and remain on him.* I would not have known him, except that the one who sent me to baptize with water told me, 'The man on whom you see the Spirit come down and remain is he who will baptize with the Holy Spirit.' I have seen and I testify that this is the Son of God."

John made these declarations about Jesus: (1) he was the one who would take away the sin of the world (making it possible for the citizens to be fully aligned with the heavenly kingdom); (2) the Spirit came down from heaven and *remained* on him (Jesus had the total sanction of the King-Father); and (3) he was the Son of God (he came directly from the King-Father and was one with him). Paul wrote, "In Christ all the fullness of the Deity lives in bodily form." God the Father, God the Son, and God the Spirit are one. The King expresses himself in three unique dimensions, which he revealed in the plan to restore humanity.

Jesus therefore possesses a dual nature—he is fully God and fully human. God the Father is the King, and Jesus Christ is the King who came in human form. The New Testament book of John says, "In the beginning was the Word, and the Word was *with* God, and the Word *was* God." Yet the King's coming as a man wasn't just a convenient way in which to coordinate his rule on both heaven and earth. His mission was to restore holiness to men and women so they could again be a suitable environment for the Holy Spirit to dwell in. As we will see, the only way he could do this was to become a human being himself.

THE ERA OF THE KING ON EARTH

In a previous chapter, I stated that Jesus began his public ministry by saying, "The time has come....The kingdom of God is near," and I posed these questions:

+ What "time" was he speaking about? And why then?

+ What was the nature of the kingdom he was referring to?

The "time" was the "day of the LORD," or the era when the King-Son would come to earth to restore the Governor to humanity. The purpose and nature of the kingdom was (1) the reconciliation of the earth's inhabitants to the King-Father, so that it was possible once more for human beings to be his children, and (2) the reign of heaven returning to earth through the Governor's presence and power operating in the lives of the King's children.

The inhabitants of the colony of earth had been ransacking the King's territory—stealing, lying, abusing, killing one another, living their lives outside the nature of the kingdom. Therefore, as the Son and heir of the King of heaven, Jesus was coming to reclaim his Father's territory. His arrival on earth marked "the day of the LORD" prophesied by Joel.

The King-Son came to reclaim his Father's property two thousand years ago as a baby born in Bethlehem. Christmas is not about a beggar coming; it's about an owner arriving. He came to reclaim the earth because, as the psalmist David, king of Israel, wrote, "The earth is the Lord's, and everything in it." He came to recover all of creation as its legal owner.

The King-Son didn't come to earth to plead with Lucifer to return his property. He treated him as a thief, saying, "The thief comes only to steal and kill and destroy; I have come that they may have life, and have it to the full." He also said, "How can one enter a strong man's house and plunder his goods, unless he first binds the strong man? And then he will plunder his house." The King-Son came to *bind* the strongman, Lucifer, so he could retake the house and give it back to the children of the household. Therefore, the man Jesus was the fulfillment of the King-Father's remarkable plan to send his Son to earth to restore the heavenly government here.

Paul called Jesus the "last," or Second, Adam. The King-Son came to fulfill what the first Adam had failed to do. He lived a life in total harmony with the King-Father, his kingdom, and the kingdom's purposes on earth. Jesus taught his disciples to pray, "Our Father in heaven, hallowed be your name, *your kingdom come, your will be done on earth as it is in heaven.*"

As the Second Adam, Jesus came to rescue us from being dominated by the kingdom of darkness led by Lucifer and to restore us to the home kingdom. He went through his life and death on earth so we could be reconciled to the King as his children.

Through Jesus, human beings can be restored as vice governors in the world, earthly kings who rule under the direction of the Spirit of the King—the Royal Governor. The kingdom of heaven is therefore *a family of kings*. This is what the nation of Israel was meant to demonstrate as a prototype: "a kingdom of priests and a holy nation." Although the Governor is equal to the King-Father and the King-Son, the Scriptures never refer to him as a King in relation to humanity, but as our Counselor or Comforter. This is because his role is to sustain and perpetuate the will and work of the heavenly kingdom in the lives of the inhabitants of earth.

THE KING-SON REINTRODUCED THE KINGDOM OF HEAVEN TO HUMANITY

Jesus's first declaration in his public ministry was essentially his mission statement: "Repent, for the kingdom of heaven is near." He continually repeated this same message for three-and-a-half years during his entire ministry on earth. Throughout the written record of his life in the New Testament writings of Matthew, Mark, Luke, and John, we find him restating his central theme of *the kingdom of heaven*. Sometimes, he would use the phrase *the kingdom of God*. While these phrases are essentially the same, you could say that the kingdom of heaven is the *place*, while the kingdom of God is the *influence*. The kingdom of heaven is the headquarters, the invisible country where the King-Father resides. The kingdom of God is the influence of that country on its territories. Here is a sample of the King-Son's other statements concerning the kingdom:

- ✦ Jesus went throughout Galilee, teaching in their synagogues, preaching the good news of the kingdom, and healing every disease and sickness among the people.

- "But if I drive out demons by the Spirit of God, then the kingdom of God has come upon you."

- "The kingdom of heaven is like a king who wanted to settle accounts with his servants…."

- "The kingdom of heaven is like a landowner who went out early in the morning to hire men to work in his vineyard…."

- "The kingdom of God will be…given to a people who will produce its fruit."

Lucifer (also called the devil or Satan) knew that the King-Son had come to overthrow him to restore the heavenly kingdom on earth. He therefore tried to tempt Jesus away from his mission by appealing to his natural human desire to exercise dominion over the earth. Notice that Lucifer tried to get Jesus to substitute the kingdoms of the world for the kingdom of heaven, which is basically the same thing with which he had tempted Adam and Eve. This would allow Lucifer to maintain his oppressive domination and destruction of the earth. Yet the King-Son was totally loyal to the kingdom. He countered Lucifer's temptation by rebuking him with the words of the King-Father, which were first given to the Israelites after they came out of Egypt. The New Testament book of Matthew records,

> The devil took him to a very high mountain and showed him all the kingdoms of the world and their splendor. "All this I will give you," he said, "if you will bow down and worship me." Jesus said to him, "Away from me, Satan! For it is written: 'Worship the Lord your God, and serve him only.'" Then the devil left him.

BAPTISM INTO KINGDOM PHILOSOPHY

Jesus's temptation by the devil occurred right after his baptism by John. Many people are confused about the true nature of baptism and why Jesus himself was baptized. While baptism is treated as a religious ritual by many people, it is actually a very practical act that is related to the will of the King and his desire for the colony of earth.

CHANGING ONE'S THINKING AND LIFESTYLE

At the time Jesus lived on earth, various rabbis, teachers, and groups (such as the Sadducees) baptized their followers. Baptism in this context meant you were publicly declaring you believed in a particular teacher and his philosophy. In fact, to a large degree, this was the significance of the baptism of John, which John referred to as a "baptism of repentance." Our contemporary connotation of the word *repentance* doesn't really convey John's meaning. In its essence, repentance does not mean crying or wailing over wrongdoing. It simply means to change your mind, to reverse your way of thinking and acting.[1] When a person was baptized, he was signaling that he was changing his thinking and actions and aligning them with the views and life of the teacher he had committed himself to follow.

This type of teacher-student relationship was not uncommon. The Old Testament makes references to "the company of the prophets," also called the "schools of the prophets." These particular prophets were closely associated with the well-known prophets Elijah and Elisha, supporting them and learning from them. In New Testament times, the Pharisees, the Sadducees, and the Herodians had disciples. Outside the biblical world, we note similar teacher-learner arrangements among the Greek philosophers Socrates, Plato, and Aristotle and their followers. A philosopher, of course, is someone who sets forth his own ideas about life. Philosophers attract people who want to learn their ideas and imitate their lifestyles, and these become their students or disciples. The Greek word we translate as *disciple* means "learner" or "pupil."[2] Disciples were personally trained by their masters in the masters' philosophies and belief systems, perhaps traveling with them as they learned to think and act like their masters.

JOINING A SCHOOL OF THOUGHT

When you became a student of a philosopher or other teacher, you joined what is called his school of thought. Schools were not originally associated with buildings. They were essentially the ideas unique to a teacher. They were the teacher's philosophical concepts and ways of thinking, which he passed along to his followers.

From this perspective, the significance of baptism is not the water or even the act of being baptized—it has to do with the *transformation* of your way of thinking and living. When you were baptized in the name of your master teacher, you were saying, "I am choosing you above every other available teacher, philosopher, rabbi, and leader, and I am publicly declaring that I am submitting to your school of thought. I'm going to be associated with you *only*, so that whenever people see me, they're going to know, 'He belongs to that teacher.'"

As I mentioned, at the time of Jesus, there were a number of teachers and philosophers, and all had their own schools of thought and their own disciples. In that culture, a man couldn't begin such a school until he was thirty years old because this was the age at which a young man could be officially designated as a master teacher.

Therefore, when the Creator of heaven and earth himself came to earth as a man, he entered the culture of the day and presented himself in a way that the people would understand the life-changing nature of his message and its requirement of total commitment to him. It was at age thirty that Jesus began his public ministry, became the ultimate Master Teacher, and welcomed those who desired to follow him. *The kingdom* was the embodiment of his teaching.

JESUS'S MESSAGE WAS IN HARMONY WITH JOHN'S MESSAGE

Note that John the Baptist had been presenting the same message about the kingdom. Jesus was fully aware of John's message when he went to him for baptism. Many people are at first surprised to read of the King-Son submitting to a master teacher for baptism. Yet he did this to demonstrate to the people of the world that his teaching was not independent of John's; rather, he was in total harmony with it. In fact, Jesus himself was the *fulfillment* of the teaching of John, who, as the faithful prophet of the King-Father, was proclaiming the message of the kingdom and preparing the way for the King-Son's appearance in the world.

John had been gaining a number of disciples, and when people came to him with a sincere desire to repent (to change their thinking and lifestyle from the kingdom of darkness to the kingdom of heaven), he baptized them. Yet when Jesus went to him for baptism, John was taken aback and said, in essence, "You should be the teacher, not me!" John recognized Jesus as the King who would send the Governor to earth. In fact, John had said to the people earlier, "After me will come one more powerful than I, the thongs of whose sandals I am not worthy to stoop down and untie. I baptize you with water, but he will *baptize you with the Holy Spirit.*"

Jesus, however, replied to John, "Let it be so now; it is proper for us to do this to fulfill all righteousness." He was saying, "I understand your reluctance to act as master teacher to me. However, in order to demonstrate to the world that I am aligned with the kingdom of heaven, I need to be identified with it through baptism. I need to publicly declare that I belong to the school of the kingdom of heaven, that I am fully integrated with the mind and ways of the kingdom."

THE KINGDOM SCHOOL TRANSFERRED TO JESUS

When a master teacher was no longer able to teach, he would decide which of his disciples would succeed him. Whoever was chosen to take his place would automatically gain his students. Jesus had to be a part of John's school in order to take over leadership of it. And John turned the whole school over to Jesus; he released his disciples to him, indicating that Jesus was the one they should follow because he was the King who would restore them to the kingdom. The New Testament book of John records,

> The next day John was there again with two of his disciples. When he saw Jesus passing by, he said, "Look, the Lamb of God!" When the two disciples heard him say this, they followed Jesus. Turning around, Jesus saw them following and asked, "What do you want?" They said, "Rabbi" (which means Teacher), "where are you staying?" "Come," he replied, "and you will see." So they went and saw where he was staying, and spent that day with him. It was about the tenth hour. Andrew, Simon Peter's brother, was one of the two who heard what John had said and who had followed Jesus.

Most importantly, we should note that the King-Father had appointed Jesus as the ultimate Master Teacher of the kingdom school. After Jesus submitted to John's baptism to show that he was immersed in the philosophy of the kingdom and in alignment with it, what happened to him? The *Holy Spirit*—the Governor—descended on him. The New Testament book of Matthew says,

As soon as Jesus was baptized, he went up out of the water. At that moment heaven was opened, and he saw the Spirit of God descending like a dove and lighting on him. And a voice from heaven said, "This is my Son, whom I love; with him I am well pleased."

The King-Father was confirming, "This one has the Holy Spirit; he is my Son, and he is fully integrated with my thoughts and ways. He is the one who will restore my Spirit to the earth." Later on, the King-Father affirmed that Jesus was the one whom his disciples were to listen to above all others, when he said, as documented in the book of Mark and elsewhere in the New Testament, "This is my Son, whom I love. Listen to him!"

Jesus had many disciples, or students, but he chose twelve to be in full-time traveling work with him and to learn from him in an intense training relationship. Among these were the notable apostles Peter, James, and John. When Jesus called various of his disciples, saying, "Follow me," he was inviting them to join the school of the kingdom of heaven.

We are followers of Jesus when we have decided to identify with the life and message of the King-Son and submit to him as our Master Teacher. Jesus said, "No one can serve two masters. Either he will hate the one and love the other, or he will be devoted to the one and despise the other. You cannot serve both God and Money." Although this statement was about money, it also has broader application. In the context of baptism, it tells us, "You cannot be in two schools. You cannot have two philosophies that are in contradiction to one another."

BAPTISM WITH FIRE

Water baptism aligned and identified Jesus's followers with his kingdom teaching. But what had John meant when he said that Jesus would "baptize…with the *Holy Spirit* and with *fire*"? The baptism with the Holy Spirit, which we will talk about in more detail in later chapters, is the consummation of identification with the King and his kingdom, as well as a reception of the *power* of the heavenly kingdom. The Holy Spirit is the personification of the heavenly government. To be baptized in this way means you are immersed in kingdom philosophy and lifestyle, and that it has total influence over your thoughts and actions.

The word *philosophy* is derived from the Greek word *philosophos*, which is a combination of two smaller Greek words. *Philos* means "fond" or "beloved," and *sophos* means "wise." So *philosophos* means a fondness for or a love of wise things.[3] Disciples of kingdom philosophy are to fall in love with the mind and will of the King, so that his mind and will become theirs, and their actions mirror his. As the wise King Solomon wrote, "As a person thinks within himself, so he is."

This process of transformation into kingdom thinking and lifestyle is absolutely necessary because the Creator-King has declared this about the rebellious inhabitants of earth: "My thoughts are not your thoughts, neither are your ways my ways.... As the heavens are higher than the earth, so are my ways higher than your ways and my thoughts than your thoughts." Our thoughts and ways need to become realigned with the Creator-King's, and we do this by identifying completely with kingdom thinking, submitting to the Master of the kingdom, and being baptized into his power.

The way to fully live out the life of the kingdom, therefore, is to be baptized with the Spirit. We are to be totally submerged in the Creator-King's frame of reference and mind-set so that we always think his thoughts, live his thoughts, and manifest his life.

The New Testament book of Luke tells us that, following his baptism by John, Jesus was "full of the Holy Spirit,...and was led by the Spirit in the desert, where for forty days he was tempted by the devil." When he emerged from that experience, having overcome each temptation, Luke further records, "Jesus returned to Galilee in the power of the Spirit," and the book of Matthew adds, "From that time on Jesus began to preach, 'Repent, for the kingdom of heaven is near.'" The message of the kingdom and the fullness and power of the Spirit are intimately connected.

THE KING-SON DEMONSTRATED THE INFLUENCE OF THE KINGDOM ON EARTH

The King-Son not only spoke the message of the kingdom, but he also lived it out. His entire life on earth was evidence of kingdom rulership. Everything Jesus said or did was the administration of the King-Father's will through the power of the Governor within him. He spoke about this reality with statements such as these:

+ My teaching is not my own. It comes from him who sent me.

+ These words you hear are not my own; they belong to the Father who sent me.

+ My Father is always at his work to this very day, and I, too, am working.

+ I and the Father are one.

+ I tell you the truth, the Son can do nothing by himself; he can do only what he sees his Father doing, because whatever the Father does the Son also does. For the Father loves the Son and shows him all he does.

+ Do not believe me unless I do what my Father does. But if I do it, even though you do not believe me, believe the miracles, that you may know and understand that the Father is in me, and I in the Father.

+ If God were your Father, you would love me, for I came from God and now am here. I have not come on my own; but he sent me.

+ I came from the Father and entered the world; now I am leaving the world and going back to the Father.

In the Old Testament accounts we reviewed in the previous chapter, we saw that what we call miracles were actually evidence of kingdom influence on earth. The same thing applies to the miracles Jesus performed. The administration of the kingdom could be seen whenever Jesus healed someone who was sick (power over the effects of humanity's rebellion), delivered someone who was possessed by an agent of Lucifer (power over the kingdom of darkness), fed thousands by multiplying small amounts of food (power over the natural world), or raised people from the dead (power to give life). These acts were confirmation of heavenly dominion over the environment of earth; they were demonstrations of kingdom power over circumstances. Jesus was saying, in essence, "What you see is what the heavenly government is doing. I'm just manifesting it."

THE KING-SON DIED TO REDEEM AND RESTORE HUMAN BEINGS TO THE KING-FATHER AND HIS KINGDOM

The King-Son's mission on earth was not only to deliver the message and demonstrate the influence of the kingdom, but also to provide a way for human beings to reenter the kingdom and be reconciled to the King-Father. The children's separation from the Father because of their rebellion had to be addressed. And the only way their holiness (integrity or internal wholeness and devotion to the Father) could be restored was through a sacrifice.

As we saw, the Old Testament animal sacrifices of the tabernacle and temple were only temporary. Animal sacrifices were not equitable blood payment for the rebellion and the culture of hatred and death that human beings had brought to earth. Animal sacrifice did not have the power to change the perpetually evil hearts of the world's inhabitants. Only human blood could make restitution for the rebellion and bloodshed of humanity. Instead of making the people pay for their rebellion with their own blood, however, the Father sent the Son to earth as a human being to pay for it with his blood. The Son took the punishment for all the inhabitants of earth, which allowed them to be reconciled to the kingdom. This was the ultimate reason for his incarnation.

The King-Son could reconcile the inhabitants to the King-Father because he was holy. Again, in his humanity, Jesus was like other human beings in all ways except one—he had no rebellion in him or double-mindedness toward the kingdom. He was fully integrated, devoted, and set apart for the King-Father. He lived within a human body because he wanted to go through every aspect of human experience—he desired to feel what we feel and experience everything about being human, without the rebellion. **Jesus demonstrated by his life what it meant to be a human being with the Governor living within. He was true humanity rightly related to the King-Father and his kingdom.**

Jesus's death on the cross at the place called Calvary (meaning "Skull") was the plan of the Father to provide for the return of the Governor. It was not a mistake, but part of the program. The earthly temple with its sacrifices would no longer be needed because the heavenly temple had arrived in Jesus's own body; the Holy Spirit was present within *him*. Again, Jesus was able to be the ultimate sacrifice because he was fully aligned with the King and lived a perfect life. Jesus explained the nature of his death before he died:

> The reason my Father loves me is that I lay down my life—only to take it up again. No one takes it from me, but I lay it down of my own accord. I have authority to lay it down and authority to take it up again. This command I received from my Father.

The King-Son laid down his life in payment for the rebellion of all humanity, past and present. When this was paid, the Father gave him authority to take up his life again, and he was raised from the dead. The Author of life chose to die because of his love for the human beings whom he had created; he desired to rescue them from the kingdom of darkness so they could live within the kingdom of heaven once more. Paul described our entrance to the kingdom through the King-Son's sacrifice as walking in "newness of life":

> Do you not know that as many of us as were baptized into Christ Jesus were baptized into His death? Therefore we were buried with Him through baptism into death, that just as Christ was raised from the dead by the glory of the Father, even so we also should walk in newness of life.

Some people wish they could go back to the day Jesus died and prevent his death. We would all want to spare anyone from that kind of death. However, his dying was necessary to fulfill the Father's restoration plan. Jesus's death wasn't forced upon him; he chose it for the express purpose of saving the world and releasing the Governor to the earth again. Once more, before he was crucified, Jesus made his choice very clear, saying,

> I am the good shepherd; I know my sheep and my sheep know me—just as the Father knows me and I know the Father—and I lay down my life for the sheep. I have other sheep that are not of this sheep pen. I must bring them also. They too will listen to my voice, and there shall be one flock and one shepherd.

Jesus told his followers beforehand that he was going to die to pay for the rebellion of humanity, even though they didn't comprehend it at the time. He said, "This is what is written [was predicted by the King's prophet]: The Christ will suffer and rise from the dead on the third day."

Jesus therefore wasn't killed as a tragic mistake. He gave up his life in sacrifice so we could be cleansed vessels for the Governor to live in. He kept moving forward with the restoration plan until everything was set in place for our reconciliation with the Father. Just before he died, he said, "It is finished." The enemies of Jesus didn't finish him. He gave up his life when he was finished with his mission. Just before his arrest, he prayed,

> Father, the time has come. Glorify your Son, that your Son may glorify you. For you granted him authority over all people that he might give eternal life to all those you have given him. Now this is eternal life: that they may know you, the only true God, and Jesus Christ, whom you have sent. I have brought you glory on earth by completing the work you gave me to do. And now, Father, glorify me in your presence with the glory I had with you before the world began.

Again, Jesus wasn't a helpless victim of jealous enemies. He is the King of glory who overcame both sin and death. Notice that he prayed to the Father, "I have brought you glory on earth by completing the work you gave me to do." The Old Testament prophet Habakkuk had foretold, "The earth will be filled with the knowledge of the glory of the LORD, as the waters cover the sea." Because Jesus completed the work of restoration, the glory (nature) of the kingdom of heaven was released and began to spread throughout the earth.

THE KING-SON DESTROYED THE SPIRIT OF INDEPENDENCE AND REBELLION IN THE COLONY

Jesus's death at Calvary, the blood that he shed on the cross, and his resurrection from the dead were required in order to break the spirit of rebellion in humanity. I use the word *spirit* because rebellion is really an attitude or nature within every human being. It's something we're born with; it is ingrained within us. This spirit is antagonistic to the kingdom of heaven. It couldn't be wished away or ignored. It had to be *broken*. And Jesus did break this power, allowing the earth's inhabitants to instead yield to the Holy Spirit. Paul wrote, "For the sinful nature desires what is contrary to the Spirit, and the Spirit what is contrary to the sinful nature. They are in conflict with each other, so that you do not do what you want. But if you are led by the Spirit, you are not under law."

Breaking a spirit of independence is very difficult, but this is what Jesus accomplished. He gave us the ability to say to the Father, as he himself said at the most difficult point in his earthly life, "Not my will, but yours be done." He provided for the spirit of rebellion to be replaced with a spirit of yieldedness to the kingdom. He gave us the ability to obey the will of the Father. In fact, Jesus said that submitting to him was the same thing as submitting to the Father, since he and the Father are one. "If you love me," he said to his followers, "you will obey what I command. And I will ask the Father, and he will give you another Counselor [the Governor] to be with you forever."

Can you imagine anyone in American politics telling the voters, "Do everything I say"? They would think he was crazy because we're taught not to trust anyone like that. But Jesus came to bring back the *perfect* government. In the kingdom of heaven, trust in the King-Son is the only way to experience life. In the kingdom of heaven, independence from the King-Son brings death, as Jesus explained to his disciples:

Remain in me, and I will remain in you. No branch can bear fruit by itself; it must remain in the vine. Neither can you bear fruit unless you remain in me. I am the vine; you are the branches. If a man remains in me and I in him, he will bear much fruit; apart from me you can do nothing. If anyone does not remain in me, he is like a branch that is thrown away and withers; such branches are picked up, thrown into the fire and burned.

Jesus was destroying the idea of independence and rebellion, showing that this leads to deadly consequences. In contrast, dependence on him leads to life because "apart from [him] you can do nothing." We are to be dependent on him so that he can help us be what we were created to be. Paul discovered this truth firsthand. Jesus told him, "My grace is sufficient for you, for my power is made perfect in weakness." Paul's response was to say, "When I am weak, then I am strong [in the power of the kingdom]."

The key, then, to being freed from the grip of rebellion, restored to wholeness and devotion to the King-Father, and released in the power and life of the Spirit is to acknowledge and receive the cleansing that the King-Son accomplished for us when he paid for our rebellion through his death. His was the ultimate sacrifice for the rebellious nature of humanity. It was a sacrifice for *all* of humanity. It is available for *all* people. Yet each human being must make a personal decision to commit to Jesus's kingdom school and enter into the kingdom by accepting his sacrifice to break the spirit of rebellion and by desiring to realign with the King. As he does this, he will receive the nature of the kingdom within.

"HE LIVES WITH YOU AND WILL BE IN YOU"

This brings us back to what Jesus told his followers about the Governor, the Spirit of the King: "He lives with you and will be in you." Jesus's followers had seen the demonstration of the Governor's power lived out in his life. The Governor's works were manifested on the earth, but no other human being besides Jesus had the Spirit living within. Jesus was promising the disciples that, through his sacrifice, the Governor would be coming back to live within them, also, just as had been promised since Genesis 3 when the rebellion occurred. This would not only *align* them with the nature and thinking of the kingdom, but it would also *empower* them to live it out just as Jesus had lived it out on earth. Soon, the Governor would be taking up his official residence again in the citizens of the kingdom on earth, as the prophet Joel had foretold.

THE KING-SON'S ULTIMATE REASON FOR COMING TO EARTH

After his resurrection, Jesus told his disciples, "I am going to send you what my Father has promised." The King-Son was restating the essential reason for his ministry. This next statement may shock a few people, but I believe it is vital for us to understand: the promise of the Father was not Jesus's sufferings, his death on Calvary, or even his resurrection. Over the centuries, the Christian church has emphasized these aspects of Jesus's ministry to the point that I believe the ultimate reason he endured them has been obscured.

Through the years, people—especially religious people—have changed the meaning of the Father's promise to humanity. Christianity has become the celebration of what Jesus did rather than a reception of the reason He did it. We have declared a message that Jesus never gave. We've changed the promise into one of leaving this earth and going to heaven, when what we're called to is restored *dominion* over the earth through the indwelling Spirit.

The result is that we have worshipped Calvary, rather than benefiting from it. Jesus's sufferings, death, and resurrection were the means to an end—the reconciliation of humanity to the King, and, ultimately, the restoration of the Spirit to humanity. They were not ends in themselves. We've made the process the purpose. The promise of the Father was the reappointment of the Spirit *as a result* of these things. The entire reason for the King-Son's coming into the world was to break the stronghold of Lucifer, destroy the grip of rebellion from human beings, and reconnect them to their King-Father so that the Governor could be restored to them.

The Spirit is what all human beings need in order to be realigned with the King and fulfill their purpose on earth. We should note that John the Baptist never emphasized the blood or death or resurrection of Jesus. He emphasized the Holy Spirit, because John was expressing the specific reason for his coming: "He will baptize you with the Holy Spirit and with fire." Humanity is not in need of a "religion." We don't need rituals and traditions. We need this promise of the Father to be a reality in our lives.

We must come to truly understand that the Holy Spirit is the heavenly government personified. He is the source of the power of the kingdom in our lives. The Old Testament experience of the priests and prophets was only a shadow of what was to come. At that time, the Holy Spirit couldn't live in human beings; he could only be among them. But now, Jesus was saying, "The Spirit of truth...lives *with* you and will be *in* you."

As I said earlier, every miracle of Jesus, every healing, every act of dominion—whether it was walking on water, casting out demons, or cleansing a leper—was not for entertainment or for making an impression; nor was it for the purpose of creating a religion or providing interesting material for preaching. These things were for the purpose of producing *evidence* to the world that the Spirit of the kingdom had returned to earth and would soon live within humanity again.

Just before Jesus died, he gave his disciples many instructions, and these instructions had important information about the Governor. He was trying to tell them, in effect, "Everything I'm about to suffer is all because of my purposes concerning the Holy Spirit in your lives and in the lives of those who will believe in the future." He told them, in essence, "I'm going to leave you, but don't panic or worry. The Governor is going to come back; he will be with you forever, and he'll never forsake you."

A striking illustration of the Governor's return occurred at the moment of Jesus's death. The curtain in the temple separating the people from the Holy of Holies tore in two from top to bottom, signaling that Jesus had made provision for human beings to be holy and receive the Spirit once more. The Spirit no longer had to be separated from them, dwelling only between the cherubim on a mercy seat that had been sprinkled with the blood of animals. Because of Jesus's ultimate blood sacrifice, the Spirit could once more be at home *within human beings*, giving them direct access to the King.

THE GOAL OF THE KING

The King's desire to restore the Holy Spirit to humanity, therefore, is what made the entire redemptive program of Jesus Christ necessary. The principal goal and primary purpose of Jesus's coming into the world was to deliver the Governor of heaven to the colony of earth. *Everything* else was a means to that end. He didn't come to bring us to heaven. He came to bring heaven to earth. This is why our Master Teacher taught us to pray, in what we call the Lord's Prayer, that the King-Father's influence, will, intent, and laws be done on earth—the colony—as they are in heaven—the home country.

THE ROMAN EMPIRE AS A TYPE OF THE HEAVENLY KINGDOM

The best time in history for the concept of the heavenly kingdom to be fully communicated to the inhabitants of earth was during the time of the Roman Empire, and this is a major reason why the King-Son, the Messiah, was born at that time. It was not a random choice by the King; it was the perfect time. Paul wrote,

When the *time had fully come*, God sent his Son, born of a woman, born under law, to redeem those under law, that we might receive the full rights of sons. Because you are sons, God sent the Spirit of his Son into our hearts, the Spirit who calls out, "Abba, Father." So you are no longer a slave, but a son; and since you are a son, God has made you also an heir.

The structure and functioning of the Roman Empire (though not its moral nature) at the time of Jesus served as a type of the kingdom of heaven. For those living under its rule in Palestine, the analogy would have been obvious. Caesar was the emperor or king in Rome, and he was a type of the heavenly King.

Caesar sent Pilate to be his procurator or governor over the region of Judea, to oversee it and create the culture of the Roman Empire there. Similarly, Jesus said that when he returned to the Father, the Governor would be released to earth, enabling the inhabitants to fulfill the will of the King on earth once more, making it into a replica of the kingdom of heaven. Jesus told his disciples, "When the Counselor comes, whom I will send to you from the Father, the Spirit of truth who goes out from the Father, he will testify about me," and "I am going to send you what my Father has promised; but stay in the city until you have been clothed with power from on high."

Political concepts familiar to the people of the time were present for them to come to understand that Jesus was talking about the return of the Governor to earth to enable them to fulfill the will and work of the kingdom of heaven. Interestingly, Jesus's enemies recognized that his message was about a kingdom, not a "religion." This kingdom demanded full loyalty to the King-Father through the King-Son. Because Jesus's enemies did not want to submit to the authority of the heavenly government, they sought to kill him. They told Pilate that Jesus was a threat to the political order of the day, saying, "We have no king but Caesar." In this way, they pressured Pilate into choosing between killing an innocent man and appearing to support a king other than Caesar. He caved to the pressure and allowed Jesus to be crucified. He was responsible for his choice, even though Jesus's death was part of the heavenly restoration plan. Every person essentially faces the same choice. Allegiance to the kingdom of heaven does not allow for any person or any thing to take the place of the King.

THE RELEASE AND RECEPTION OF THE GOVERNOR

After the King-Son's life on earth, a process unfolded by which the Governor was given to his followers. First, of course, the Holy Spirit dwelled within the body of Jesus—the first human being to have the Spirit within him since Adam and Eve. When Jesus died on the cross, eyewitness and disciple John recorded that he "gave up his spirit." Although this term can be a description for taking one's last breath, I believe it also has a deeper significance here. The Greek word for "give up" means to "yield up."[4] Therefore, I think this term means that Jesus also *released* the Holy Spirit back to the Father in heaven at his death.

When Jesus was resurrected, he was raised by the power of the Spirit, and the Spirit again dwelled in him. Paul wrote, "And if the Spirit of him who raised Jesus from the dead is living in you, he who raised Christ from the dead will also give life to your mortal bodies through his Spirit, who lives in you." Just as the King-Son was raised from death by the Spirit, and the Spirit dwelled in him, those who enter the kingdom through the King-Son's sacrifice will also receive the Spirit.

At Jesus's resurrection, then, the Spirit was now poised to return to humanity and rescue lives that had lived in rebellion, confusion, and despair under the kingdom of darkness. Just as the Spirit had brought life out of emptiness and order from chaos at the creation of the earth, he would transform the earth once more into a colony of heaven through the return of the kingdom in the lives of its citizens.

CHAPTER FIVE STUDY QUESTIONS

QUESTIONS FOR REFLECTION

1. Have you made resolutions to obey God but continually failed to live up to them? If so, what do you think is the reason for this?

2. Is the kingdom of God a central focus of your life? How much of your thinking and lifestyle is influenced by the purposes of the kingdom?

EXPLORING PRINCIPLES AND PURPOSES

3. How was the Spirit of the King directly involved in the King's coming to earth as a human being?

4. In what way did the Governor return to earth when the King-Son was born?

5. As God the Son, the King-Son was fully _____. As the man Jesus, the King-Son was fully _____.

6. How was the man Jesus different from other human beings?

7. What did John the Baptist say about the measure to which the Spirit of the King was in Jesus? What can we conclude by this?

8. What was the purpose and nature of the kingdom the King-Son came to bring?

   (1)

   (2)

9. How did the King-Son refer to Lucifer, and what did he intend to do to him?

10. What was the central theme of Jesus's message throughout his three-and-a-half year ministry?

11. How and why did Lucifer try to tempt Jesus away from his mission? How did Jesus overcome this temptation?

12. When can we be considered followers of Jesus?

13. John the Baptist said Jesus would "baptize...with the Holy Spirit and with fire" (Matthew 3:11). What is the nature of the baptism with the Holy Spirit?

14. Why is a process of transformation into kingdom thinking and life-style absolutely necessary for the inhabitants of earth?

15. What was Jesus's entire life on earth evidence of?

16. What are some specific ways the administration of the kingdom of heaven was demonstrated in Jesus's life?

17. What was the ultimate reason for the King's incarnation?

18. What was the result of Jesus's completing the work of restoration for humanity?

19. Though Jesus paid the penalty for the rebellion of all humanity, what is the responsibility of each person in receiving the results of Jesus's sacrifice?

20. What is the Holy Spirit the source of in our lives?

21. For a kingdom citizen empowered by the King's Spirit, what is the essential meaning of this phrase in the Lord's Prayer: "Our Father in heaven, hallowed be your name, *your kingdom come, your will be done on earth as it is in heaven*" (Matthew 6:9–10, emphasis added)?

APPLYING THE PRINCIPLES OF KINGDOM LIVING

THINKING IT OVER

+ Have you made a solid decision to be a disciple in Jesus's kingdom school, so that you *know* you have forever chosen him above all other possible teachers and philosophies on earth? Why or why not?

+ It is essential to remember and be thankful for the sacrifice Jesus made on the cross to enable us to be restored to the Father. Yet have you moved beyond a contemplation of Christ's ultimate sacrifice and entered into the reason for which he made it? Have you allowed the Holy Spirit to fill your life so you are living according to the mind and heart of God and in the power of his Spirit?

ACTING ON IT

+ Dr. Munroe reminded us that the word *repentance* does not specifically refer to emotions and crying, but it means "to change your mind, to reverse your way of thinking and acting." Has this been your attitude concerning areas in your life that are not in alignment with the kingdom of God? Write about how you would think and act differently in your life, based on true repentance.

+ As a student enrolled in Jesus's kingdom school, read a portion of Jesus's words or actions from one of the four Gospels every day. Then apply its teaching, wisdom, or directives to your own life.

PRAYING ABOUT IT

+ Make this the prayer of your heart every day to the King-Father: "Our Father in heaven, hallowed be your name, your kingdom come, your will be done on earth as it is in heaven" (Matthew 6:9–10).

The only way to live the life of the kingdom is to be submerged in the mind-set of the King.

SIX

A KING'S LOVE FOR HIS CITIZENS

LOVE IS THE NATURE OF THE KING AND HIS KINGDOM.

LOVE'S VOLUNTARY LIMITATION

To fully understand the nature of the kingdom we have an opportunity to enter, we must see that the King-Son's motivation for coming to earth was unqualified love for its inhabitants. He loved the people of the world so much that he voluntarily limited himself in significant ways in order to restore them to the kingdom. The New Testament writer John penned one of the best-known statements from the gospel writings: "For God so loved the world that he gave his one and only Son, that whoever believes in him shall not perish but have eternal life." Love is the nature of the King-Father and the King-Son.

Jesus is the perfect representation of God in human form. He came to show us what God is like and to take away our fear of Him, enabling us to call him not only our King, but also our Father again, because we have the same Spirit within us.

THE GOVERNOR'S LIMITATION

The King-Son's voluntary limitation of himself was prompted by the limited way in which the Governor had been able to work with the earth's inhabitants since the rebellion of humanity. As we noted earlier, the Governor could only come *upon* people in Old Testament times to do the work of the kingdom in specific instances; he could not work from *within* them yet. When the Son came to earth as the man Jesus, the Spirit could now live on earth within his body. Yet the Governor still could not dwell in all of humanity. The King-Father's plan was for the Governor to eventually be released into all human beings who would receive him through the provision of the King-Son.

THE KING-SON LIMITED HIMSELF IN ORDER TO BECOME UNLIMITED

Jesus's teachings were filled with seeming paradoxes that contain great truths. For example, he taught that in order to live eternally, one had to die to oneself; in order to be strong in kingdom power, one had to be weak in oneself. He lived out a paradox by voluntarily limiting himself so that he could become unlimited in the lives of his followers—those who became children of the King and received the Governor within them. Jesus limited himself in the following ways. He…

- emptied himself so that we could be full; became poor so that we could be rich.

- placed himself under the restrictions of a world of space and time so that we could be connected to the eternal kingdom.

- subjected himself to law so he could free those under it.

- submitted to physical death so we could have eternal life.

Paul wrote to the kingdom citizens in Philippi that Jesus,

being in the form of God, did not consider it robbery to be equal with God, but made Himself of no reputation, taking the form of a bondservant, and coming in the likeness of men. And being found in appearance as a man, He humbled Himself and became obedient to the point of death, even the death of the cross.

All the above are demonstrations of the King-Son's powerful love for the inhabitants of earth. He did these things so that he could send the Governor back to us—and *in* us—without limitations. The Holy Spirit *continues the ministry of Jesus on earth.* Jesus told his disciples,

And I will ask the Father, and he will give you another Counselor to be with you forever—the Spirit of truth. The world cannot accept him, because it neither sees him nor knows him. But you know him, for he lives with you and will be in you.

Let's take a closer look at the ways in which the King-Son limited himself for our sakes.

LIMITED HIMSELF FROM GLORY

In a letter to the followers of Jesus in Corinth, Paul wrote, "For you know the grace of our Lord Jesus Christ, that though he was rich, yet for your sakes he become poor, so that you through his poverty might become rich." The King-Son emptied himself of his heavenly power, glory, and riches to live as a physical, earthly being dependent on the King-Father for everything through the Spirit. Jesus said, "I tell you the truth, the Son can do nothing by himself; he can do only what he sees his Father doing, because whatever the Father does the Son also does."

When the Son became a man, he temporarily set aside his former glory. Just before his death, Jesus prayed, "Father, glorify me in your presence *with the glory I had with you before the world began.*" Only three of Jesus's disciples were given a glimpse of this glory when he was on earth, when he was "transfigured" by the Father for a short time:

> Jesus took with him Peter, James and John the brother of James, and led them up a high mountain by themselves. There he was transfigured before them. His face shone like the sun, and his clothes became as white as the light. Just then there appeared before them Moses and Elijah, talking with Jesus. Peter said to Jesus, "Lord, it is good for us to be here. If you wish, I will put up three shelters—one for you, one for Moses and one for Elijah." While he was still speaking, a bright cloud enveloped them, and a voice from the cloud said, "This is my Son, whom I love; with him I am well pleased. Listen to him!"

The effect of this experience on Peter, James, and John was overwhelming. The Son had set aside this magnificent glory to fulfill his mission on earth.

LIMITED HIMSELF TO TIME AND SPACE

The eternal King-Son also allowed himself to become restricted by time. He who owns the universe limited himself to a small region on a small planet during an earthly life of thirty-three years, where he could be in only one place at a time. He lived there, died there, rose again there, and even ascended to heaven from there. Eternity allowed itself to be limited within time, so that those in time could be reconnected to the eternal kingdom.

LIMITED HIMSELF UNDER LAW

Paul wrote, "When the time had fully come, God sent his Son, born of a woman, born *under law, to redeem those under law,* that we might receive the full rights of sons." The law of Moses and the sacrificial system had been instituted for those who were disconnected from the King. Jesus had full access to, and total communion with, the heavenly Father; yet he submitted himself to all the requirements of the law so that he could perfectly fulfill them. Then, when we receive his perfect sacrifice on our behalf, we are enabled to obey God through the indwelling Holy Spirit. The book of the prophet Ezekiel says,

> I will give them an undivided heart and put a new spirit in them; I will remove from them their heart of stone and give them a heart of flesh. Then they will follow my decrees and be careful to keep my laws. They will be my people, and I will be their God.

Jesus also submitted himself to the laws of nature in this physical world. Can you imagine God having a tired body? Being thirsty? Hungry? The God who created the whole world and all its oceans, lakes, and rivers had to ask someone else for a drink of water. The God who made the trees and their ability to bear fruit had to stop to pick fruit to eat. The God whom the psalmist said "neither slumbers nor sleeps" had to rest. In fact, Jesus was once so tired that he kept sleeping in the middle of a violent storm! He temporarily submitted himself to physical limitations in order to give back dominion power to humanity.

LIMITED HIMSELF BY DEATH

The Author of life had to look into the eyes of death. He met it face-to-face and submitted to it. Then he conquered it, taking away its sting from humanity. The prophet Isaiah said it pleased the King-Father for the King-Son to suffer and die. Why would it please him to have the Son experience agonizing suffering and death? Again, it is because he didn't want the earth's inhabitants to experience spiritual death as a result of their rebellion, and therefore the King-Son willingly died in our place. He allowed himself to be limited in a physical human body, and to be limited by the experience of death, because only another human being could be a viable substitute for humanity. Paul wrote, "The wages of sin is death, but the gift of God is eternal life through Jesus Christ our Lord." Jesus had no sin, but he took all our sins on himself, and that is why he—the perfect man, the Second Adam—died.

Yet Jesus was resurrected, never to be limited by death again. In the same way, when we enter into the kingdom, we receive eternal life, and death can't keep our bodies in the grave forever. Again, Paul wrote, "By his power God raised the Lord from the dead, and he will raise us also." The Son's limitation of death brought unlimited life for us! Death has no ultimate claim on us because Jesus paid the punishment of death for us. As Paul said, "God made him who had no sin to be sin for us, so that in him we might become the righteousness of God"—so that we could receive eternal life and be in right standing with the kingdom again.

This is another clear difference between the heavenly King and the human leaders we are familiar with. You don't hear of presidents or prime ministers dying in office for the purpose of freeing their citizens. A leader may be assassinated for standing up for a cause or because of someone's hatred or insanity. But to *choose* to die for his citizens? This is unheard of in our experience. Remember the words of the disciple John: "For God so loved the world that he gave his one and only Son, that whoever believes in him shall not perish but have eternal life." Jesus compared his sacrifice for humanity to a shepherd laying down his life for his sheep: "I am the good shepherd; I know my sheep and my sheep know me—just as the Father knows me and I know the Father—and I lay down my life for the sheep." His death was a demonstration of pure love for his people.

THE PROMISE OF UNLIMITED KINGDOM INFLUENCE

Jesus's limiting of himself made possible the return of unlimited kingdom influence on earth. I've heard some people say longingly that they wish Jesus Christ were on earth today. They believe that if he were, and they met him personally, their lives would be different. Perhaps you wish for the same thing. I used to, also. But I've come to see that this is a bad wish; it's not in our best interests. The transformation of our lives is possible *because* Jesus is no longer physically on earth.

Why is this so? First, let's consider the logistics of it. If Jesus were physically here, and you wanted to visit him, you'd have to pay for the plane fare to Palestine. After you arrived, you'd have to make your way through all the crowds just to try to get near him. And then, you couldn't expect him to spend all his time with you. Think of the millions or billions of people who would also want to meet with him every day. Even so, we seem to hold on to the idea that Jesus's physical presence on earth is what we need. This is because we haven't realized that the Governor is now available to all people at all times.

Jesus's disciples made the same error we do. When the King-Son told his followers he was leaving earth to go back to the King-Father in the heavenly home country, they became depressed. They had become attached to Jesus's physical presence in their lives, and they were afraid to lose it. Yet let's look at Jesus's response to this perspective:

> Now I am going to him who sent me, yet none of you asks me, "Where are you going?" Because I have said these things, you are filled with grief. But I tell you the truth: it is for your good that I am going away. Unless I go away, the Counselor will not come to you; but if I go, I will send him to you.... In a little while you will see me no more, and then after a little while you will see me.

Jesus was saying that he *had* to return to heaven so that he could send the Governor to be with them always. They would not see Jesus after he went away, but when he sent the Governor from heaven shortly thereafter, they would be indwelled with the Holy Spirit, who would guide them into all truth and remind them of everything Jesus had said to them.

When the Governor came, he wouldn't be with them only in a limited way, such as Jesus had to be when he was ministering to someone else or alone praying to the Father. He would be with them continually, day and night, in all situations. Before, if Jesus was in Samaria, he couldn't be in Galilee. If he was in Jerusalem, he couldn't be in Bethany.

We should be glad that he has returned to heaven because now the kingdom can be all over the world at the same time through the Holy Spirit, who lives in all kingdom citizens. Jesus assured his disciples, in essence, "My going away is for your good. The Governor is *with* you now, but he will be *in* you." It wasn't Jesus's purpose to physically remain on the earth because this would have stopped the King's plan of restoration right before its culmination in the return of the Governor.

When Jesus was arrested and crucified, Lucifer thought he had won the victory over the King that he had been looking for. Actually, he was being set up for total defeat. If Jesus hadn't gone to the cross and been resurrected, we would still be trapped in rebellion and in the kingdom of darkness. If Jesus hadn't returned to the heavenly home country and sent the Governor to fill us, the kingdom of God would not have been able to fully return to the earth. Jesus had said, in effect, "If I go to the cross, I will be able to draw all people to me and into the kingdom. I will be able to release billions of people into their original purpose of kingdom rulership and dominion."

Jesus limited himself, in the many ways that he did, out of self-sacrificial love and devotion to the estranged children of the King. He made reconciliation and restoration possible for all the inhabitants of the world.

A PRICELESS GIFT FOR HUMANITY

We have seen all along that the most important person on earth is the Holy Spirit, the Governor of the heavenly kingdom. He is a priceless gift to humanity, and it delighted the King-Father to restore the Governor to us. Luke the physician recorded Jesus as saying to his disciples, "If you then, though you are evil [controlled by the kingdom of darkness], know how to give good gifts to your children, how much more will your Father in heaven [Ruler of the kingdom of light] give the Holy Spirit to those who ask him!" He also said, "Your Father has been *pleased* to give you the kingdom."

In the next chapter, we will see how the Governor returned to earth.

CHAPTER SIX STUDY QUESTIONS

QUESTIONS FOR REFLECTION

1. Do you tend to feel assured and confident in your relationship with God or fearful of him? Why?

2. How would you describe God's character?

EXPLORING PRINCIPLES AND PURPOSES

3. What was the King-Son's motivation for coming to earth? What did the King-Son choose to do as a result of this motivation?

4. Jesus is the perfect _____ of God in human form.

5. What is the essential nature of the King-Father and the King-Son?

6. In what four ways did the King-Son limit himself so he could send the Governor back to us—and *in* us—without limitations?

    (1)

    (2)

    (3)

    (4)

7. How did the King-Son limit himself from glory?

8. How did the King-Son limit himself to time and space?

9. How did the King-Son limit himself under law?

10. How did the King-Son limit himself by death?

11. What did the King-Son do that is virtually unheard of in our experience of human leaders?

12. In what way did the King-Son's limitation of death and subsequent resurrection bring unlimited life for us?

13. How did the King-Son's absence from the earth, when he returned to the King-Father after his resurrection, bring unlimited kingdom influence to the earth?

14. Where would we be if the King-Son had not died for us and been resurrected?

15. Where would we be if the King-Son had not returned to the heavenly home country and sent the Governor to us?

16. How did the King-Father feel about restoring the kingdom to human beings again through the Holy Spirit?

17. Of what value is the Holy Spirit as a gift to humanity?

APPLYING THE PRINCIPLES OF KINGDOM LIVING

THINKING IT OVER

+ What have you learned from this chapter about the nature of God the Father and God the Son?

+ Describe God's attitude toward you. Has your perspective on this changed at all since reading chapter six and doing this study? If so, in what ways?

ACTING ON IT

+ Do you often feel things would be better for you if Jesus was living on earth today? In what ways is your life better with Jesus in heaven and the Holy Spirit living within you?

+ Jesus provided unlimited kingdom influence for the world through the gift of the Holy Spirit in the lives of kingdom citizens. What do you think you are meant to do with this gift? Record some of your ideas, below.

PRAYING ABOUT IT

+ Thank your heavenly Father for the priceless gift of the Holy Spirit in your life, and ask the Father to use you to spread his kingdom influence in the world.

+ Do you struggle with accepting God's unqualified love for you? Ask him to enable you to both understand and receive his love, so you may live in the sure knowledge of it as you help spread the message of the kingdom through his Spirit.

Love is the nature of the King and his kingdom.

SEVEN

RESTORING THE CONNECTION

THE FUTURE OF A PLANT IS IN STAYING ATTACHED TO THE SOIL.

The King-Son had promised his disciples concerning the Governor, "He lives with you and will be in you." He would connect them to the Father through the Spirit. After his resurrection, the work of *preparing* humanity to receive the Governor was complete. The spirit of rebellion and independence from the kingdom was broken. Any human being who personally received the sacrifice of Jesus, applying it to his own life, was now cleansed and qualified to be a residence for the Governor.

THE BREATH OF JESUS

Jesus's life, ministry, death, and resurrection therefore led up to his most important act on earth: the giving of the Governor. Shortly after his resurrection, Jesus came to the room where his disciples had gathered, and said, "'As the Father has sent me, I am sending you.' And with that he breathed on them and said, 'Receive the Holy Spirit.'"

Note that Jesus *breathed* on them. Does that act seem familiar? It was very similar to what the Creator did when he first made Adam a living being: "The LORD God formed the man from the dust of the ground and breathed into his nostrils the breath of life, and the man became a living being." But in this life-giving act, the King-Son specifically explained what this meant. He didn't just say, "Receive the breath of life." He said, "Receive the Holy Spirit."

The breath of life *is* the Holy Spirit; the Governor *is* the life of humanity. Without Him, even though our bodies may be physically alive for a limited length of time, we are dead to the kingdom, to the heavenly influence we were created to live in, and to the Creator-King himself.

In other words, when the Creator first breathed into Adam, he was essentially saying, "*Ceive* the Holy Spirit." Now, Jesus was saying to his disciples, as the first human beings (besides himself) to be filled with the Spirit, "Re-ceive the Holy Spirit." In the English language, we don't use the word *ceive* as a verb, but the English word *receive* comes from the Latin *re-* (again) and *capere* (to take).[1] When Adam rebelled, he lost the Spirit he had been given. So when Jesus brought the disciples together after the resurrection, he was saying, in effect, "Humanity, take the Spirit *again*, as Adam did." He was giving human beings back what they had lost.

In breathing on his disciples, Jesus reconnected humanity to the kingdom of heaven. He was literally bringing his disciples into identity with heaven's government. He was renewing human beings' standing and authority in the kingdom. They were restored to their original assignment as vice governors of earth. So the disciples of Jesus were the first human beings after Jesus to receive the Governor resident within them again.

The return of the Holy Spirit is the most important act of redemption in God's program for humanity. At that moment, the kingdom of God returned to earth because the Spirit lived within humanity once more!

Note that, after his resurrection, Jesus's message continued to be the kingdom. Luke the physician wrote,

> In my former book…I wrote about all that Jesus began to do and to teach until the day he was taken up to heaven, after giving instructions through the Holy Spirit to the apostles he had chosen. After his suffering, he showed himself to these men and gave many convincing proofs that he was alive. He appeared to them over a period of forty days *and spoke about the kingdom of God.*

Some people question whether the kingdom of heaven is on earth right now. The answer is absolutely yes. In order to understand why, we have to remember the nature of kingdoms. Wherever the Governor is, the kingdom is present. Wherever the Spirit of the King is, the kingdom is. The Governor is the presence of the absent King. Luke recorded Jesus's response when he was asked about this very question:

Once, having been asked by the Pharisees when the kingdom of God would come, Jesus replied, "The kingdom of God does not come with your careful observation, nor will people say, 'Here it is,' or 'there it is,' because the kingdom of God is within you."

The kingdom of God is within you when the Governor is resident within you. And when the Governor is resident within you, the kingdom of heaven is present on earth. Jesus told his followers, "I tell you the truth, some who are standing here will not taste death before they see the kingdom of God come with power." According to Luke's account in his second book, Acts, about one hundred twenty disciples were present when the Governor was poured out and fully reinstated on earth.

WAITING FOR THE FIRE

Jesus's purpose was to reintroduce the government that had been recalled from earth by humanity's rebellion. After he had completed his mission of providing a way for the inhabitants to be holy again, he returned to the heavenly kingdom. The ascension of Jesus was evidence of his finished work on earth, indicating that all was in readiness for the Governor's full return. The gospel of Mark records, "After the Lord Jesus had spoken to [his disciples], he was taken up into heaven and he sat at the right hand of God." I believe he reported to the Father at this time that everything was in place for the Governor to be poured out on the inhabitants of earth. Jesus had instructed his disciples about how they would receive this power from the Governor. On various occasions, he had made these statements to his disciples:

> And I will ask the Father, and he will give you another Counselor to be with you forever—the Spirit of truth. The world cannot accept him, because it neither sees him nor knows him. But you know him, for he lives with you and will be in you.

> The Counselor, the Holy Spirit, whom the Father will send in my name, will teach you all things and will remind you of everything I have said to you.

I am going to send you what my Father has promised; but stay in the city until you have been clothed with power from on high.

On one occasion, while he was eating with them, he gave them this command: "Do not leave Jerusalem, but wait for the gift my Father promised, which you have heard me speak about. For John baptized with water, but in a few days you will be baptized with the Holy Spirit.... But you will receive power when the Holy Spirit comes on you; and you will be my witnesses in Jerusalem, and in all Judea and Samaria, and to the ends of the earth."

Jesus had already breathed the Spirit on his disciples. They had received the Governor into their lives and were connected to the kingdom. But they still needed to be connected to the kingdom's *power*, which the King would soon send them. This is what John meant when he said Jesus would baptize them with the Holy Spirit and with fire. After Jesus returned to the heavenly kingdom, the "fire" would come, and his mission of both reconnection and restored power would be fully realized.

In other words, Jesus was saying, "For the last three-and-a-half years, I have been telling you that the influence of the heavenly government is coming. Every time I talked about the kingdom, I was referring to the Governor's influence in your lives and on the world. Now, stay here in Jerusalem because you're about to receive the fullness of the promise my Father made to you."

Jesus told them they would be clothed with power from "on high." This point is vital: we are to receive our power from the heavenly country, from a place *outside* this world, because this world is controlled by the kingdom of darkness. Again, the King-Son sent the Governor to earth *from the throne of the Father*, just as a royal governor was sent to a colony from the throne of the king to carry on the work of the sovereign there.

THE HOLY SPIRIT POURED OUT AT PENTECOST

After Jesus ascended to heaven, his disciples, along with over one hundred other followers, met together and awaited the coming of the Governor. His arrival occurred on the day of Pentecost, which means "fiftieth" in Greek.[2] Pentecost was a harvest feast held on the fiftieth day after the Passover feast. Jesus appeared to his followers over a period of forty days after his resurrection, and they waited ten days from his ascension for the coming of the Spirit. These fifty days bring us exactly to the day of Pentecost. Luke the physician recorded,

> When the day of Pentecost came, they were all together in one place. Suddenly a sound like the blowing of a violent wind came from heaven and filled the whole house where they were sitting. They saw what seemed to be *tongues of fire* that separated and came to rest on each of them. All of them were filled with the Holy Spirit and began to speak in other tongues [languages] as the Spirit enabled them.

When Jesus's followers were *filled* with the Holy Spirit, they were given power to speak in the variety of languages spoken by the Jewish people who had come to Jerusalem, from a number of countries, to celebrate the feast of Pentecost. The heavenly government gave them the ability to communicate the message that the kingdom of God had fully come so that people of many nations could hear this momentous news. Their speaking in these languages was an evidence that they were connected to the King and their assignment to bring the kingdom of heaven to earth. As recorded in the book of Mark, Jesus had previously told his disciples, "And these signs will accompany those who believe: In my name they will…speak in new tongues…."

Luke reported that the people who heard them said, in essence, "Why are you speaking like this; what is going on with you?" The disciple Peter responded,

> Fellow Jews and all of you who live in Jerusalem, let me explain this to you; listen carefully to what I say. These men are not drunk, as you suppose. It's only nine in the morning! No, this is what was spoken by the prophet Joel: "In the last days, God says, I will pour out my Spirit on all people. Your sons and daughters will prophesy, your young men will see visions, your old men will dream dreams. Even on my servants, both men and women, I will pour out my Spirit in those days, and they will prophesy."… God has raised this Jesus [King-Son] to life, and we are all witnesses of the fact. Exalted

to the right hand of God, he has received from the Father [King-Father] the promised Holy Spirit [Governor] and has poured out what you now see and hear.

Once again, we see the promise of the Father announced; but this time, the news was that the promise was now fulfilled in the return of the Governor. Peter was telling them they were witnessing the influence of the government of heaven through the arrival of the Holy Spirit.

When Jesus's disciples received the Holy Spirit, and then were filled by the Spirit when he was poured out at Pentecost, this signaled a seismic change on earth. The way was now open, for all people who received the cleansing Jesus provided, to receive the presence and power of the Governor. What separates the kingdom of heaven from all other philosophies, belief systems, and religions is that its citizens have within them the Holy Spirit. Religions have doctrines, tenets, and lists of *dos* and *don'ts*, but they don't have the indwelling Spirit.

THE POWER OF ABSENCE

As we saw in the previous chapter, while the Holy Spirit once dwelled only in Jesus, now He is able to dwell in millions of people throughout the world. He's back home in the colony so that the whole planet can be filled with the glory of the King. Now that he has been poured out, he can be all over the world at the same time. He lives in people of all races and skin colors. He lives in both men and women. The physical Jesus had only two hands with which to bless children and break bread for the hungry and relieve the sick. Now, through the Spirit dwelling in the lives of his followers, there are millions of hands doing the work of the kingdom. While Jesus's ministry was once limited to the area of Palestine, it can now be in Australia, China, the United States, the Bahamas, and all over the world at the same time. His purpose is to spread the kingdom of God on earth through a multitude of people, in a multitude of ways, in all spheres of life.

For example, if the Spirit lives within you, then, when you are at your job, the heavenly government is also present there. He wants you to bring about his influence in your workplace by your kingdom value system, attitude, forgiveness, love, and patience. If anyone asks you, "Why are you so different?" your answer can be the same as Jesus's: "My kingdom is not of this world." The King wants you to represent his kingdom in the midst of the kingdom of darkness, so others can be reconciled to the heavenly government, also.

GREATER WORKS ON EARTH

John recorded this statement by Jesus, which he made shortly before his death and resurrection: "I tell you the truth, anyone who has faith in me will do what I have been doing. He will do even greater things than these, *because I am going to the Father.*" How could we do greater works than Jesus did on earth?

The word *greater* here has to do with magnitude, not quality.[3] We could never improve on the quality of the works of Jesus. But when we are aligned with the mind and will of the Father, and his purposes are foremost in our lives, Jesus promised, "And I will do whatever you ask in my name, so that the Son may bring glory to the Father." The nature of the heavenly government will be spread throughout the colony, and this will bring due honor to the King of both heaven and earth. All who have received his Spirit will collectively multiply his works in the world.

The power of the Governor is that he makes the reality of heaven on earth possible. This is why *everybody* needs the Holy Spirit. He is the only one who can connect us to the King and, through us, dispel the kingdom of darkness with his kingdom of light. He is the most important person on earth.

CHAPTER SEVEN STUDY QUESTIONS

QUESTION FOR REFLECTION

1. Do you often find you have the desire but not the ability to spread God's kingdom in the world? What do you think might be hindering you?

EXPLORING PRINCIPLES AND PURPOSES

2. Jesus's life, ministry, death, and resurrection led up to his most important act on earth. What was that act?

3. How was the Holy Spirit initially given to Jesus's disciples?

4. How was this giving of the Spirit similar to another momentous event in human history?

5. What did Jesus indicate by the words he used when he gave the Spirit to his disciples?

6. What did this initial giving of the Spirit to Jesus's disciples signify?

7. How do we know the kingdom of heaven is on earth right now?

8. Even though Jesus had already breathed the Spirit on his disciples and they had received the Governor in their lives and been reconnected to the kingdom, what did they still need to be connected to?

9. What is significant about the disciples receiving the power of the Governor from "on high"?

10. Describe how the Governor was poured out on Jesus's followers after he ascended to heaven—"on high."

11. Why were Jesus's followers given the ability to speak in other languages after they were filled with the Holy Spirit?

12. What were these languages an evidence of?

13. What separates the kingdom of heaven from all other philosophies, belief systems, and religions?

14. Why does the King want us to represent his kingdom on earth?

15. What is the meaning of Jesus's statement, "I tell you the truth, anyone who has faith in me will do what I have been doing. He will do *even greater things* than these, because I am going to the Father" (John 14:12, emphasis added)?

APPLYING THE PRINCIPLES OF KINGDOM LIVING
THINKING IT OVER
+ Do you exhibit clear evidence of the influence of the heavenly government in your life? If so, in what ways?

ACTING ON IT
+ If the Spirit lives within you, then the influence of the heavenly government is present wherever you are. Write how you can bring the influence of the heavenly government to your home (family); workplace; school; friends; people you meet at stores, restaurants, appointments, and the like; and church.

PRAYING ABOUT IT
+ Ask your heavenly Father to help you exhibit the influence of his kingdom wherever you go.

+ Pray for someone specifically this week who needs to be reconciled to the King-Father and enter the kingdom of heaven.

"The kingdom of God is within you."
—Luke 17:21

EIGHT

REINSTATING THE GOVERNOR

A PUZZLE REMAINS A PUZZLE UNTIL ALL THE PARTS ARE IN PLACE.

Our entrance into the kingdom of heaven, also called the "new birth," results in the restoration of our legal authority as rulers on earth. Then, our baptism in the Holy Spirit results in the restoration of our power or ability to carry out that authority. Understanding these two concepts will enable us to be effective as we live out the culture of the kingdom on earth, for both have to do with the reinstatement of the Governor to his place and role in the lives of human beings.

Let us now take a closer look at these two concepts, comparing the new birth to a well of water, and the baptism in the Spirit to the power of a moving river.

THE NEW BIRTH: REINSTATING THE AUTHORITY OF THE KINGDOM

John the disciple recorded these words of Jesus regarding the restoration of the Governor within humanity: "Whoever drinks the water I give him will never thirst. Indeed, the water I give him will become in him *a spring of water welling up* to eternal life." Water in this context is a symbol of the Holy Spirit. The reality of the new birth is that there is now a continuous reservoir of God's Spirit within us. Picture a spring forever bubbling up with fresh, clean, life-giving water. As we continually drink deeply from this water of the Spirit within us, we will constantly be connected to the life of the kingdom.

The following is how the Governor restores the life of the kingdom to us through the new birth.

RECONNECTS HUMAN BEINGS TO THE GOVERNMENT

When we initially receive the breath of the Holy Spirit—the return of the Governor within us—we are given what theologian Paul of Tarsus referred to several times in his writings as a "deposit" showing that we

now belong to the King and that he gives us an inheritance in his heavenly
kingdom:

> Now it is God who makes both us and you stand firm in Christ.
> He anointed us, set his seal of ownership on us, and put his Spirit
> in our hearts as a deposit, guaranteeing what is to come.

> Now it is God who has made us for this very purpose and has
> given us the Spirit as a deposit, guaranteeing what is to come.

> And you also were included in Christ when you heard the word
> of truth, the gospel of your salvation. Having believed, you were
> marked in him with a seal, the promised Holy Spirit, who is a
> deposit guaranteeing our inheritance until the redemption of
> those who are God's possession—to the praise of his glory.

RESTORES HUMAN BEINGS' CITIZENSHIP IN HEAVEN

Whereas, before, we were merely inhabitants of the earth, we have
become children of the King and full citizens in the realm. Paul wrote,
"Consequently, you are no longer foreigners and aliens, but fellow citizens
with God's people and members of God's household." Our citizenship in
heaven has been conferred on us by the King himself, with the full rights
and privileges that encompasses.

REINSTATES THE KINGDOM ON EARTH THROUGH HUMANITY

Because the Governor is resident in the kingdom citizens who live
on earth, the kingdom of God itself is on earth. This reinstatement first
occurred with the King-Son's coming to live as a human being in the world,
and first returned to fallen humanity when Jesus breathed the Holy Spirit
on his disciples. The heavenly government has representatives on earth again
through the new birth. The more inhabitants of earth who enter the kingdom of heaven, the more the kingdom influence should be felt in the world.

RESTORES INTER-REALM COMMUNICATION AND ACCESS TO THE UNSEEN WORLD

The new birth restores two-way communication from heaven to earth
and earth to heaven. It is what I earlier called inter-realm communication.

Humanity had perfect communication with the King-Father in the beginning, but we lost it when we lost the *means* of that communication, the Governor. With the reestablishment of our relationship with the King, he is now able to have direct access to and contact with us, and we are able to have direct access to and contact with him. The new birth means that we have admittance to the unseen world in which the King dwells, and even have *influence* there as we pursue the purposes of the kingdom. This is what Jesus meant by the following statement, which we noted earlier:

> I tell you the truth, whatever you bind on earth will be bound in heaven, and whatever you loose on earth will be loosed in heaven. Again, I tell you that if two of you on earth agree about anything you ask for, it will be done for you by my Father in heaven. For where two or three come together in my name, there am I with them.

RESTORES THE NATURE OF THE KING WITHIN HUMANITY

This concept is what Jesus taught to Nicodemus, the Pharisee, who was trying to understand the meaning of the new birth. Jesus told him, "I tell you the truth, no one can enter the kingdom of God unless he is born of water and the Spirit. Flesh gives birth to flesh, but the Spirit gives birth to spirit. You should not be surprised at my saying, 'You must be born again.'"

This account is the only reference to the term "born again" in the Scriptures, yet the expression has become almost a catchphrase today so that we have lost its meaning. Being born again means that we have received the Governor and have therefore been given a new nature that enables us to be citizens in the territory of the kingdom. We become "imitators of God" once more, as Paul wrote: "Be imitators of God, therefore, as dearly loved children and live a life of love, just as Christ loved us and gave himself up for us as a fragrant offering and sacrifice to God." Because we are children of the King, we have his nature in our spiritual "DNA" and can now reflect it in the world.

THE BAPTISM IN THE HOLY SPIRIT: REINSTATING THE POWER OF THE KINGDOM

The new birth, or conversion, prepares us for heaven—for reconnection with the heavenly government and restored relationship with the

King. The baptism in the Spirit, on the other hand, prepares us for earth—for our restored dominion assignment to make the earth into a replica of heaven. I want to contrast these encounters with the Spirit because they are distinct experiences.

Just before the King-Son returned to the Father in the heavenly government, he told his disciples, "You will receive power when the Holy Spirit comes on you." The Greek word translated as *power* here is *dunamis*, which means "miraculous power."[1] Remember our earlier discussion about what we call "miracles." They are merely the manifestation of the influence of the kingdom of heaven on earth. So this power comes directly from another world, the heavenly government, to enable us to exercise authority on behalf of the King in the world.

The book of John records these words of Jesus: "If anyone is thirsty, let him come to me and drink. Whoever believes in me, as the Scripture has said, *streams of living water will flow from within him.*" John added, "By this he meant the Spirit, whom those who *believed* in him were *later* to receive. Up to that time the Spirit had not been given, since Jesus had not yet been glorified."

The Spirit already dwells within us at conversion. The baptism in the Holy Spirit is our yielding to the King and allowing him to release in power what is already inside us. While the new birth is like a continuous well, the baptism is like a forceful river; it is like waterpower that is harnessed as energy to run equipment, such as in a mill, for the betterment of humanity and its needs.

Let's look at how the baptism in the Holy Spirit restores to our lives the power we lost at humanity's rebellion.

RESTORES THE POWER OF DOMINION

While the new birth restores us to the heavenly government, the baptism gives us the ability to carry out the authority that the government has given back to us. Remember that power refers to our ability to influence and control circumstances. This is the power we must have to exercise dominion over the physical earth and the various situations we will encounter in the world.

RESTORES HUMANITY'S ABILITY TO REPRESENT THE GOVERNMENT

It is one thing to be recommissioned as a representative of the heavenly government, but it's another to demonstrate proof that you have been sent by that government. The baptism gives you the power to prove the claims of your King. This is where the gifts of the Spirit become important. As we will see in chapter thirteen, the context of the gifts is governmental administration on earth. The Governor empowers us to fulfill the assignments given to us by the heavenly government. So the gifts are not some strange supernatural manifestations but very practical endowments.

Jesus said, "If I drive out demons by the Spirit of God, then the kingdom of God has come upon you." He was saying that driving out demons was *evidence* that the heavenly kingdom had returned to earth. The same is true for all the gifts of the Spirit, whether we are talking about faith, healing, or miracles. The gifts are evidence of the presence, authority, and power of the government of God on earth. This is what Jesus was referring to when he answered John the Baptist's questions about whether he was indeed the King-Son who had come to earth to bring back the Governor. The book of Matthew records,

> When John heard in prison what Christ was doing, he sent his disciples to ask him, "Are you the one who was to come, or should we expect someone else?" Jesus replied, "Go back and report to John what you hear and see: The blind receive sight, the lame walk, those who have leprosy are cured, the deaf hear, the dead are raised, and the good news is preached to the poor."

Jesus was giving John proof that he had come from the heavenly government and was exercising kingdom dominion in the earth. He referred to everything in terms of the kingdom, and since this was also John's message, Jesus knew he would understand his reference.

ENABLES HUMAN BEINGS TO PROVE THE KING'S CLAIMS AND DEMONSTRATE THE KINGDOM'S PRESENCE

The book of Matthew also records this statement of Jesus: "And this gospel of the kingdom will be preached in the whole world as a *testimony* to all nations." The word *testimony* generally refers to speaking as a witness to the truth about a situation. The word in the original Greek in the above statement means "something evidential, i.e. evidence given."[2] Exercising power through the baptism is a means of presenting the truth to the world about the reality of the kingdom and its purposes.

GIVES HUMAN BEINGS THE ABILITY TO DISPLAY THE GLORY OF THE KING AND HIS KINGDOM

The power of the baptism enables us to demonstrate both the characteristics and works of the almighty Creator of heaven and earth. The psalmist King David wrote,

> The heavens declare the glory of God; the skies proclaim the work of his hands. Day after day they pour forth speech; night after night they display knowledge. There is no speech or language where their voice is not heard. Their voice goes out into all the earth, their words to the ends of the world.

The glory of God as demonstrated in nature transcends language. People of all races and nations and backgrounds see it; it is a continual and articulate testimony to the Creator of the world. In a similar way, the works that kingdom citizens do through the power of the Governor transcend human language and culture. If you were to go to another country where you don't speak the language, and the Governor were to use you to bring healing to a man who had been paralyzed for years, it wouldn't matter if he could understand your words; he would understand your action. The word *glory* refers to the essential nature of something. The man would come to realize that it is the nature of the King to be concerned about his personal needs, and that he has the power to meet them. He would be open to hearing about this King and his kingdom. As Jesus told his disciples, "Let your light shine before men, that they may see your good deeds *and praise your Father in heaven.*"

GIVES HUMAN BEINGS THE ABILITY TO DEMONSTRATE HEAVENLY CITIZENSHIP

In line with this, the power demonstrated through the baptism proves that we are citizens of a heavenly kingdom. It is like a passport; it both identifies us as belonging to the King and gives us credibility in carrying out the work of the kingdom. Just *trying* to do the works of the kingdom is not enough; you must have the authority to back up your work. This is what the sevens sons of Sceva, written about in the book of Acts, found out the hard way. They noticed Paul driving out demons in the name of Jesus, so they thought they would try it, too. But they weren't a recognized authority of the heavenly kingdom:

> Seven sons of Sceva, a Jewish chief priest, were doing this [trying to expel demons in Jesus's name]. One day the evil spirit answered them, "Jesus I know, and I know about Paul, but who are you?" Then the man who had the evil spirit jumped on them and over-powered them all. He gave them such a beating that they ran out of the house naked and bleeding. When this became known to the Jews and Greeks living in Ephesus, they were all seized with fear, and the name of the Lord Jesus was held in high honor.

Paul was an authorized citizen of heaven, and his authority in the heavenly kingdom was respected and obeyed by agents of the kingdom of darkness. The power of the heavenly kingdom is never to be used lightly, but only by those authorized by the King through his indwelling Spirit.

RECEIVING THE GOVERNOR IN YOUR LIFE

In coming chapters, I will be discussing more about the power that comes through the baptism in the Holy Spirit. Right now, I would like you to consider how to receive the Governor in your own life, because this first step will reconcile you to the King-Father and enable you to receive the authority of his kingdom.

Reconciliation through the new birth is the best news you could ever hear! It means you can approach the King without fear. Jesus has paid the penalty for your rebellion and independent spirit. When Jesus's disciple Peter spoke to the crowds who had gathered on the day of Pentecost, and explained to them what was happening, the people asked him what their response should be. He answered, "Repent and be baptized, every one of you, in the name of Jesus Christ for the forgiveness of your sins. And you will receive the gift of the Holy Spirit." Therefore, to receive the new birth, you are to...

First, *repent*. Change your mind about how you have been living and desire to live by the standards of the heavenly kingdom.

Second, *receive the forgiveness provided through Jesus's sacrifice*. One of the greatest problems of humanity today is a heavy weight of guilt for the wrong things we have done, for the actions we have committed that are contrary to the nature of the King and his kingdom. To forgive means to release from accountability and guilt. So, in order to live in the freedom of the kingdom, you must accept the forgiveness provided for you through Jesus, and then walk, as Paul wrote, in "newness of life."

Once you have gone through the above steps, you will *receive the gift of the Holy Spirit* within you. This is the "deposit" and proof of your entrance into the kingdom. Offer thanks to your King-Father for giving you this priceless gift.

Note that we are also instructed to *be baptized in water*. Being baptized in water in the name of Jesus shows that you are submitted to Jesus's kingdom school, acknowledges that your allegiance and identification from this time on is to him as your Master Teacher, and demonstrates that you have received full forgiveness for your rebellion.

The new birth means you no longer have to try to figure out life on your own. The King has removed that burden and stress from you. Just as a colony relies on the kingdom to build its roads, supply its water, and so forth, a kingdom citizen has all his needs supplied as he puts the priorities of the King first in his life. This is why Jesus said:

> Do not worry, saying, "What shall we eat?" or "What shall we drink?" or "What shall we wear?" For the pagans [people outside the heavenly kingdom] run after all these things, and your heavenly Father knows that you need them. But seek first his kingdom and his righteousness, and all these things will be given to you as well. Therefore do not worry about tomorrow, for tomorrow will worry about itself.

This is the kingdom life: seeking the good of the kingdom first and allowing the King to provide for all your needs as you serve him in the authority and power he gives you through the heavenly Governor.

CHAPTER EIGHT STUDY QUESTIONS

QUESTIONS FOR REFLECTION

1. Do you generally feel connected or disconnected from God? Explain why you feel this way.

2. How would you present the claims of the kingdom of God to someone of another culture?

EXPLORING PRINCIPLES AND PURPOSES

3. After entering into the kingdom of heaven, or the new birth, how can we be constantly connected to the life of the kingdom?

4. What did Paul mean when he referred to the Holy Spirit as a "deposit" in our lives?

5. The new birth prepares us for restored relationship with the Father. What does the baptism in the Holy Spirit prepare us for?

6. While the new birth is described as a well of water springing up, what is the baptism in the Holy Spirit described as? What is the significance of this word picture to heavenly influence on earth?

7. The baptism in the Holy Spirit restores the power of _____.

8. What is the definition of power?

9. What enables kingdom citizens to give evidence of the presence, authority, and power of the government of God on earth?

10. The baptism in the Holy Spirit enables human beings to _____ the claims of the King.

11. The works that kingdom citizens do through the power of the Governor... [choose one]

    (a) will never be understood by other people

    (b) could be understood only in the first-century

    (c) are limited to certain languages and cultures

    (d) transcend human language and culture

12. How can the baptism be compared to a passport?

13. Who is the one who can exercise the power of the heavenly kingdom?

14. Who respected and obeyed Paul's authority as an authorized citizen of heaven?

15. What steps did Dr. Munroe present, based on Peter's instructions to the crowds at Pentecost, for being reconciled to the King-Father and receiving the Governor?

    (1)

    (2)

16. What is the kingdom life?

APPLYING THE PRINCIPLES OF KINGDOM LIVING

THINKING IT OVER

+ Are you trusting in God to supply all your needs in life as you pursue the purposes of the kingdom? If not, what prevents you from doing this?

ACTING ON IT

+ Have you taken the first step to be reconnected to your heavenly Father? If you haven't, decide today to repent (desire to live according to the kingdom) and receive the forgiveness provided through Jesus's sacrifice. Then, accept the gift of the Holy Spirit and thank God for sending him to live within you.

+ Are you seeking the kingdom first? Which areas of your life can you offer to God to use in his kingdom purposes?

PRAYING ABOUT IT

+ Dr. Munroe wrote that, with the new birth, there is a continuous reservoir of God's Spirit within us, much like a spring forever bubbling up with fresh, life-giving water. As we continually drink deeply from this water of the Spirit within us, we will constantly be connected to the life of the kingdom. If you are feeling spiritually dry, ask God to enable you to drink deeply of this water by drawing on the love and power of the Spirit, who dwells within you.

+ Paul wrote in Ephesians 5:1–2, "Be imitators of God, therefore, as dearly loved children and live a life of love, just as Christ loved us and gave himself up for us as a fragrant offering and sacrifice to God." Ask your heavenly Father to enable you to be an imitator of him by reflecting his nature in the world.

The new birth prepares us for heaven.
The baptism in the Spirit prepares us for earth.

NINE

RESULTS OF RECONNECTION

THE SUCCESS OF A FISH IS STAYING IN WATER.

Without the Governor, a person cannot be a citizen of the heavenly kingdom. In his gospel, John documented this statement of Jesus: "I tell you the truth, no one can enter the kingdom of God unless he is born of water and the Spirit. Flesh gives birth to flesh, but the Spirit gives birth to spirit."

A person may do many beneficial things and be involved in a number of good causes and even have a religious background, but if he doesn't have the Spirit of the kingdom, he's not in the kingdom. The King of heaven is not interested in religious practices and rituals. Just as DNA pinpoints the identity of a person, the Spirit of God within a person identifies him as a citizen of the kingdom. There is no margin of error.

Yet when you are connected to the King through his Governor, an entirely new and remarkable life opens up for you. Before we discuss specific ways in which we are trained by the Governor in the lifestyle of the kingdom, and to partner with him in exercising dominion over the earth, let's review the initial transformation and benefits that occur when we receive the Governor into our lives.

RESTORED RELATIONSHIP WITH THE KING-FATHER

The first result of reconnection is a restored relationship with the King-Father. When human beings declared independence from the heavenly government, we cut ourselves off from our source of life; we became broken and confused, and this is why life on earth today is filled with such destruction, violence, grief, and lost potential. The earth is like somebody who has big plans—but no money to pay for them.

When the Governor enters a person's life, he connects that person to his source of life and gives him a relationship with his Creator—not just as his King, but also as his heavenly Father. He belongs to the King's immediate household now, with all the rights and privileges of a member of the heavenly royal family.

When we become realigned with our King-Father, we are acknowledging, "I came from you, and I must be sustained by you; I depend on you." We place the obligation for our sustenance upon God. As the prophet Isaiah said, the government is on the King's shoulders. He is responsible for leading his people. The names by which he is called indicate not only his responsibility, but also his ability, toward us, such as Wonderful Counselor, Mighty God, Father Who Lives Forever, Prince of Peace.

ENTRANCE INTO A NONDISCRIMINATORY, NONPARTISAN KINGDOM

The second result of reconnection is entrance into a nondiscriminatory and nonpartisan kingdom. Earlier, we looked at the words of the prophet Joel, who described the coming of the promise of the Father:

> And afterward, I will pour out my Spirit on all people. Your sons and daughters will prophesy, your old men will dream dreams, your young men will see visions. Even on my servants, both men and women, I will pour out my Spirit in those days.

This was the prophecy that Peter quoted on the day of Pentecost. For the people listening to Peter's comments, this would have been a radical change from the life they knew, because the coming of the Governor affirmed the worth and value to the kingdom of every citizen on earth, whether male or female, young or old. In the past, it had only been the high priest who could be in the presence of God's Spirit in the Holy of Holies, and only after he had been cleansed by the blood of sacrifice. In addition, only males could be priests. Yet here was Peter, quoting Joel, saying that the Spirit would be poured out on *all* people.

No longer would people have to go through priests to receive forgiveness from God. No longer would they depend only on prophets to deliver the word of the Lord to them. The Spirit would be poured out on them, and they would have direct access to the King himself.

Today, many people still engage in customs that I call "pre-Lord's Day practices." These are practices that the coming of the Governor has made obsolete. For example, some people believe they can have their sins forgiven only if they confess them to a priest. That's basically the way it was in the day of Joel. Only one person could go in to the presence of God in the Holy of Holies and enable you be in right standing with God again, and that was the priest. Joel was saying, however, that there would be a day when the King-Son was going to make this program obsolete because his sacrifice would make full atonement for our rebellion and sin. Everybody who received forgiveness through his substitutionary death would be able to come in to the King-Father's presence. No one would have to enter in to the Holy of Holies because the Holy of Holies would be *in* them in the person of the Governor! Nothing else—not our penitence, our memorization of Bible verses, our chanting, or our going to church meetings makes us acceptable to God. Only the King-Son's sacrifice cleanses us from *all* sin and enables the Governor to reside within us.

In addition, under the previous system, no woman would have imagined ever being a priest. Yet Joel told us that when the day of the Lord arrived, the King was going to give the Governor to everybody, regardless of gender. He said, "Your sons and daughters will prophesy." Why were "daughters" mentioned? This was to show the nature and extent of the kingdom. Joel prophesied, in effect, "I see the day coming when the King will arrive on earth, and he will destroy our categorizing of people according to gender." Both sons and daughters would prophesy, which means they would begin to speak the mind and heart of the home country to the colony of earth. The Greek word translated as *prophesy* means to "foretell events," "tell forth," or "speak under inspiration."[1] It means to speak forth on behalf of God. Both men and women are meant to communicate heaven's thoughts. Paul wrote,

> You are all sons of God through faith in Christ Jesus, for all of you who were baptized into Christ have clothed yourselves with Christ. There is neither Jew nor Greek, slave nor free, male nor female, for you are all one in Christ Jesus. If you belong to Christ, then you are Abraham's seed, and heirs according to the promise.

The next statement in Joel is, "Your young men will see visions, your old men will dream dreams." He didn't say, "Young *priests* will see visions" or "Old *priests* will dream dreams." All people who have the Governor are eligible. It doesn't matter if you are a child, a teenager, a middle-aged person, or a senior citizen, you can receive the Governor into your life, and he will involve you in kingdom purposes. There's no age discrimination in the kingdom of heaven.

Then, just in case we missed the point, Joel said, "Even on my servants, both men and women, I will pour out my Spirit in those days." The King repeated himself, as if to say, "All the human cultural prohibitions regarding gender, age, and social status have disappeared. When I pour out my Spirit on the territory of earth, everybody can be filled."

Again, the King desires to pour out his Spirit on *all people*. Everyone on earth needs the Governor. Those without the Holy Spirit feel the lack of him, whether they realize it or not, and are inadvertently seeking him as they try to fill the void in their lives. The atheist is ultimately seeking the Holy Spirit. So are the agnostic, the Buddhist, the Hindu, and the Muslim.

When the Spirit was poured out on the day of Pentecost, Peter told the people,

> Repent and be baptized, every one of you, in the name of Jesus Christ for the forgiveness of your sins. And you will receive the gift of the Holy Spirit. The promise is for you and your children and for all who are *far off—for all whom the Lord our God will call.*

Later, in his second letter to kingdom followers of Jesus, Peter wrote, "The Lord is not slow in keeping his promise, as some understand slowness. He is patient with you, not wanting anyone to perish, but everyone to come to repentance." All human beings lost the Holy Spirit when humanity rebelled, but God desires everyone to be reconciled to him and to be filled with the Governor. Some people seem to want to hoard the knowledge of the Governor for themselves. Yet the Holy Spirit is meant for every human. Receiving him into your life doesn't make you better than anyone else. It makes you a *steward* of kingdom authority and power. Paul wrote, "For it is by grace you have been saved, through faith—and this not from yourselves, it is the gift of God—not by works, so that no one can boast."

We should want others to receive the Spirit, as well, especially since the kingdom is to cover the whole earth. The power to live a life in alignment with the kingdom is everybody's privilege, because the King-Son died to give all people that right. John the disciple, in his first letter to new kingdom citizens, wrote, "He is the atoning sacrifice for our sins, and not only for ours but also for the sins of the whole world." Telling others about realignment with the Father through Jesus, and the promise of the Father, then, gives other people the opportunity to receive the precious gift of the Spirit.

RESTORED ABILITY TO INFLUENCE

Third, reconnection gives us a restored ability to influence the world around us. Remember our definition of power from earlier in this book? It is the ability to influence and control circumstances. This is what governments are largely about, and this is what the coming of the Governor to earth means.

A governor's job in a colony was to influence its way of life and to regulate activities in it. The world had been influenced and dominated by the kingdom of darkness since humanity's first rebellion, and it was only through the power of the Governor that life on earth could be set right again. As Paul wrote to first-century kingdom followers, "The kingdom of God is…[a matter of] righteousness, peace and joy in the Holy Spirit, because anyone who serves Christ in this way is pleasing to God and approved by men." The Governor gives us the kingdom authority we need to influence the colony of earth so that it reflects the nature of the King.

DELEGATED-AUTHORITY AND ABILITY-AUTHORITY

As we began to discuss in the previous chapter, there are two kinds of kingdom authority: (1) legal or delegated-authority, and (2) ability-authority. One gives you the right to do something. The other gives you the power and wherewithal to back up the authority by accomplishing the mandate.

The royal governor in a colony had delegated-authority, which was given to him by the king. When I was at the reception with the royal governor of the Turks and Caicos islands, the governor was really the only physical evidence in the colony that the queen was present there. Yet everyone treated him with great respect, bowing, shaking his hand, and calling him "Your Excellency." Why? Because, in the Turks and Caicos, he *was* the government of Great Britain. He was the monarchy. He was backed up by the authority of the kingdom of Great Britain.

The royal governor in colonial times also had ability-authority, which meant he was empowered by the king to *act*. A king gave ability-authority by providing people and material support that the Governor needed to fulfill his assignment. The governor was therefore backed up with the resources of the kingdom. This is a vital point because if you have delegated authority but not ability-authority, you probably won't see much accomplished. The power to act means that whatever the governor needed, the king made available to him. For example, in the days when Jesus lived on earth, Pilate, as Rome's procurator in Palestine, had the Roman army as a resource to back up his authority.

Yet, with the kingdom of God, the heavenly King grants legal authority and ability-authority that have more influence than any human institution or power. When Jesus was brought before Pilate, the Roman governor threatened Jesus with death, essentially saying, "I have the authority to take your life or to give it to you." Pilate was a governor, but he didn't comprehend that Jesus was a King with all the power of the heavenly government within him. He had infinitely more power than Pilate had. At his arrest, Jesus told Peter that he could have called twelve legions of angels [warriors of the King] to rescue him. Jesus therefore replied to Pilate, in effect, "You would have no authority over me unless it was given to you by the heavenly government. I have at my disposal all the resources of my kingdom to execute whatever I need on earth. However, my purpose is not to free myself but to reconcile humanity to the Father through my sacrifice." His being handed over by Pilate to be crucified wasn't about a lack of power on his part; he was fulfilling his kingdom mission on earth.

After his resurrection, Jesus told his followers that, as King, he had the power to give them both delegated-authority *and* ability-authority to carry out their work of realigning people with the kingdom. His words are recorded in the book of Matthew:

All authority in heaven and on earth has been given to me. Therefore go and make disciples of all nations, baptizing them in the name of the Father and of the Son and of the Holy Spirit, and teaching them to obey everything I have commanded you. And surely I am with you always, to the very end of the age.

The Greek word for *authority* used here is "in the sense of ability" and the "power to act."[2] We saw earlier that, when Jesus told his disciples, "You will receive power when the Holy Spirit comes on you," the word for *power* is *dunamis*, which means "miraculous power," "force," "might," and "strength."[3] His followers would have all the resources of heaven to carry out their assignment. This ability-authority would come with the outpouring of the Governor in their lives at Pentecost.

POWER IN THE NAME

The authority of a royal governor was in the name of the sovereign of the country he was serving. He used that name to exercise authority in getting things done. His own name had no real weight; he had to speak in the name of the monarch.

The King-Son operated on earth in terms of authority, and he showed us how we are to use his name in exercising dominion. He said, "I did not speak of my own accord, but the Father who sent me commanded me what to say and how to say it." The Governor functions on earth in a similar way. When Jesus was about to return to the heavenly kingdom, he said of the Spirit,

But the Counselor, the Holy Spirit, whom the Father will send in my name, will teach you all things and will *remind you of everything I have said to you.*

But when he, the Spirit of truth, comes, he will guide you into all truth. *He will not speak on his own;* he will speak only what he hears, and he will tell you what is yet to come. He will bring glory to me by taking from what is mine and making it known to you. All that belongs to the Father is mine. That is why I said the Spirit will take from what is mine and make it known to you.

We are therefore to act in the *name* of Jesus, the King-Son to whom all authority has been given by the Father, when we work on behalf of the kingdom. When Jesus was ready to leave to go back to the Father, he said in this regard,

> Now is your time of grief, but I will see you again and you will rejoice, and no one will take away your joy. In that day you will no longer ask me anything. I tell you the truth, my Father will *give you whatever you ask in my name.* Until now you have not asked for anything in my name. Ask and you will receive, and your joy will be complete.… In that day you will ask in my name. I am not saying that I will ask the Father on your behalf. No, the Father himself loves you because you have loved me and have believed that I came from God. I came from the Father and entered the world; now I am leaving the world and going back to the Father.

Under colonial rule, the royal governor of the Bahamas had a seal with the name of Elizabeth II on it. It was a sign to those who saw it that the one who used it was backed up by the authority and power of Great Britain. Whatever he sealed in the Bahamas was sealed in Great Britain, also. He had been given that authority by the queen.

Remember that Jesus gave his followers a similar authority when he said, "I will give you the keys of the kingdom of heaven; whatever you bind on earth will be bound in heaven, and whatever you loose on earth will be loosed in heaven." If we are rightly aligned with the King, the Governor confirms that we are legal agents of the kingdom by backing us up with the power of the heavenly government.

RESTORED DOMINION

In one sense, the Governor returning is not really the ultimate issue of the King's purpose on earth. It is his intent that *humanity* should again have dominion in the world. This was his plan in the beginning, and the plan of redemption was put into effect to reclaim that purpose. I believe that we keep missing this point and stopping short of where the King wants us to be. Again, we aren't reclaimed for the kingdom just to go to heaven. We have been reclaimed for our assignment of earth.

Some Christians spend their lives focused only on Jesus's sacrifice on the cross and haven't understood that God wants them to receive the promised outpouring of the Spirit in their lives. Others have received the promised baptism in the Holy Spirit but do not fully understand its relationship to kingdom life. All of us need to move on to the main point: exercising rulership on earth for the kingdom of God. This was God's original assignment for humanity, and it is not temporary but eternal. Once Lucifer and the kingdom of darkness are totally defeated by the King of heaven, we will have what is, in essence, "Genesis II." The King has promised that there will be a new heaven and earth, in which we will fully reflect the glory of the heavenly kingdom. Below are statements from both Peter and John about this new kingdom environment:

> But in keeping with his promise we are looking forward to a new heaven and a new earth, the home of righteousness.

> Then I saw a new heaven and a new earth, for the first heaven and the first earth had passed away, and there was no longer any sea. I saw the Holy City, the new Jerusalem, coming down out of heaven from God, prepared as a bride beautifully dressed for her husband. And I heard a loud voice from the throne saying, "Now the dwelling of God is with men, and he will live with them. They will be his people, and God himself will be with them and be their God. He will wipe every tear from their eyes. There will be no more death or mourning or crying or pain, for the old order of things has passed away." He who was seated on the throne said, "I am making everything new!"

A TRANSFORMED OUTLOOK ON LIFE

Fourth, it is impossible to really be in the kingdom of God and not experience change. There is a realignment of the proper functioning of a person's spirit, soul, and body because anyone who has the Spirit of God has become truly human again.

For example, a major transformation occurs in the way we think. As we saw earlier, before the rebellion, Adam's intellect was a servant of his spirit. Afterward, when his spirit became dead to the kingdom of God, his intellect and senses took over and became dominant. All human beings who are not aligned with the King and have not received his Spirit find themselves in this same situation.

This is why, when the Governor comes to live within a person, the Governor immediately attacks the false mind-set with which the person has been influenced by the kingdom of the world. This is also why we are instructed by the Scriptures—what we can call the Constitution of the kingdom of heaven—with admonitions such as the following:

> For the sinful nature desires what is contrary to the Spirit, and the Spirit what is contrary to the sinful nature. They are in conflict with each other.

> Live by the Spirit, and you will not gratify the desires of the sinful nature.

> We demolish arguments and every pretension that sets itself up against the knowledge of God, and we take captive every thought to make it obedient to Christ.

All these statements refer to the critical conflict between the mind-set of the kingdom of heaven and the mind-set of the kingdom of darkness.

Our outlook is to be transformed by a thorough understanding and reception of the mind and ways of the King, and through being receptive to the Governor's instructions and leading in our lives. If we try to deal with life from the mind-set we're used to, we'll fall back on thinking that is not in line with the kingdom. We need the Governor to teach us the ways of the King.

The Governor changes our inner culture by teaching us a new way to live. He reveals to us the thoughts and ways of the King so that we may understand and follow them. Remember that the King declared, "My thoughts are not your thoughts, neither are your ways my ways.... As the heavens are higher than the earth, so are my ways higher than your ways and my thoughts than your thoughts." The word *ways* here means "a road (as trodden); figuratively a course of life or mode of action."[4] In other words, it's talking about lifestyle, and we need to change our mind-set if we are to have the same lifestyle as the King in order to help rule the earth. Then we will be able to live according to the heavenly government, rather than in the old culture of the kingdom of darkness.

We talked earlier about how a colony's citizens were made to learn the history of the kingdom they were now under. In a similar way, the King wants you to forget your former life outside his kingdom. He wants you to build a new history for yourself in the kingdom of heaven. Our history as the human race and as individuals is one of rebellion, fallenness, distorted and lost purpose, and death. But when we are born anew into the kingdom of heaven, we have a history of being redeemed. We now have purpose and potential again. Our history is one of *life*—eternal life. The Governor encourages us to thoroughly learn our history, so that we can say, as Paul said, "If anyone is in Christ, he is a new creation; the old has gone, the new has come!'"

This means that we are supposed to be educated completely out of our history of sin. The book of Hebrews records, "'This is the covenant I will make with them after that time, says the Lord. I will put my laws in their hearts, and I will write them on their minds.' Then he adds, 'Their sins and lawless acts *I will remember no more*.'" The King is saying, "Look, your sins are blotted out. Just remember that you were rescued from the kingdom of darkness."

The kingdom's history of "righteousness, peace and joy in the Holy Spirit" is your own. Whenever Lucifer accuses you, saying, "You're a sinner," you can reply, "I was redeemed by the blood of the King-Son. He cleansed and washed away my wrongdoing."

The book of Hebrews continues, "Let us draw near to God with a sincere heart in full assurance of faith, having our hearts sprinkled to cleanse us from a guilty conscience." Even our *consciences* are cleansed by the blood of our Redeemer. Again, if another person brings up your past, you can say, "You're talking about someone who is dead. I've been raised in newness of life!" So the Governor teaches you your new kingdom history, for this is the will of the King for your life.

Paul wrote, "Do not conform any longer to the pattern of this world, but be transformed by the renewing of your mind." Your mind is to be transformed so that you will no longer have a mind-set filled with rebellion, guilt, depression, fear, confusion, and frustration, but rather righteousness, peace, and joy in the Holy Spirit.

Remember that the Governor is the presence and nature of the kingdom of God on earth. This means that if you receive the Holy Spirit, you should be able to say, as Jesus did, "He who has seen me has seen the Father." We will explore our transition into the Governor's culture in more detail in chapter eleven.

NEW COURAGE AND CONFIDENCE

Jesus's disciple John taught first-century kingdom citizens what he had learned from the Master Teacher: "You, dear children, are from God and have overcome [the kingdom of darkness], because the one who is in you [the Governor] is greater than the one who is in the world [Lucifer and his followers]." When the Spirit lives within you, heaven is your home country, and you have its authority and power. There is nothing or no one in the world who has more power and resources than the King. Therefore, you don't need to be threatened by anyone on earth who tries to intimidate or harm you. Luke the physician recorded Jesus's teaching on this:

> My friends, do not be afraid of those who kill the body and after that can do no more. But I will show you whom you should fear: Fear him who, after the killing of the body, has power to throw you into hell. Yes, I tell you, fear him. Are not five sparrows sold for two pennies? Yet not one of them is forgotten by God. Indeed, the very hairs of your head are all numbered. Don't be afraid; you are worth more than many sparrows. I tell you, whoever acknowledges me before men, the Son of Man will also acknowledge him before the angels of God.

The fear of man is a snare to us as kingdom citizens because it will cause us to live by a mind-set and standards other than the kingdom's. We won't be acting in authority and power but in worry and timidity. Paul wrote that the King has not given us the spirit of fear but of power, love, and a sound mind. We can be composed in all circumstances because we know that the King lives within us through the presence of the Governor.

RECONNECTION TO LIFE'S PURPOSE

When the Governor comes to live within a person, he helps connect him to the assignment for which he was born. The prophet Joel talked about old men dreaming dreams, young men seeing visions, and sons and daughters prophesying the King's will. I define a dream as something you can see being accomplished in the future, even though you may not live to see it fully completed. A vision is something you can see to do, which you can complete in your lifetime.

Paul wrote, "For we are God's workmanship, created in Christ Jesus to do good works, which God prepared in advance for us to do." We are newly created when the Governor comes to dwell in us. We can therefore start over in the kingdom to do good works, which the King planned for us to accomplish even before we were born. The Governor gives back to older people the dreams for the future they thought they had lost. He gives young people visions for their lives to help them stop wasting their time and energy on useless things. He makes us all rulers in the realms of our particular giftings.

Some people mistake the meaning of the Governor's presence in their lives. As we have seen, they think he came just to make them "feel good," or that he came to give them abilities that they can use to draw attention to themselves. Instead, he came to give us a vision or a dream of something that only we can help accomplish, because he has given it to us as our special work on earth. He came to give us *power* so that this particular work can be realized.

In addition, you can be cleansed and receive the Governor, but not understand that he wants to give you power for *living* the kingdom life. You therefore spend all your time fighting against attitudes and desires that are contrary to the kingdom, instead of overcoming them through the authority and power of the Spirit, so that you can do the important work for which you were born. His power should work through you so you can show evidence that your life is under the influence of the kingdom. The Governor came to empower you for *work*. He is here to impact the earth for heaven through *your* vision or dream.

COMMUNICATION WITH THE HEAVENLY GOVERNMENT

Finally, but very importantly, the return of the Governor gives us the ability to communicate with the heavenly government. We can bring the kingdom of heaven to earth and have dominion over the earth only if we are receiving clear instructions from the King. A kingdom can function in delegated authority only if the purpose, will, and intent of the King are being transmitted to that delegated authority.

What the King intends for earth is to be transmitted by the Governor to his vice governors, and to be executed on earth through their rulership. Whenever the Governor is not present, or the communication of the Governor is *ignored*, the practical rulership of the King is absent on earth. Some presence of the government has to exist. This is why the Holy Spirit is the key to the kingdom of heaven on earth. The Governor is the agent of the revelation of God's mind to the earth through humanity's dominion.

ACCESS TO THE KING

Let me try to illustrate how vital the Governor is to our communication with the King. In the colonial period in the Bahamas, if anybody, and I mean *anybody*, whether members of Parliament, local commissioners, or the bishop, wanted to go to Great Britain to see the queen, they couldn't get close to her without going through the royal governor first. This was true even for the premier of the colony.

A similar process applies in our relationship with the King-Father. Some people think they can have access to the heavenly throne because of their level of education or how wealthy they are, or how much they have done for the poor. We can't have an audience with the King-Father, however, unless we go through the King-Son, who opened the way for us by his substitutionary death, and unless we do so through the power of the Governor, who is our means of speaking with and hearing from the Father.

When you went to the governor in the Bahamas for permission to see the queen, the governor would send a message concerning you to England, and if the governor in Nassau cleared you, you were in. Likewise, when the King-Son clears you, and when you are relying on the Governor to communicate your requests and desires, you can go straight to the King-Father's throne room in the inner courts of the palace. As the writer of the book of

Hebrews wrote, "Let us then approach the throne of grace with confidence, so that we may receive mercy and find grace to help us in our time of need."

I've heard that when John F. Kennedy was the president of the United States, he was sitting in the Oval Office having a meeting with his cabinet. They were discussing the most dangerous situations in the world at that time, the Bay of Pigs issue with Cuba and the Soviet Union's nuclear weapons. This was the most serious meeting they had held up to that point in the administration. The story goes that the door suddenly swung open, and a little boy ran across the room, around the cabinet members, and landed in the lap of the president. All the important members of the cabinet were suddenly silent. This little boy looked up at his father—the most powerful leader in the world—and said, "Daddy, who are these people?" And President Kennedy said, "These are my Cabinet, son." The boy looked at this powerful group of men; then he pointed to his father and said, "This is my daddy." At that moment, it didn't matter who the president was meeting with. The son had complete access to the father. And the same is true in our relationship with our King-Father.

HEARING THE WILL OF THE KING

When a king wanted to communicate with his citizens, the Governor was also involved in this process. For example, any time the queen came to the Bahamas to visit, she didn't announce her visit directly to the people. She told the royal governor, and he told the people. In a similar way, whenever the King of heaven is going to do anything on earth, he communicates it through the Governor, who tells it to us. As Paul wrote, "Who among men knows the thoughts of a man except the man's spirit within him? In the same way no one knows the thoughts of God except the Spirit of God." The presence of the Governor in our lives enables us to hear and know the will of the King for us.

Hearing from the King is actually a very practical thing for a kingdom citizen, and was modeled for us by Jesus. The New Testament tells us that Jesus often went off by himself to hear the King-Father's instructions. Prayer was his means of dealing with government business. You have to be able to receive instructions from the heavenly government before you can accurately represent it. Jesus said to his disciples, "*When* you pray...."

Prayer, therefore, is not an option; it is daily government communication. We need to ask the King, with the help of the Governor, "What do you want done today?" And we have to be ready to listen and respond.

KEEPING IN RIGHT RELATIONSHIP

Worshipping the King is another form of communication with the heavenly government. Many people have made worship into a ritual, when it's really about keeping in right relationship with the King. It is a means by which we remain in constant connection and communion with our Sovereign and honor his government.

Worship protects us from establishing our own kingdoms on earth, rather than the heavenly government's, because we acknowledge and confirm to the King that his desires and will are paramount. We affirm that his government's interests are the ultimate reason for our existence.

The significance of our connection to the kingdom through the Governor will become even clearer in coming chapters as we explore the nature and role of the Holy Spirit and his impact on the culture of our individual lives, as well as the culture of earth.

CHAPTER NINE STUDY QUESTIONS

QUESTION FOR REFLECTION

1. How has your outlook on life changed since you became a kingdom citizen? Are there any areas that have stayed the same that you think should better reflect the mind-set of the kingdom?

EXPLORING PRINCIPLES AND PURPOSES

2. What is the first result of reconnection with the heavenly kingdom?

3. When the Governor enters a person's life, with what specifically does he connect that person?

4. What is the second result of reconnection with the heavenly kingdom?

5. Receiving the Holy Spirit into your life makes you… [choose one]

    (a) better than other people

    (b) able to hoard the knowledge of the kingdom for yourself

    (c) a steward of kingdom authority and power

    (d) not responsible for telling others about the kingdom message

6. What is the third result of reconnection?

7. What are the two kinds of kingdom authority, and how are they defined?

    (1)

    (2)

RESULTS OF RECONNECTION 159

8. Dr. Munroe explained that the authority of a royal governor was in the name of the sovereign of the country he was serving. His own name had no real weight. He used the King's name to exercise authority in getting things done. How does our influence and authority as kingdom citizens under the Governor function in a similar way?

9. What statement did Jesus make to his followers showing that the Governor would confirm their authority as legal agents of the kingdom by backing them up with the power of the heavenly government?

10. What did the King-Father promise would happen when Lucifer and the kingdom of darkness are totally defeated?

11. What is the fourth result of reconnection?

12. With a transformed outlook, there is a realignment of the proper functioning of a person's _____, _____, and _____.

13. What is the fifth result of reconnection?

14. Why is the fear of man a snare to kingdom citizens?

15. What is the sixth result of reconnection?

16. How did Dr. Munroe define a dream? A vision?

    Dream:

    Vision:

17. The King makes us all rulers in the _____ of our particular
    _____.

18. True or False:

    The Governor came to give you a vision or a dream that only you can
    help accomplish, as well as the power to accomplish it, as your special
    work on earth.

19. What is the seventh result of reconnection?

20. What two avenues give us complete access to the Father and enable us
    to know his will for us?

    (1)

    (2)

21. List several aspects of the nature of worship in relation to the King-
    Father and the outworking of his government on earth.

APPLYING THE PRINCIPLES OF KINGDOM LIVING
THINKING IT OVER

+ How much have you thought about the authority you have been
  given to carry out the work of the kingdom—that you have both
  delegated-authority and ability-authority? How would a true
  understanding of these types of authority in your life change the
  way you live and interact with others?

+ We have seen that whenever a communication of the Governor is
  ignored by a kingdom citizen, the practical rulership of the King
  is absent on earth. In what ways might you be ignoring the clear
  communication of the Holy Spirit regarding kingdom purposes?
  How can you restore the practical rulership of the King in your
  life?

ACTING ON IT

+ What steps are you taking to renew your mind according to the nature of the kingdom? Regularly reading the Scriptures—the Constitution of the kingdom—enables us to learn the King's will and "take captive every thought to make it obedient to Christ" (2 Corinthians 10:5). Write what you are doing and would like to do in renewing your mind:

+ Another way to renew our minds is to take on the history of the kingdom rather than allowing our past sins and failings to defeat us. Our history as the human race and as individuals is one of rebellion, fallenness, distorted and lost purpose, and death. But when we are born anew into the kingdom of heaven, we have a history of redemption, forgiveness, love, hope, vision, and life. Our sins are blotted out, and God does not remember them any longer. We now have purpose and potential. Which history are you choosing for yourself? How will you take on the history of the kingdom in your life?

PRAYING ABOUT IT

+ Dr. Munroe said the King-Father gives us visions of what we can accomplish in our lifetimes, and dreams of what we can see being accomplished in the future, even though we may not live to see them fully completed. What vision or dream do you have? Ask the Father to clarify this for you and show you how to fulfill his purposes for your life. Allow the Governor to empower you to impact the earth for heaven through *your* vision or dream.

> *"If you remain in me and my words remain in you,*
> *ask whatever you wish, and it will be given you."*
> —John 15:7

PART 3

UNDERSTANDING THE GOVERNOR

TEN

THE NATURE OF THE GOVERNOR

A PERSON LEFT TO HIMSELF WILL SELF-DESTRUCT.

We have seen that the presence of the Governor is essential for transforming the world into the kingdom of heaven. It is now vital that we consider in more depth the nature of the Holy Spirit because, though the Governor is the most important person on earth, he is also the most misunderstood and ignored.

People who are not yet in the kingdom don't understand the Holy Spirit's indispensable role in their lives because they've been led to believe that he is mysterious and unknowable. Or they think he is a kind of apparition because of our modern connotation of the word *spirit* and the use of the term *Holy Ghost* for Holy Spirit in the King James Version of the Bible. Even people who have received the Governor have misconceptions regarding who he is. I said earlier that some think he's a sensation or a thrill whose purpose is to make them feel good. Let's explore the nature of the Governor beginning with what he is *not*.

WHAT THE HOLY SPIRIT ISN'T

NOT AN "IT"

The Holy Spirit is not an "it" or a "thing." Some people refer to him as a nonpersonal object, saying, "Do you feel it?" or "Do you have it?" The Holy Spirit is a person with a personality. We will discuss more of his personal characteristics in the next section.

NOT A UNIVERSAL "FORCE" OR "COSMIC MIND"

The Holy Spirit is also not a kind of force or cosmic mind that we can "tap into" to receive the power and knowledge of the universe. He is not the sum total of the consciousness of the inhabitants of earth. To some

166 THE PURPOSE AND POWER OF THE HOLY SPIRIT

people, these metaphysical ideas have become synonymous with God's Spirit. However, no one can control the Holy Spirit or "siphon off" his knowledge or power. Neither is he part of our consciousness. He is a distinct Being who grants us knowledge and power when we have a relationship with the King and are yielded to the will of the kingdom. Instead of demanding it or taking it for granted, we are to be grateful for the power with which he works in our lives to further the purposes of the kingdom and to strengthen us as children of the King.

NOT A CLOUD OR MIST

Some people think of the Holy Spirit as just a kind of smoke or mist or cloud that comes in to a place and sometimes causes people to fall down on the floor. I'm not saying that there aren't legitimate times when the Holy Spirit will manifest his presence in a physical way, but I believe that people who are always looking for such manifestations are susceptible to imaginings and fabrications.

Rather than referring to the Spirit as a kind of ethereal mist, Jesus talked about the Spirit using the word *he*. In fact, this statement of his could not be clearer:

> But when *he*, the Spirit of truth, comes, *he* will guide you into all truth. *He* will not speak on his own; *he* will speak only what *he* hears, and *he* will tell you what is yet to come. *He* will bring glory to me by taking from what is mine and making it known to you.

Jesus could have said, "When the Holy Spirit comes." He kept repeating the word *he*, however, as if he wanted to make sure we knew the Holy Spirit is not just a force or cloud.

NOT A FEELING OR SENSATION

The Holy Spirit is also not just a "feeling." Again, I think we have often relegated him to a kind of strange, goose-pimple-raising experience. I think part of the reason for this is that some people come to corporate worship experiences so pent up with frustration about their lives that, when they can't take it anymore, but they sense an accepting environment, they run around screaming, roll on the ground, and call it the Holy Spirit. They are simply releasing tension.

You don't need to make a lot of noise to experience the Holy Spirit. You don't need loud drums and cowbells and screaming and shouting. If you read the Bible carefully, most of the time when the Spirit manifested himself, it was in quietness, not in exuberance. The prophet Elijah had this experience:

> A great and powerful wind tore the mountains apart and shattered the rocks before the LORD, but the LORD was not in the wind. After the wind there was an earthquake, but the LORD was not in the earthquake. After the earthquake came a fire, but the LORD was not in the fire. And after the fire came a gentle whisper. When Elijah heard it, he pulled his cloak over his face and went out and stood at the mouth of the cave. Then a voice said to him, "What are you doing here, Elijah?"

Let me add this statement, however: The Holy Spirit is not a feeling, but his presence can certainly affect your emotions as you experience his peace, joy, and comfort.

WHO IS THE HOLY SPIRIT?

THE HOLY SPIRIT IS GOD EXTENDED

The most important thing we must know about the nature of the Holy Spirit is that he is God. I like to use the term "God extended." He is God extended to a person and/or situation to work the purpose and will of his kingdom in the person's life or in the circumstance.

ONE WITH GOD

Earlier, we talked about the fact that Jesus is fully God, even though he is also fully human. God the Son became Jesus of Nazareth for the purpose of his redemptive task in the world. His dual nature never diminished His oneness and equality with the Father. The Scripture says that Jesus, "being in the form of God, did not consider it robbery to be equal with God, but made Himself of no reputation, taking the form of a bondservant, and coming in the likeness of men."

You don't need to grasp for something that you already have. Jesus is equal with God, even though he is distinct in personality and function from God the Father and God the Spirit. The Scripture tells us that Jesus was sent from the Father through the Spirit. The heavenly messenger told Mary, the mother of Jesus, "The Holy Spirit will come upon you, and the power of the Most High will overshadow you. So the holy one to be born will be called the Son of God." And Jesus spoke of his oneness with the Father, saying, "I and the Father are one," and "If anyone loves me, he will obey my teaching. My Father will love him, and *we* will come to him and make *our* home with him."

The word *Father* in relation to God doesn't mean father the way one is related to a human father, or in the sense of someone who is "greater" or "older." God is not "older" than Jesus Christ. Jesus is eternal, as God the Father is eternal. Rather, the word *Father* refers to God's being the Source from which Jesus was sent.

Likewise, the Holy Spirit is God, and he is equal to the Father and the Son. John wrote in his gospel, "God is spirit, and his worshipers must worship in spirit and in truth." Jesus spoke of the Spirit as *"another* Counselor" who would continue his work on earth. So God is one, but he expresses himself in three distinct personalities and dimensions.

Jesus told his disciples, "When the Counselor comes, whom I will *send to you from the Father*, the Spirit of truth who *goes out from the Father….*" Both Jesus and the Spirit proceeded from the Father to accomplish the work that needed and still needs to be done on earth. Jesus was sent by the Father to redeem us; the Spirit was sent by Jesus to empower us. Jesus was sent to restore us; the Spirit was sent to release us into a new kingdom life.

I like to describe the concept of the triune God by the analogy of water. Water, in its liquid state, is like God the Father; it is the natural source. If you were to take some water and freeze it, it would become solid ice. Ice is like Jesus, the Word who became flesh; he was tangible, someone who could be seen, heard, and touched. If you were to take the same ice, put it in a pot, and heat it to boiling, it would become steam. Steam is like the Holy Spirit, the invisible influence that generates power. Ice and steam can return to their original liquid state. All three are in essence water, although in different forms.

RECEIVES THE SAME HONOR AS GOD

Another confirmation that the Holy Spirit is God is Jesus's statement about the consequences of blaspheming him. "I tell you the truth, all the sins and blasphemies of men will be forgiven them. But whoever blasphemes against the Holy Spirit will never be forgiven; he is guilty of an eternal sin." The only sin Jesus said you can never be forgiven of is a sin against the Holy Spirit. Why did he say this? I believe that he was saying it is the Holy Spirit who (1) convicts people of their need to be cleansed from sin by the work of Christ, and (2) who enables us to be spiritually reborn and brings us into the heavenly kingdom. Therefore, if someone totally hardens himself to the Spirit and his work, he won't be drawn to forgiveness through Christ, and he won't be able to receive the regenerating work of the Spirit in his life.

Jesus Christ cleanses us, the Father forgives us, and the Spirit renews us. The writer of the book of Hebrews wrote, quoting Psalm 95, "As the Holy Spirit says: 'Today, if you hear his voice, do not harden your hearts as you did in the rebellion.'" In other words, if you hear his voice, if you feel his conviction, if you hear him saying, "It's time," then do not harden your heart because there is going to come a day when he will stop calling you. The Scriptures speak about God as longsuffering or patient; it doesn't say that he is *forever*-suffering. He will allow foolishness for a long time, but only for so long.

The term *apostate* refers to someone who has entered a state where he can't hear the Spirit of God anymore. You don't want the Holy Spirit to stop convicting you. If the Holy Spirit convicts you about your need to repent, receive forgiveness, and enter the kingdom of God, you should run to him! Why? Because that means you are still in good relationship with him, and he is able to talk to you. Don't let your pride prevent you from responding because you wonder what people will say. You should rather worry that the Spirit will stop talking!

I hope that you will listen to the most important person from heaven, who is the most important person on earth! He is vastly more important than angels, which many people hope to see. Angels, however, work for the government, but he *is* the government.

THE HOLY SPIRIT IS A PERSON WITH QUALITIES, CHARACTERISTICS, AND A WILL

So the Holy Spirit is first of all "God extended." Second, as we have seen, the Holy Spirit is a *person*. A person has qualities and characteristics that distinguish him from others, so that he is a separate being. The Governor has a distinct personality, characteristics, and will. As the Representative of heaven, the Resident Governor in the colony, his main desire is for us to fulfill the King's purposes on earth.

Jesus described the person and work of the Holy Spirit, revealing at various times that among his characteristics are his abilities to teach and guide. A feeling or a force cannot be a governor. A mist can't teach or guide. Most citizens of the kingdom have no real relationship with the Governor because they haven't realized they have someone invaluable dwelling in them. Some*one*.

THE HOLY SPIRIT HAS SPIRITUAL SENSES

The Holy Spirit also has "senses" that are part of his personality. By this, I mean that he has spiritual senses similar to the way human beings have physical senses. Spiritually speaking, the Holy Spirit sees, hears, feels, and smells or discerns in his dealings with the earth and its inhabitants.

THE HOLY SPIRIT HAS FEELINGS OR EMOTIONS

Paul wrote, "Do not grieve the Holy Spirit of God, with whom you were sealed for the day of redemption." We can grieve the Spirit when we actively resist him, behave in ways that are contrary to the kingdom of heaven, or neglect him.

I want to focus on the area of neglect. Think about this: When you ignore someone, he generally stops talking to you. And the more you ignore him, the more he will ignore you. For example, if you don't acknowl-edge me, eventually I will come to the conclusion that I'm not important to you and that you don't have any regard for me. Or, if you keep ignoring me when I talk to you, then, eventually, I should have a little sense to say, "He really doesn't want to listen to me." Jesus said that the Holy Spirit will teach us all things. I used to be a teacher in the classroom, and let me tell you, there is no worse experience for a teacher than to have a group of students who have no interest in learning.

We must realize that the Holy Spirit is a person who knows when we are ignoring him. If we disregard his teaching and leading, we aren't treating him with the respect and devotion he deserves. We also miss opportunities to learn and serve in the kingdom. And it is not only we who are negatively affected by this. Suppose the Governor prompts you five times to bring food to a neighbor. Finally, he stops speaking to you about it. Two things happen: You miss a blessing, and your neighbor may go hungry.

Or suppose the Governor prompts you during the night to get up and pray for someone, but you say, "I'm tired, and I've had a long day, so I need to sleep." The Holy Spirit says, "Yes, but someone is in need of help, and I need a human vessel through whom to intercede because this is the way the kingdom of heaven works on earth." You think, "That's just my imagination; I'm tired." So you stay in bed and no longer sense his prompting. You find out the next day that someone was in a dangerous or troubling situation, and your prayers were urgently needed.

We listen to other people more than we listen to the Spirit of God. We seek other people's advice more than we seek his. Sometimes, he withdraws our sense of his presence in order to get our attention.

Some people have not heard the voice of the Holy Spirit for a long time. Why? They get up in the morning and don't acknowledge him at all before plunging into the day. They never refer to him when they make decisions, invest their finances, work at their jobs, run their businesses, or go to school. Therefore, he's quiet toward them.

You literally have to learn to fellowship with and listen to the Holy Spirit. He speaks to us through the Scriptures, through our thoughts, and through promptings and impressions. We need to practice hearing his voice and not ignore him, but acknowledge him as a person who is intimately interested in who we are, what we do, and how we fulfill our role in the kingdom.

THE GOVERNOR'S NATURE EXPRESSED TO US

Let us now look at how the Governor attends to us in fulfillment of his nature. The Scriptures describe and define particular roles and responsibilities of the Holy Spirit on earth. Again, in all his works, the Governor acts only according to the word of the King. "The Spirit of truth," Jesus said, "...will not speak on his own; he will speak only what he hears, and he will tell you what is yet to come. He will bring glory to me by taking from what is mine and making it known to you."

COUNSELOR AND COMFORTER

Jesus told his disciples,

But the Counselor, the Holy Spirit, whom the Father will send in my name, will teach you all things and will remind you of everything I have said to you.

And I will ask the Father, and he will give you another Counselor to be with you forever.

The Greek word for *Counselor* in both these statements is *parakletos*, which means "an intercessor, consoler," "advocate, comforter."[1] Some Bible translations use the word "Helper." It refers to one who comes right alongside us to assist us. Jesus promised his followers that he would return to be with them in the person of the Governor to enable them to live the life they were called to: "In a little while you will see me no more, and then after a little while you will see me."

I've heard people say, "I want to become a believer [citizen of the kingdom], but I'm not strong enough. When I have enough strength to stop doing this and start doing that, I'm going to commit to the kingdom." These people still haven't made a commitment because they think they have to be strong *first*. You may be struggling with the same issue because you're trying to change yourself on your own. The King is telling us, "Look, if you're going to learn kingdom culture, you need help from the home country." Receiving the Governor into your life will enable you to change. He will show you how to transform your thinking and how to live.

Likewise, some of you are discouraged because, even though you are citizens of the kingdom of heaven, you feel as if you keep falling back into the attitudes and actions of the kingdom of darkness. But the Governor says to you, "I'm going to help you up again." This is his job! He won't give up on you.

Jesus emphasized the King's commitment to you through his analogy of a shepherd who leaves his ninety-nine sheep in the fold while he goes off to look for the one that is lost. This doesn't give us a license to keep going back to the behavior of the kingdom of darkness. Once we're in the kingdom of heaven, we're not supposed to keep returning to our old ways intentionally. Some people purposely do what is contrary to the kingdom, and then they want to be automatically forgiven by the King. This does not reflect a true transformation into a kingdom citizen. If we really desire to live by heavenly standards, even though we sometimes may slip up, the Governor will help us to live them out. He wants us to succeed.

GUIDE AND TEACHER

Jesus also said about the Governor,

But when he, the Spirit of truth, comes, he will guide you into all truth. He will not speak on his own; he will speak only what he hears, and he will tell you what is yet to come.

As we have seen, governors were placed in colonies not just to give information, but also to train the citizens to think, act, and live the standards, the customs—the entire culture—of the home country. This involved both general teaching and individual training.

Because the governor of a colony was sent from the throne of the sovereign, he knew the sovereign's intent. In the same way, the Governor from heaven is the only one who can enable us to understand the truth of the statements that Jesus made and the instructions he left for us. The Holy Spirit is the only one who can reconnect us to original information about the King and his kingdom. He protects us from error and from others' opinions that are not according to the mind of the King.

One of the jobs of a governor in a colony is to interpret for the citizens what the sovereign means by the words he delivers to them. We saw in the last section that the Holy Spirit is called the Counselor. The word *counsel* has to do with one who interprets law, and the Governor reveals and explains the laws of the King to us, bringing those words to life.

The prophet Isaiah said of Jesus, "The Spirit of the LORD will rest on him—the Spirit of wisdom and of understanding." We, too, have this Spirit of wisdom and understanding living within us. Knowledge is information, and wisdom is how to apply it. In other words, wisdom is the proper use of knowledge. The Governor shows us how to take our knowledge and apply it to life. He is the one who makes us practical people in the world. In some religious circles, this has been reversed. The Holy Spirit is considered to be the one who makes people act in strange ways. However, the Governor couldn't be more sensible. He shows us how to apply our knowledge to family, business, community, national, and worldwide issues.

HELPER AND ENABLER...

When the King-Son was on earth, he quoted from the prophet Isaiah concerning himself,

> The Spirit of the Lord is on me, because he has anointed me to preach good news to the poor. He has sent me to proclaim freedom for the prisoners and recovery of sight for the blind, to release the oppressed, to proclaim the year of the Lord's favor.

When a sovereign declared what he wanted for a colony, it was the governor's job to make sure it happened, encouraging the citizens to work toward its fulfillment. As the Holy Spirit carries out the will of God in the world, we are to be in unity with his desires and intent for the earth in carrying out our role as vice governors over the territory. We are not here to establish *our* kingdoms. We are here to establish the kingdom of our Sovereign, whom we represent.

IN FULFILLING THE PURPOSES OF THE KINGDOM

The above passage from the book of Isaiah emphasizes the focus of the kingdom on earth: telling the inhabitants about the promise of the Father, freeing them from the kingdom of darkness, and showing them the nature of the kingdom and how to enter in to it. It is the Governor who helps us to do all these things.

It is the King's ultimate purpose, as spoken through the prophet Habakkuk, that "the earth will be filled with the knowledge of the glory of the LORD, as the waters cover the sea." We can take this statement as an instruction concerning the kingdom. Again, the glory of God refers to the nature of God. Jesus said that, under the Governor's direction, we are to "go and make disciples of all nations, baptizing them in the name of the Father and of the Son and of the Holy Spirit, and teaching them to obey everything [Jesus has] commanded." In this way, the prophecy will be fulfilled.

The Governor calls upon us to bring the culture of the kingdom into the foreign culture that has taken over the earth—the culture of the kingdom of darkness. We saw earlier that to disciple means to teach kingdom philosophy and values, so that the students are immersed in the mind-set of the King. The term *nations* in Jesus's statement about making disciples is the Greek word *ethnos*, referring to races or people groupings.[2] Every special grouping of people on earth is to be converted into kingdom culture.

The royal governor of the Bahamas used to appoint local commissioners, or council people, from the colony, and he would empower them to do different improvement projects, such as fixing the roads. Likewise, the Governor empowers us to do good works in the world on behalf of the government. As Paul wrote, "For we are God's workmanship, created in Christ Jesus to do good works, which God prepared in advance for us to do."

IN RECONNECTING TO OUR GIFTS

Every human being is born with gifts from God, but in order for these gifts to reach their maximum potential in service for the kingdom, they need to be reconnected to their original source. No one really knows the true essence of his gifts unless he reconnects with the Spirit of the Creator. Moreover, the Governor activates our gifts to a level that we wouldn't naturally bring them. Paul wrote, quoting the prophet Isaiah, "'No eye has seen, no ear has heard, no mind has conceived what God has prepared for those who love him'—but God has revealed it to us by his Spirit. The Spirit searches all things, even the deep things of God."

The Governor reconnects you to the source of your gifts so that you can understand what you have been given—not just the value of your gifts, but also the magnitude of them. In other words, no one's intellect alone can discern or understand the gifts that the King has placed within him for the purposes of the kingdom. This is why, if you want to know what the Spirit of God really created inside you, you have to connect to the Governor.

Paul also said, "We have not received the spirit of the world but the Spirit who is from God, that we may understand what God has freely given us." This statement tells us that we don't even realize what we *have* until the Holy Spirit reveals it to us. Knowing this truth is vital for fulfilling your purpose and potential. There are things about yourself that you will never know unless the Holy Spirit reconnects you to the deep things in the mind of the Creator and enables you to use your gifts most effectively.

Paul likewise wrote, "The man without the Spirit does not accept the things that come from the Spirit of God, for they are foolishness to him, and he cannot understand them, because they are spiritually discerned." Without the Governor, we can never recognize what has been placed deep within us. We cannot know who *we* are without the Spirit of God. This is why many of us are living far below our potential.

We should note here that there are gifts we are born with and additional gifts that we are given when we receive the Spirit. I believe there is a distinction between these two types of gifts, and we'll talk more about "gifts of the Spirit" in coming chapters. However, the gifts I'm referring to here are the gifts you were born with to fulfill a specific purpose on earth for the kingdom. And the Holy Spirit empowers us to execute these gifts. This empowerment is not necessarily to give us the ability to *do* them because that ability already exists within us. Rather, he empowers us by revealing them to us fully and introducing us to gifts we didn't even know we had. Moreover, he shows us how to use them for the kingdom rather than for selfish purposes because the gifts our King gives us are always given to benefit other people.

CONVICTER

Jesus told his disciples concerning the Governor,

When he comes, he will convict the world of guilt in regard to sin and righteousness and judgment: in regard to sin, because men do not believe in me; in regard to righteousness, because I am going to the Father, where you can see me no longer; and in regard to judgment, because the prince of this world now stands condemned.

The word *world* in the above statement is not referring necessarily to people but to a *system* or *mind-set*. It's the system based on the kingdom of darkness that influences the behavior of humans. Therefore, it is the Governor who convicts those outside the kingdom that they need to be forgiven and connected to their Father in the heavenly government. He also convicts the citizens of the kingdom of attitudes and actions that are contrary to the nature of the kingdom. It is the Governor who works through our consciences so that we will choose to live according to kingdom standards.

We should realize that the Holy Spirit is not given to us to "take over" our lives. He prompts us, but he never forces us. In other words, he makes all the citizens *conscious* of the expectations, the standards, the laws, the regulations, and the customs of the kingdom, and he also convinces them of the benefits of these things.

The King-Father is not in the business of controlling his citizens. He wants his children to *desire* what he desires. He respects our wills. The Governor shows us what the Father's will is and helps us to fulfill it as we look to him for wisdom, strength, and power.

DRAWER TO GOD

In accordance with being Convicter and Convincer, the Holy Spirit is heaven's divine attraction to the throne of the King. As the Governor works in people's lives, he draws them to the Father in a gentle way. Again, he is not overbearing. The prophet Hosea gave a beautiful illustration of this approach when he recorded these words of the King to his people: "I led them with cords of human kindness, with ties of love."

COMMUNICATOR

A true governor would never communicate anything to the people that violated the king's wishes. Likewise, as we have seen, the Holy Spirit communicates only what comes from the heavenly throne. Jesus said, "He will not speak on his own; he will speak only what he hears, and he will tell you what is yet to come."

This statement reminds me of a practice we observed when the Bahamas was still under the kingdom of Great Britain. Every year, the people would gather at Clifford Park in Nassau to hear the royal governor read a document, sent from the queen in England, known as The Speech from the Throne. To ensure that everyone heard the speech, the whole country had a holiday; everything was shut down.

The royal governor would sit in a chair, surrounded by local government officials, and he would read the mind of the queen of England for our colony. That speech became the plan and the mandate for the new year. We were gathered together to be reminded of the sovereign's desires for the kingdom and the colony, and her expectations from the colony. It was a review of the laws, customs, and standards of the kingdom, and it also expressed her plans for the future of the colony.

Similarly, the Holy Spirit regularly brings us The Speech from the Heavenly Throne as we set aside the busyness of life to listen to him. The Governor's words will never disagree with the King's words or bring a message that is contrary to them. The Governor will remind us of what the King has already said and what he desires, and he will also speak prophetically of the future of the kingdom.

SANCTIFIER

Paul wrote to the first-century kingdom citizens in the city of Thessalonica, "From the beginning God chose you to be saved through the sanctifying work of the Spirit and through belief in the truth."

As Sanctifier, the Governor helps free us from things in our lives that are contrary to the nature of the King and that diminish our capacity to maximize our gifts for the kingdom. Earlier, we saw that to be sanctified or holy means to be both pure (integrated, whole) and set apart. The Holy Spirit therefore eliminates hindrances to our development and progress.

The Governor also sanctifies us in the sense of setting us apart for the service of the heavenly kingdom, and for the day when the King will once more return to the earth to live forever with his people with the creation of a new heaven and earth. When the queen of England was going to visit the Bahamas, the royal governor would require everyone to prepare for it. We would have to sweep the roads, clean the lampposts, and plant trees and flowers. We even had to mow our own private yards, even though the queen would never see them. It is the Holy Spirit's job to prepare every aspect of our lives for the King's coming.

These, then, are the major ways in which the Governor attends to us according to his nature. In the next chapter, we'll take a closer look at the culture of the kingdom that the Governor desires to instill in us.

CHAPTER TEN STUDY QUESTIONS

QUESTION FOR REFLECTION

1. What is your conception of the Holy Spirit's nature and qualities? What did you think the Holy Spirit was like when you were growing up or when you first became a Christian?

EXPLORING PRINCIPLES AND PURPOSES

2. What is the most important thing we must know about the nature of the Holy Spirit?

3. God is one, but he expresses himself in three distinct _____ and _____.

4. How do we know that the Holy Spirit has feelings or emotions?

5. When we neglect or ignore the Holy Spirit, what will he sometimes do in order to get our attention?

6. How can we learn to have fellowship with and listen to the Holy Spirit?

7. There are seven distinct ways in which the Governor attends to us in fulfillment of his nature. What is the first of his roles and responsibilities toward us?

8. What analogy did Jesus use to emphasize the King's commitment to us, which also lets us know the Holy Spirit will never give up on us?

9. What is the second of the Holy Spirit's roles and responsibilities toward us?

10. Why is the Governor our most important teacher?

11. How does the Governor make us practical people in the world?

12. What is the third of the Holy Spirit's roles and responsibilities toward us?

13. What are the two general arenas in which this help is given?

14. What is the fourth of the Holy Spirit's roles and responsibilities toward us?

15. How does the Holy Spirit exercise this role with those outside the kingdom of heaven?

16. How does the Holy Spirit exercise this role with those who have already entered the kingdom of heaven?

17. What is the fifth of the Holy Spirit's roles and responsibilities toward us?

18. In what manner does the Holy Spirit fulfill this role, and what Scripture from Hosea illustrates it?

19. What is the sixth of the Holy Spirit's roles and responsibilities toward us?

20. What is the nature and content of the words or messages the Governor brings us?

21. What is the seventh of the Holy Spirit's roles and responsibilities toward us?

22. What are the two main ways the Holy Spirit fulfills this role?

APPLYING THE PRINCIPLES OF KINGDOM LIVING
THINKING IT OVER

- Have you thought of the Holy Spirit as an impersonal object, a feeling, or a force? Have you realized *whom* you have living within you? How does this knowledge change the way you think of the Holy Spirit, and how will it change your relationship with him?

- Have you hesitated to make a commitment to the kingdom because you think you have to overcome sin and wrong attitudes *first*? Or have you struggled, even as a kingdom citizen, because you're trying to change your false mind-sets and behavior on your own?

Remember that the King is saying to us, "If you're going to learn kingdom culture, you need help from the home country." Receiving the Governor first into your life will enable you to change. Recognize that he will show you how to transform your thinking and how to live for the kingdom. The King sent him to us for this very purpose.

ACTING ON IT

+ Has the Holy Spirit been prompting you that it is time to repent, seek forgiveness, and enter the kingdom of God? Have you been resisting that prompting? Run to him now! As one of the New Testament writers reminded us, "Today, if you hear his voice, do not harden your hearts as you did in the rebellion" (Hebrews 3:15). God is long-suffering (patient), but he is not forever-suffering. We must respond to him when he calls us or it may become too late to respond.

+ Take each of the roles and responsibilities of the Holy Spirit we have explored in this chapter and meditate on them until you come to a thorough understanding of the way the Governor works in your life. You may want to focus on one per day, week, or month.

PRAYING ABOUT IT

+ Do you seek the advice of people without ever consulting the Holy Spirit—your Teacher and Guide? Do you go through your day without acknowledging him or referring to him as you make decisions, invest your finances, work at your job or business, or go to school? Make a decision to acknowledge and inquire of the Holy Spirit every morning and throughout the day. This will help you to build a relationship with him, learn to hear his voice, and fulfill the will of God in your life.

The Holy Spirit's presence in our lives is indispensable.

ELEVEN

THE GOVERNOR'S CULTURE

YOUR CULTURE REVEALS YOUR ORIGIN.

THE GOVERNOR'S QUALITIES OF THE KING

We should always keep in mind that the culture of the kingdom of heaven is synonymous with the nature of the King. When we talk about the characteristics of the Holy Spirit and his culture, we are talking about the qualities of the King himself. Since the role of a governor is only to represent the king, we should be able to look at a governor's temperament and the way he acts, and conclude what the king is like. Likewise, since the Holy Spirit reflects the qualities of the heavenly King, his characteristics are the personification of the King's nature.

This concept is familiar to us from everyday life. If we sit down to eat in a restaurant and the waiter is rude and inattentive, it will negatively affect our perception of the whole environment of the restaurant. However, if we go into a shoe store and find an extremely knowledgeable and patient salesperson who helps us find exactly what we need, we will have a favorable attitude toward the company he represents. The manner in which a person serves on behalf of another person, business, or institution inevitably contributes to the perception we have of that person, business, or institution.

THE KING'S CHARACTER DETERMINES THE STATE OF THE KINGDOM

A country's culture may be summed up as its *national character*. It is the combination of its beliefs, attitudes, values, conventions, practices, and characteristics. In a kingdom, the monarch's character and characteristics were vastly important because they influenced and often determined the state of the environment over which he ruled. They created what life was like in the kingdom. The wise King Solomon wrote,

Like a roaring lion or a charging bear is a wicked man ruling over a helpless people. A tyrannical ruler lacks judgment.

When the righteous increase, the people rejoice, but when a wicked man rules, people groan.

In other words, when the character of a leader is a certain way, it can affect the experience of his whole country. We see this played out in the Old Testament in the history of the nation of Israel, which eventually split into the kingdoms of Judah and Israel. The character of various kings influenced the people for evil or for good. For example, in the first book of Kings, we read, "Nadab son of Jeroboam became king of Israel..., and he reigned over Israel two years. He did evil in the eyes of the LORD, walking in the ways of his father and in his sin, *which he had caused Israel to commit.*" The epitaph about Jeroboam was that his actions "provoked the LORD, the God of Israel, to anger." Jeroboam had caused the people of Israel to worship idols rather than the Lord, and he had appointed as priest anyone who wanted to be one, rather than appointing only Levites, as God had commanded. His son Nadab clearly followed in his footsteps.

We also read in the first book of Kings that another king,

Ahab...did more evil in the eyes of the LORD than any of those before him. He not only considered it trivial to commit the sins of Jeroboam..., but he also married Jezebel daughter of Ethbaal king of the Sidonians, and began to serve Baal and worship him. He set up an altar for Baal in the temple of Baal that he built in Samaria. Ahab also made an Asherah pole and did more to provoke the LORD, the God of Israel, to anger than did all the kings of Israel before him.

The things that Jeroboam had done, which had so angered the Lord, Ahab considered trivial, and he did more evil than any of the kings who had preceded him! Evil leadership continued through the line of the kings of Israel, and the people also continued to do evil. The second book of Kings reports that the people experienced only misery as a result: "The LORD had seen how bitterly everyone in Israel, whether slave or free, was suffering; there was no one to help them."

In Judah, however, we see the example of King Hezekiah, whom the second book of Kings describes in this way:

> He did what was right in the eyes of the LORD, just as his father David had done…. Hezekiah trusted in the LORD, the God of Israel. There was no one like him among all the kings of Judah, either before him or after him. He held fast to the LORD and did not cease to follow him; he kept the commands the LORD had given Moses. And the LORD was with him; he was successful in whatever he undertook.

The book of 2 Kings gives an account of how the Lord delivered the people of Judah from a boastful, vengeful enemy, and how the people listened to Hezekiah when he told them how to deal with the situation. If they hadn't trusted Hezekiah and his example of faithfulness to the Lord, they would have fallen into their enemy's trap.

The key to a successful kingdom is the good character of its king. Likewise, the character of the heavenly Governor determines the environment of the kingdom of God on earth. Again, his character is exactly the same as the character of the King. He represents the nature and manners of the King in the colony.

The King wants us to understand the nature of his kingdom, so that we can trust it and what it means to live in it. This is one reason why the King-Son kept giving his followers descriptions of what he is like. He would say things such as these:

> I am the good shepherd. The good shepherd lays down his life for the sheep.

> I am the bread of life. He who comes to me will never go hungry, and he who believes in me will never be thirsty.

> Come to me, all you who are weary and burdened, and I will give you rest. Take my yoke upon you and learn from me, for I am gentle and humble in heart, and you will find rest for your souls. For my yoke is easy and my burden is light.

Jesus wanted to emphasize his nature because other kings and leaders of his day exhibited the opposite character. For example, his disciples were once disputing about which of them was the greatest and deserved the highest honors. Jesus used this argument as an occasion to explain the nature of the heavenly kingdom. This is his statement from the book of Matthew:

> You know that the rulers of the Gentiles lord it over them, and their high officials exercise authority over them. Not so with you. Instead, whoever wants to become great among you must be your servant, and whoever wants to be first must be your slave—just as the Son of Man did not come to be served, but to serve, and to give his life as a ransom for many.

In this way, and in many other ways, Jesus kept trying to teach them that the kingdom of God was radically different from the kingdom of darkness they had been living under. He wanted to express the qualities and characteristics of the King to thoroughly acquaint them with their benevolent Ruler.

The whole idea of knowing the nature of the King is critical to Jesus's statement, "The kingdom of heaven is near." He is inviting us to become citizens of a specific kingdom, and he wants to reassure us of the nature of this kingdom.

THE QUALITIES OF THE HOLY SPIRIT: GROWING KINGDOM CULTURE

Paul desired to instill the nature of the heavenly kingdom in the lives of its first-century citizens, who were learning what it meant for them to be realigned with the King. In his letter to kingdom citizens in Galatia, he made a list of essential qualities that make up the character of the King:

- Love
- Joy
- Peace
- Patience
- Kindness
- Goodness
- Faithfulness
- Gentleness
- Self-control

Any true manifestation of the kingdom of God on earth will have these characteristics. Paul referred to these qualities as "the fruit of the Spirit." He was saying that, wherever the Governor was, these qualities should be evident, indicating that the culture of the King was present.

Paul used this particular analogy of fruit because fruit doesn't appear overnight; it develops over time, and he wanted them to know that they would have to *cultivate* the culture of the King in their lives, under the example and leading of the Governor. First, the Governor teaches us the nature of the original government in heaven. Then he shows us that, because he lives within us, we have this original nature and need to manifest it in our lives.

When you receive the Holy Spirit, you also receive the seed of kingdom nature. You develop this seed by putting into your life the kingdom elements that allow it to grow. For example, an apple tree doesn't have to "work" to produce its fruit. The seeds of the fruit are within it, and eventually, through a process of maturity, enabled by elements such as the nutrients in the ground and sunlight, what is on the inside of the tree becomes manifested on its branches. The spiritual nutrients that enable the fruit to grow in our lives are maintaining a continual connection with the King, learning the Constitution of the kingdom, which is the Scriptures, and yielding to the direction of the Governor in our lives.

Just as apples are a natural outgrowth of apple trees, the fruit of the Spirit becomes a *natural* development in the life of a kingdom citizen because he is reflecting the *nature* of his King. For example, one of the fruits of the Spirit is goodness. It is therefore natural for us to be good if we're in the kingdom. If we are not good, we are unnatural. The Governor connects us to our original nature, which is true life for us as human beings.

The qualities or fruit of the Spirit embody the King's culture so that, first of all, we see that it is a culture of love, a culture of joy, and a culture of peace. Imagine a culture filled with all the qualities in the above list! It's our culture to be faithful—to be loyal to our commitments. It's our culture to be gentle. We're never brash or rude with other people. As Jesus said, "Blessed are the meek, for they will inherit the earth." It's our culture to be self-controlled. We never lose control of our tempers or our desires.

No matter what happens in our lives, we still live out and exhibit all these qualities.

When we have the Royal Governor resident within us, therefore, he renovates our lives by enabling us to reflect the nature of the King. He changes our personal culture by giving us a new perspective on life and a new "kingdom educational curriculum"; he causes us to have the mind-set of the King. He retrains us in how to think, how to talk, and how to walk.

CULTURE REVEALS ORIGIN

Your culture should reveal your origin. The way you behave, the way you respond to others, the way you react to problems, and the way you deal with disappointments should all reveal the culture of heaven. The qualities of the Spirit within you define the uniqueness of your nature. Your unique nature then links you to your heavenly heritage.

Earlier, we talked about how people's distinct mannerisms and traits lead us to instantly recognize what country they are from. You see someone and you say, "That person is an Australian." The same thing is true for citizens of any country. There are certain things that only Australians would say or do in a certain way. People should have the same experience in regard to those who represent heaven on earth. They should look at our behavior and be able to say, "You come from the heavenly kingdom." Jesus said, "By their fruit you will recognize them." Being in the kingdom is a matter of dynamic change into the nature of the King. If the Governor lives in you, you cannot enjoy living in rebellion against the King. Doing so feels uncomfortable and unnatural.

CULTURE CLASH

When you become realigned with the kingdom of heaven, you essentially now live in two worlds or kingdoms. The invisible kingdom of God lives within you through the presence of the Governor. The human kingdom, the kingdom of darkness fueled by Lucifer, is all around you. In addition, remnants of the rebellious nature are still present in your life and need to be rooted out.

We are therefore faced with a choice of which kingdom and its culture we are going to yield to. Paul encouraged the first-century kingdom citizens in Philippi to keep their focus on the heavenly kingdom because "our citizenship is in heaven." Following his list of the fruit of the Spirit, he told the Galatians, "Those who belong to Christ Jesus have crucified the sinful nature with its passions and desires. Since we live by the Spirit, let us keep in step with the Spirit." The disciple John encouraged Jesus's followers, "The one who is in you is greater than the one who is in the world." In other words, the power of the Governor within you exponentially exceeds the power of the kingdom of the world around you.

We often experience a clash of these cultures, especially within our own families. Let me illustrate with another example from kingdom and colony. The majority of the people who live in Caribbean nations are black. Many are related because their ancestors came from the same villages in Africa when they were brought to the Caribbean as slaves. People from the same family were often separated, sold to owners in different colonial kingdoms. So you have people who belong to the same family, but depending on what kingdom they fell under, they took on the language and customs of that kingdom so that, today, the descendants of a single family can't even communicate with one another. They don't know each other's language.

While this was a tragic consequence of colonialism, you may have a similar experience when you enter the kingdom of God and take on an entirely different culture. Because you exhibit the evidence of a changed life, your own family members—people you grew up with—may no longer understand you or why you act in the way you do. They notice that you've changed your language, your attitude, and your friendships. They see that you've stopped doing things that are against the heavenly kingdom. The proof that you are in the kingdom is that you are living the lifestyle of a different culture.

LIVING BY THE SPIRIT

Sometimes, we try to have one foot in the kingdom of heaven and one foot in the kingdom of the world. We want the Governor to look the other way while we behave according to a culture that is foreign to the King's. Yet Paul wrote to the Galatians,

Live by the Spirit, and you will not gratify the desires of the sinful nature. For the sinful nature desires what is contrary to the Spirit, and the Spirit what is contrary to the sinful nature. They are in conflict with each other, so that you do not do what you want. But if you are led by the Spirit, you are not under law.

Paul went on to catalog the culture of the rebellious nature:

The acts of the sinful nature are obvious: sexual immorality, impurity and debauchery; idolatry and witchcraft; hatred, discord, jealousy, fits of rage, selfish ambition, dissensions, factions and envy; drunkenness, orgies, and the like. I warn you, as I did before, that those who live like this will not inherit the kingdom of God.

The word *inherit* here implies living in or experiencing the kingdom. The culture of heaven and the culture of the world are opposites; you cannot experience the kingdom of heaven if you are living according to a foreign culture.

Since the Governor's role is to convert the citizens to live as the King does, when we act according to the culture of darkness, he rebukes and corrects us. He does this in two ways. First, he uses the internal warning system of our consciences. Second, he reminds us of the teachings of the King. He brings to our minds what is recorded in the Constitution of the kingdom, or the written record of the King's words and ways, the Scriptures. Paul wrote that we no longer live "under law." In other words, our trying to follow strict *dos* and *don'ts* doesn't work. Only a changed nature causes us to live as the King lives. And the Governor gives us this new nature and enables us to follow it.

Remember "The Speech from the Throne," through which the royal governor would read the queen's will for the Bahamas for the coming year? The Scriptures are a major component of The Speech from the *Heavenly* Throne, and as we become familiar with them, the Governor teaches and reminds us of the King's will. He tells us, "You're planning to do this, but that's not what the King says is good for you. That's not written in the Speech from the Throne." The Holy Spirit will only speak in accordance with what is in the Speech because it's the King's mind. And again, our job is to say, "Not my will, but yours be done." Jesus said, "The Spirit gives life;

the flesh counts for nothing. The words I have spoken to you are spirit and they are life."

You must remember that you are under a new Master Teacher, Jesus Christ. You are under a new philosophy of life. You are a student of a new curriculum. You are a steward of a new ideology. You have abandoned all other schools and have submitted yourself totally to the kingdom school. And the Governor is your private teacher, enabling you to internalize and manifest the teaching of the King. He is like a royal tutor, instilling the nature of the kingdom into the king's children. We have to be trained in what it means to be heirs in the heavenly kingdom.

The Governor begins by teaching us to relate to the Creator as our Father again, so that we can call him, "Abba, Father," just as the King-Son did. This relationship enables us to be remade in the image of our Creator. It is because of the rebellion that we lost our capacity to manifest his nature. That nature has been distorted in us because of our former association with the kingdom of darkness. The Governor has the challenging job of teaching us to be what we were originally created to be.

The qualities, or fruit, of the Spirit that we have been looking at are not only what the King *does*; they are what he *is*. The King doesn't only *act* in love; he *is* love. He doesn't only *demonstrate* peace; he *is* peace. And every aspect of the King's nature is what we are to be in our essence, as well. This is what Jesus meant when he said, as recorded in the book of Matthew, "Be perfect, therefore, as your heavenly Father is perfect."

Realizing that we are to reflect the nature of our King-Father causes us to watch what we allow to enter the personal culture of our spirits, souls, and bodies. Paul wrote to the kingdom citizens in the city of Corinth, "Do you not know that your body is a temple of the Holy Spirit, who is in you, whom you have received from God? You are not your own; you were bought at a price. Therefore honor God with your body." Paul was saying, in effect, "Don't you know that your body is the Governor's mansion? He is holy, and he lives in you; therefore, you need to keep the residence clean for him and in accordance with his nature. Jesus paid for the redemption of your spirit, soul, and body, so that the Governor could live within you. Therefore, as steward of the Governor's mansion, you should honor it by taking care of it."

Jesus taught, "Your eye is the lamp of your body. When your eyes are good, your whole body also is full of light. But when they are bad, your body also is full of darkness." The culture of the world enters our lives through our eyes and ears. Whatever we watch on television or the Internet, or read in a book, affects the quality of our inner, personal culture. Whatever we keep listening to influences our lives. We must not allow a destructive culture to invade and destroy our lives and our work for the heavenly kingdom.

Being a kingdom citizen requires that we exist in some degree of tension because we live in the midst of a culture of rebellion and death. Our old culture is fighting with the demands of the new culture. Yet we live here for the purpose of spreading the kingdom of light and pushing back the kingdom of darkness. This is why Jesus prayed to the Father, just before he died, "My prayer is not that you take them out of the world but that you protect them from the evil one. They are not of the world, even as I am not of it…. As you sent me into the world, I have sent them into the world."

Even as we live in this tension, therefore, we live in the reality of the love, joy, peace, patience, kindness, goodness, faithfulness, gentleness, and self-control of the heavenly kingdom. Paul wrote to the kingdom citizens living in Ephesus,

> You were dead in your transgressions and sins, in which you used to live when you followed the ways of this world and of the ruler of the kingdom of the air, the spirit who is now at work in those who are disobedient. All of us also lived among them at one time, gratifying the cravings of our sinful nature and following its desires and thoughts. Like the rest, we were by nature objects of wrath. But because of his great love for us, God, who is rich in mercy, made us alive with Christ even when we were dead in transgressions—it is by grace you have been saved. And God raised us up with Christ and seated us with him in the heavenly realms in Christ Jesus…. For we are God's workmanship, created in Christ Jesus to do good works, which God prepared in advance for us to do.

Though we live on earth, we are also seated in the heavenly realms with the King, who has brought us to live in his heavenly kingdom, and we have all the resources of this kingdom to enable us to live out the culture of the kingdom on earth. Jesus told his disciples, "Let your light shine before men, that they may see your good deeds and praise your Father in heaven."

THE GIFTS OF THE SPIRIT: THE POWER OF KINGDOM CULTURE

When the Spirit was poured out on the day of Pentecost, kingdom citizens were given the Governor's power, with various kingdom abilities, to promote kingdom culture on earth. These abilities are known as "the gifts of the Spirit." The *fruit* has to do with the character of the King. It is the development of the King's nature within us. The *gifts* have to do with the power of the King. One is character, the other is ability, but both are necessary for the kingdom life. Some of these abilities are the gifts of wisdom, knowledge, faith, healing, miracles, and prophecy. We will take a closer look at these gifts in chapter thirteen. However, we should note here that while character develops over time, ability-power from the Governor can be received immediately after a person realigns with the King and receives the outpouring of the Spirit in his life.

With these gifts of power comes great responsibility. Character is more important than power because it protects our use of that power. It keeps us from using it for the wrong motivations and purposes. It prevents us from using our power to hurt others rather than to help them. Everyone wants power, and when we are offered it, we don't often think about the need to regulate it. Many people seek the power without realizing how critical it is for them to develop the essential qualities of the kingdom at the same time. It is easier to receive the gifts of the Spirit than it is to develop the fruit of the Spirit. It is easier to obtain the power of God than it is to develop the character of God. Therefore, we must develop the qualities—such as love, kindness, and self-control—because they will moderate our use of the gifts.

Both the qualities and the gifts are important, therefore, but the qualities are vital because power without character is dangerous. A balance between the two is a challenge for all kingdom citizens. I believe this is why Jesus spent three-and-a-half years teaching his disciples how to live, how to think, and how to act as kingdom citizens. He trained them first, and then they received the power of the heavenly government through the outpouring of the Spirit at Pentecost. He also told them that, after he had returned to the Father, the Governor would continue to train them because being transformed into the culture of the kingdom is an ongoing, lifelong process.

THE INFLUENCE OF CULTURE

Ultimately, culture is spread through influence, and the qualities and gifts of the Spirit are the influence of the kingdom on earth. As we allow the Governor to transform our lives into the nature of the King, and as we demonstrate his power, our lives will have an effect on others. This is how the kingdom of heaven will spread on the earth. When Peter explained that the outpouring of the Spirit at Pentecost was the fulfillment of the King's promise, the impact on the people who had gathered there was powerful:

> Those who accepted [Peter's] message [about the kingdom] were baptized, and about three thousand were added to their number that day. They devoted themselves to the apostles' teaching and to the fellowship, to the breaking of bread and to prayer. Everyone was filled with awe, and many wonders and miraculous signs were done by the apostles. All the believers were together and had everything in common. Selling their possessions and goods, they gave to anyone as he had need. Every day they continued to meet together in the temple courts. They broke bread in their homes and ate together with glad and sincere hearts, praising God and enjoying the favor of all the people. And the Lord added to their number daily those who were being saved.

That is quite a picture of cultural transformation! The public impact of the believers' love, sharing, teaching, and demonstrations of kingdom power, as a reflection of the culture of the kingdom, led to their having favor with all the people who witnessed their new kingdom lifestyle. And the influence of the kingdom of heaven on earth grew daily.

As vice governors under the Royal Governor, we serve as ambassadors of kingdom culture. Kingdom influence will grow from personal commitment to community transformation to national impact to worldwide conversion. But it begins with one person who exchanges the culture of darkness for the kingdom of life and light. With which kingdom are you aligned right now?

CHAPTER ELEVEN STUDY QUESTIONS

QUESTION FOR REFLECTION

1. How have you seen the environment of an organization, school, business, family, or nation influenced by the character of its leaders?

EXPLORING PRINCIPLES AND PURPOSES

2. A country's culture may be summed up as its national character. How is national character defined?

3. Why were a monarch's character and characteristics vastly important to his kingdom?

4. What notable statement about rulers did Jesus make to his disciples that shows the kingdom of heaven is radically different from the kingdom of darkness—and earthly kingdoms that are influenced by it? How would you define the central theme of this statement?

5. What essential qualities did Paul list as the nature of the heavenly King and his kingdom?

6. When you receive the Holy Spirit, you also receive the seed of kingdom nature. How do you develop this seed in your life?

7. Explain the statement "Your culture should reveal your origin" in terms of the kingdom of heaven.

8. When you become realigned with the kingdom of heaven, what two worlds or kingdoms do you now live in?

9. We are continually faced with the choice of which of these kingdoms and its culture we will yield to. What instruction do we find in the New Testament to help us remain aligned with the kingdom of heaven?

10. What is the first thing the Governor teaches us? Why?

11. Realizing that we are to reflect the nature of our King-Father, what should we carefully watch in our lives?

12. What is our purpose for being on earth while it is still influenced by the kingdom of darkness?

13. The fruit of the Spirit has to do with the _____ of the King, and the gifts of the Spirit have to do with the _____ of the King.

14. While the fruit and the gifts are both essential for kingdom living, why is character more important than power? What is power without character?

15. Being transformed into the culture of the kingdom is an _____, _____ process.

APPLYING THE PRINCIPLES OF KINGDOM LIVING
THINKING IT OVER

+ The way you behave, respond to others, react to problems, and deal with disappointments should all reveal the culture of heaven. What aspects of the fruit of the Spirit do you most need to develop, with the guidance and help of the Governor?

+ Have you experienced a "culture clash" with members of your family, friends, or others who have not yet entered the kingdom of heaven? How have you responded to it? Have you asked the Governor to help you to respond according to the nature of the King?

ACTING ON IT

+ Dr. Munroe wrote that sometimes we try to have one foot in the kingdom of heaven and one foot in the kingdom of the world. Yet we have seen that the culture of the kingdom of heaven and the culture of the kingdom of darkness are totally incompatible. The kingdom of darkness can never reflect the nature of the King. In what areas of your life are you attempting to live in both kingdoms? Note these areas, surrender them to the Governor, and commit yourself to him for transformation into the nature of the King.

+ Are you watching what you are allowing into the personal culture of your spirit, soul, and body? Review what you are watching on television, viewing on the Internet, listening to, and reading, and evaluate these things according to a healthy kingdom life.

PRAYING ABOUT IT

+ As you become conformed to the nature of the King, make this your daily meditation and prayer: "May the words of my mouth and the meditation of my heart be pleasing in your sight, O Lord, my Rock and my Redeemer" (Psalm 19:14).

"Let your light shine before men, that they may see your good deeds and praise your Father in heaven."
—Matthew 5:16

PART 4

THE ROLE AND IMPACT OF THE GOVERNOR

TWELVE

MANIFESTING KINGDOM CULTURE

THE ABSENCE OF AN INTERNAL GOVERNMENT ALWAYS DEMANDS MORE EXTERNAL LAW.

As we have seen, every nation manifests itself in unique cultural and social expressions. There are specific ways that people from certain countries act, speak, and look, so that you can recognize, "That's a Bahamian," "That's an Italian," or "That's a Russian." After you have been around people from various countries or regions long enough, you begin to recognize their distinguishing mannerisms, attitudes, and speech.

The previous chapter emphasized that, as citizens of the heavenly kingdom, we should begin to take on the distinguishing characteristics of our new country. While we are still surrounded by the kingdom of darkness, we are to live from the *inside out* rather than from the outside in. Since we're not used to living in this way, we depend on the Governor to instruct and empower us in all the ways of the kingdom—its mind-set, lifestyle, and customs—so that what is within us can be manifested in our attitudes, words, and actions.

In this chapter, I want to explore an aspect of kingdom culture that is vital to all other aspects of it; in fact, it often leads to and is associated with the gifts of the Spirit, which we will discuss in more depth in chapter thirteen.

To begin, let's look at the characteristics of all human nations, or kingdoms.

CHARACTERISTICS OF ALL NATIONS

There are certain characteristics that nations must have to become established and to maintain themselves as nations. They must have...

1. Land (territory)

2. Culture (what the nation stands for; its ideals)

3. Values (the standards the people of the nation live by)

4. Language (a common form of communication)

For example, what makes the United States of America a nation is not a particular ethnicity or standard of living. It is the land, the foundational beliefs and tenets found in its Constitution and other important national documents, the values that are drawn from those foundational beliefs, and its common language, English.

THE POWER OF LANGUAGE TO A KINGDOM

Of the above four characteristics, *language* is the primary and greatest manifestation of a nation's culture.

Why is language so important to a nation?

LANGUAGE IS THE KEY TO NATIONAL IDENTITY

First, language is the key to national identity. When the British Empire took over the Bahamas, the first thing they did was make the people learn to speak English. Language is powerful because it gives people a shared perspective not only on life, but also on how that life is expressed. It could be said that culture is *contained* in language, because it shapes it. If you and I can't speak the same language, we can never have the same culture because we can't communicate with one another. So the key to community is language. A country is really not a country until all the people speak in the same tongue.

LANGUAGE CREATES NATIONAL UNITY

Second, language creates national unity. When a nation doesn't have a common language, the unity of the people begins to break down. In fact, the United States is currently facing a challenge with this issue. Some of the people want the nation to be officially bilingual because of the many immigrants who have come from Spanish-speaking nations. A number of these immigrants don't seem to want to learn English, so signs and literature are being printed in Spanish.

In past generations, when immigrants came to America, such as those from Ireland and Italy, there were also segments of the population who spoke another language. However, most of these immigrants wanted to learn English, and they wanted their children to speak English, too, so the situation was somewhat different. They were not asking that their languages be recognized officially but were interested in assimilating into American culture by learning English. The current question of a bilingual nation has prompted some in the Congress of the United States to propose legislation declaring English the official language.

Historically, Americans have agreed that their language is English, the French have agreed that their language is French, and people from Spain and Latin American countries have agreed that their language is Spanish. If you emigrate to another country, it's supposed to be your responsibility to make sure you adopt the country's language. Otherwise, it encourages disharmony. Therefore, every nation embraces a common language because it is the key to unity.

LANGUAGE IS THE KEY TO EFFECTIVE COMMUNICATION

Third, language is the key to effective communication. National culture, values, history, goals, needs, and desires can be transmitted only if a nation's leaders and citizens are able to effectively communicate these things to each other and subsequent generations. A common language is essential to accomplish this, especially in helping to ensure the accuracy of the transmission.

LANGUAGE IS THE KEY TO EFFECTIVE EXPRESSION

Fourth, language is the key to effective expression. You won't be able to articulate what you desire to say if you lack the words to do so. Such a lack makes it difficult for people to participate in a nation as full-fledged citizens.

LANGUAGE SIGNIFIES A COMMON HERITAGE

Fifth, language is the key to common heritage. It identifies the original home country of those who speak it. For example, if a man from Portugal met a man from Brazil, they would recognize their common heritage because they both speak Portuguese, even though there might be regional differences in their respective expressions of the language.

LANGUAGE IS THE KEY TO GENERATIONAL TRANSFER

Sixth, language is the key to generational transfer. When families emigrate from a nation, and the parents preserve the language and customs of the home country but their children do not, you eventually have situations in which grandchildren are unable to speak with their grandparents and lose contact with their heritage. This means that, if I want to pass along my values, beliefs, and family traditions to my children, I have to be able to communicate with them in a common language. Language therefore preserves family heritage throughout generations.

LOSS OF UNITY AND COMMUNICATION WITH THE KINGDOM

These points about the power and value of language have implications for kingdom culture on earth. When human beings rebelled against their King and lost the Governor, the clear lines of communication between the heavenly kingdom and the inhabitants on earth were disrupted. In this sense, we could say that heaven and earth no longer had a "common language." Human beings then tried to use their human language to further disassociate themselves from the King. Let's examine how this transpired.

The book of Genesis records, "Now the whole world had one language and a common speech. As men moved eastward, they found a plain in Shinar and settled there." We learn in Genesis 3 that after Adam and Eve were expelled from the garden of Eden, the entrance to the eastern side of the garden was specifically guarded so they couldn't return there. Apparently, they left from the east side, and humanity continued to move eastward as the earth's population grew.

In Genesis 11, we find that the people were still spreading out eastward, and that they had retained a common language. This is the chapter that describes how the people decided to build a city with an immense tower. The incident shows the power of language. The people wanted to build a tower that would reach to the heavens, and they said, in effect, "We will build a tower and make a name for ourselves." God's response was, "If as one people speaking the same language they have begun to do this, then nothing they plan to do will be impossible for them." Note that he said, "If as one people *with the same language*," indicating that a key to power is language.

The people's desire to build, however, was an indication of their separation from the home country. When you build something just for your own honor and purposes, even while using the mind, talent, and material the King gave you, and you call it your own, this is the same as idol worship. Anything that is more important to us than the King is an idol. So the people were about to build a tower that was more important to them than their Creator-King was.

The King was not against people building cities or towers. In fact, he wants us to build the dreams that are in our hearts, which he put there. Rather, he was against their selfish pursuit of fame, and their arrogance. We are to do everything for the sake of the King's glory, not our own. If it's not for his glory, it will eventually be to our detriment.

Again, the key to their ability to build this tower was their unified language. "If as one people speaking the same language they have begun to do this, then nothing they plan to do will be impossible for them." The power of language is its ability to produce. Today, we see that the language barrier prevents many countries from working together on projects, and it can cause communication problems for companies who try to build in other nations.

Since the whole world at that time had one language, we can say that the whole world had powerful potential. But they used that power of language to build something for themselves, and the King said, in essence, "This is wrong. Everything you're using is mine. The ground is mine. The water is mine. The straw is mine. The nails and the hammers are all made from materials I created." And so, his response was, "Come, let us go down and *confuse their language* so they will not understand each other." He didn't say, "Let us destroy the tower," because that wasn't necessary. If they couldn't talk to one another, the tower couldn't be completed.

The Genesis account continues, "That is why it was called Babel—because there the LORD confused the language of the whole world." This incident is where we get the word *babble*. *Babble* means "confusion."[1] When we say someone is babbling, we mean that what he is saying is incomprehensible. The tower was not originally called the Tower of Babel. That was just what it was called after the King destroyed the people's ability to communicate with one language.

Confounding humanity's language was the King-Father's way of protecting us until he would one day restore our unity and communication with him and one another through the return of the Governor. Expelling human beings from the garden had protected humanity from eating from the Tree of Life and living in an eternal state of rebellion and separation from God, with no hope of redemption. Similarly, confusing humanity's language helped to guard human beings from the self-destruction of pursuing their goals only for selfish pursuit. The action was for their ultimate good.

If the key to power is one language, then the key to weakness is many languages. I believe this is one reason why the United Nations is so ineffective. Different languages, and the cultures they create, inevitably promote misunderstanding and disunity, and it isn't possible to change this fundamental issue, even through well-meaning organizations.

The rebellion of human beings, therefore, damaged their unity and communication with God and one another until the King-Son could put them back in the position to reconnect once again through the Governor. Significantly, this restoration of communication and unity was characterized by a capacity to speak in heaven-given languages, an ability given by the Holy Spirit. Once again, we can see why the key to bringing back kingdom culture to earth is the Governor.

HEAVEN-GIVEN LANGUAGES

One of the first things the Governor gives us after we receive his infilling is the ability to speak in heaven-given languages. He may give an earthly language that the speaker does not understand. Or he may give a heavenly language that is unknown on earth. Through heaven-given languages, the Governor enables human beings to once more share a "common tongue," so to speak, with the heavenly King, showing they belong to his kingdom. After Jesus had accomplished his mission of restoration, he told his disciples, "You will receive power when the Holy Spirit comes on you." But he also said, "These signs will accompany those who believe: In my name they will drive out demons; *they will speak in new tongues;*…they will place their hands on sick people, and they will get well." Jesus was outlining the evidence of lives that have been connected to the heavenly kingdom.

The promise of the Father was not just for kingdom *power*, therefore, but it was also for kingdom *language*. According to Jesus, when you receive citizenship, you receive "new tongues." The Governor gives you languages from the heavenly kingdom. Let's review what happened when the Spirit was poured out on the day of Pentecost:

> When the day of Pentecost came, they [the one hundred twenty followers of Jesus at that time] were all together in one place. Suddenly a sound like the blowing of a violent wind came from heaven and filled the whole house where they were sitting. They saw what seemed to be tongues of fire that separated and came to rest on each of them. All of them were filled with the Holy Spirit and began to speak in other tongues [or languages] as the Spirit enabled them. Now there were staying in Jerusalem God-fearing Jews from every nation under heaven. When they heard this sound, a crowd came together in bewilderment, because each one heard them speaking in his own language. Utterly amazed, they asked: "Are not all these men who are speaking Galileans? Then how is it that each of us hears them in his own native language? Parthians, Medes and Elamites; residents of Mesopotamia, Judea and Cappadocia, Pontus and Asia, Phrygia and Pamphylia, Egypt and the parts of Libya near Cyrene; visitors from Rome (both Jews and converts to Judaism); Cretans and Arabs—we hear them declaring the wonders of God in our own tongues!"

"All of them were filled with the Holy Spirit and began to speak in other tongues as the Spirit enabled them." Suddenly, those one hundred twenty people, who had gathered together to worship the King-Father and wait for the outpouring of the Spirit, were enabled by the Governor to speak in other languages. In this particular case, the God-given languages included human languages that the international crowd could understand. The King was communicating his plan of restoration through a special gift of language given to his kingdom citizens. This was a sign of the fulfillment of his promise. It showed that the communication lines between heaven and earth were open once more through the return of the Governor. It was also an indication that God desires to restore unity among the people of the world.

Peter told those who witnessed their speaking in tongues, "God has raised this Jesus to life, and we are all witnesses of the fact. Exalted to the right hand of God, he has received from the Father the promised Holy Spirit and has poured out *what you now see and hear.*" When the Governor indwells our lives, we're supposed to *hear* his presence, not just see it. It's supposed to be manifest in the evidence of language.

Let's note the beauty of this occurrence. At the incident of the Tower of Babel, God confused the people with multiple languages so he could weaken them. Here, he gave his people the gift of languages in order to strengthen them in their new kingdom life and enable them to communicate the promise of the Spirit to other inhabitants who needed to hear this message. This gift of languages also served to unite kingdom citizens as one people belonging to the King-Father.

I have traveled to over seventy countries, mostly to speak at conferences but sometimes to visit. I don't understand the languages of many of these nations. However, when I have attended conferences in a number of these places, something unique has happened that illustrates the oneness between people that comes from receiving heaven-given languages.

For example, I was recently ministering in Ukraine, where twenty thousand people had gathered in an auditorium. I don't understand Ukrainian. However, we started worshipping, and the whole place seemed to explode with heaven-given languages. When I heard twenty thousand Ukrainian-speaking people begin to speak in tongues, and I joined them, I thought, "We're one now!" I suddenly felt at home. This reminded me again that the power of unity is in language.

In a similar incident, my wife and I went to Germany some years ago, and we went to a Pentecostal church where I was to speak. Of course, everybody was speaking German. Then they started worshipping and speaking in tongues. All of a sudden, I had that same feeling of being home. To hear them speak in tongues was to feel, "We are one family." The barriers dropped away. We realized that we are all citizens of the kingdom, and that we have a common heritage. It was tongues that did it. Then, when the worship portion ended and the people began to speak in German, I didn't understand a word anymore and I felt more like a stranger again. Heaven-given languages are more powerful than many of us realize.

PURPOSES OF SPEAKING IN TONGUES

The purpose of the Governor is to train us in the ways of our home country; and language, as we've seen, is the most crucial characteristic of a country. Let's review several ways in which speaking in tongues is important to us.

PROVIDES KINGDOM IDENTITY

Speaking in tongues is a key element of our kingdom identity. Again, following our reconciliation with the King, our being given the ability to speak in heavenly tongues means the Governor is enabling us, as it were, to share a heavenly "language" with our King-Father.

GIVES DIRECT COMMUNICATION WITH THE KING

Tongues also enables humanity to once more communicate directly with the King-Father. For example, there are times when we find it difficult to express our desires and needs to the heavenly government while speaking in our earthly languages. Paul wrote that, at these times, the Governor speaks for us and through us to the Father, through spiritual communication.

> In the same way, the Spirit helps us in our weakness. We do not know what we ought to pray for, but the Spirit himself intercedes for us with groans that words cannot express. And he who searches our hearts knows the mind of the Spirit, because the Spirit intercedes for the saints in accordance with God's will.

The Governor provides us with heaven-given languages so that, along with other communication, it becomes possible for us to express our crucial needs and requests to the King.

A SIGN WE ARE CONNECTED WITH THE KING

When Jesus's followers first spoke with "new tongues" as the Holy Spirit was poured out upon them, it was a sign to the thousands of people gathered for the feast of Pentecost that these disciples were connected to the heavenly kingdom. As Paul taught, "Tongues, then, are a sign, not for believers but for unbelievers; prophecy, however, is for believers, not for unbelievers."

AN EVIDENCE OF OUR CITIZENSHIP IN THE KINGDOM

There is an incident in the book of Acts where the Holy Spirit was poured out on new kingdom citizens in the city of Caesarea as Peter was explaining the gospel of the kingdom to them. Peter and the other believers recognized that these were fellow citizens, "for they heard them speaking in tongues and praising God." Their speaking in tongues was clear evidence of their citizenship in the heavenly kingdom.

COMMON QUESTIONS ABOUT TONGUES

Inevitably, in a discussion about tongues, people have certain questions, such as…

+ Are tongues real?

+ Were tongues only for the time of Jesus and his early followers?

+ Is it necessary to speak in tongues in order to live the life of a kingdom citizen?

Let's address these questions.

ARE TONGUES REAL?

Tongues are actual spoken communications between heaven and earth. Many people wonder if tongues are real because speaking in tongues has been put into a context of something that is strange or abnormal. The early followers of Jesus spoke in tongues, as Jesus had said they would. Kingdom citizens throughout the last two millennia have spoken with the King using this means. If we realize that tongues are what comes natural to citizens of the kingdom, their strangeness disappears and their true purpose becomes clear.

WERE TONGUES ONLY FOR THE TIME OF JESUS AND HIS FOLLOWERS?

Tongues were given to kingdom citizens to assist them in kingdom purposes, and we are still living in a time when we need this assistance on earth. Their value to the first-century kingdom citizens is their value to us today—communication with the King-Father as we carry out his will in the world.

MANIFESTING KINGDOM CULTURE 211

Yet some misunderstanding and conflict between people concerning speaking in tongues is not surprising. We read in the Genesis account concerning the tower of Babel,

> The LORD said, "If as one people speaking the same language they have begun to do this, then nothing they plan to do will be impossible for them. Come, let us go down and confuse their language so they will not understand each other." So the LORD scattered them from there over all the earth.

As we just discussed, when people don't understand each other, they tend to separate themselves. We all like to be with people we understand. This is why, generally, all the English-speaking people group together, all the French speakers stay together, all those who speak Spanish join together, and so on. Language creates differences, and differences can create feelings of competition, pressure, and conflict. When you come down to it, war is often created by language differences.

Therefore, when some kingdom citizens don't understand the value of the gift of tongues and have not received it, then misunderstanding and conflict inevitably occur between them and other kingdom citizens, and this is regrettable. I believe that heaven-given languages are a powerful unifier among those who have received them, and this is why Lucifer fights against the baptism in the Holy Spirit and the outpouring of heavenly gifts to the children of the King. He encourages some kingdom citizens to create doctrines against the gift of tongues; in this way, he tries to make sure that not all kingdom citizens will speak a common, unifying "language." This is, to a large degree, why we have theological positions against tongues, such as that tongues are not real or that they were only for the first followers of Jesus. We have seminaries that teach that these God-given languages don't exist anymore. Unfortunately, these schools are teaching ignorance. But the real damage is that this opposition to the baptism in the Spirit and tongues prevents some citizens of the King from having all the power they need to exercise the kingdom life.

The devil knows that he is in trouble when we start speaking in tongues. Tongues are our key to overcoming obstacles in many areas of our lives. For example, I used to be an F student. After I started speaking in tongues when I was in high school, I became a top student in the school and even graduated at the head of my class. Tongues, therefore, are given for renewing the lives of individual kingdom citizens and enabling them to exercise power for kingdom purposes.

IS IT NECESSARY TO SPEAK IN TONGUES TO BE A KINGDOM CITIZEN?

You can be a kingdom citizen without speaking in tongues. However, you will have problems communicating with the kingdom and, as I said, you will lack the power you could have in living the kingdom life. Here is an illustration to show you that the gifts of the Spirit, and tongues, in particular, are very practical.

In my church, I have members and visitors who come from a variety of countries. There are people from the Philippines who speak Filipino. There are people from Haiti who speak Creole. There are people from Mexico who speak Spanish. If a woman from the Philippines prayed the Lord's Prayer in Filipino, most of us wouldn't understand her. However, would she be making sense? Yes, to other people from her original country. If a man from Haiti spoke a psalm in Creole, he wouldn't make any sense to us, but he would make sense to people in Haiti. The same thing would apply to someone from Mexico who spoke in Spanish.

Now, just because we wouldn't understand them, would that make their languages invalid? Would you be able to say that their languages weren't real? Or, would your belief or disbelief in what they said change the fact that their languages were genuine? No. Whether we understood or agreed with them, the languages would still be authentic. Paul wrote,

> Undoubtedly there are all sorts of languages in the world, yet none of them is without meaning. If then I do not grasp the meaning of what someone is saying, I am a foreigner to the speaker, and he is a foreigner to me.

Now, suppose one of those church members or visitors learned English. Since it is not his country's language, when he picked up the phone to call relatives at home, he would shift into his country's tongue. Therefore, if he wanted information from the Bahamas, he would speak English, but if he wanted information from home, he would speak the language of his homeland.

In a similar way, when you speak in tongues here on earth, it's as if you've picked up a phone to call your home country and are speaking in your original language. The Scripture says, "For anyone who speaks in a tongue does not speak to men but to God. Indeed, no one understands him; he utters mysteries with his spirit." In regard to prayer, we are to pray in tongues more than we pray in our human languages. This is because we don't want a weak communication of our intent when we're speaking to heaven. The Scripture tells us that the Governor knows the mind and will of God. Therefore, when we pray in the Spirit, we know that the King hears us and that we have the things we have asked him for, because the Governor helps us to pray according to the will of the government. We need a direct line to heaven, and tongues are that direct line. When you are filled with the Holy Spirit, you can speak in tongues at any time of the day, anytime you need to communicate with your King-Father. This is why you and I should earnestly *desire* spiritual gifts, as Paul said. They are important resources from the heavenly kingdom.

Some people refer to speaking in tongues as babbling. In fact, the reverse is true. Heaven-given languages communicate the thoughts and requests of the heart more clearly than any earthly language. With tongues, we're not speaking with our minds but through our spirits, and the Spirit communicates every need. For me, speaking in English can interfere with my ability to pray. That's why I pray in tongues much of the time. I love praying in tongues because my prayers don't have to be "translated."

I would even conclude that speaking in tongues is not really an option for a citizen of the kingdom of heaven. Perhaps you grew up in a church where speaking in tongues isn't believed in or practiced. Your theology or your church doesn't give you a relationship with God, however. The sacrificial work of Jesus and the Holy Spirit within you enable you to have this relationship. The Holy Spirit brings you into the kingdom and gives you the ability to speak in tongues so that you can better communicate with your King-Father.

DIFFERENT MANIFESTATIONS OF TONGUES

Two distinct forms of tongues are described in Scripture. These differences only demonstrate the versatility of language, as well as how communication changes depending on those with whom we are communicating.

FOR DIRECT, PERSONAL COMMUNICATION WITH THE KING

For the most part, what we have been discussing in this chapter is the first type of communication in tongues, which is for direct, personal communication with the King. Paul wrote, "Anyone who speaks in a tongue does not speak to men but to God. Indeed, no one understands him; he utters mysteries with his spirit [or, by the Spirit]."

FOR HEAVENLY COMMUNICATION TO OTHER KINGDOM CITIZENS

The second type of communication in tongues is not for personal but corporate communication. Paul taught the first-century kingdom citizens that ministry spiritual gifts, in contrast to personal spiritual gifts, are for the building up of *all* those in a local gathering of kingdom citizens. They include the public declaration of the King's will in a heaven-given language(s), with accompanying interpretation in the language of the people who are gathered, to assure that everyone understands the message. Paul wrote,

> Now to each one the manifestation of the Spirit is given for the common good. To one there is given through the Spirit the message of wisdom,…to another speaking in different kinds of tongues, and to still another the interpretation of tongues.

> Now you are the body of Christ, and each one of you is a part of it. And in the church God has appointed first of all apostles, second prophets, third teachers, then workers of miracles, also those having gifts of healing, those able to help others, those with gifts of administration, and those speaking in different kinds of tongues. Are all apostles? Are all prophets? Are all teachers? Do all work miracles? Do all have gifts of healing? Do all speak in tongues? Do all interpret?

> When you come together, everyone has a hymn, or a word of instruction, a revelation, a tongue or an interpretation. All of these

must be done for the strengthening of the church. If anyone speaks in a tongue, two—or at the most three—should speak, one at a time, and someone must interpret.

For this reason anyone who speaks in a tongue should pray that he may interpret what he says.

Paul was teaching that a special gift for communicating the will of the King through heaven-given language is given to someone whom the Governor helps to speak the mind of the King, in order to present it to the citizens. Notice that Paul said this gift is for the "common good" rather than individual edification. It is to help all the citizens to know the will of the King and to be comforted and encouraged by his words. Paul concluded, "Therefore, my brothers, be eager to prophesy, and do not forbid speaking in tongues. But everything should be done in a fitting and orderly way." We should encourage public declaration of tongues and interpretation, as long as it is done according to the guidelines set forth in the Constitution of the kingdom.

TEN REASONS TO SPEAK IN TONGUES

There is more to being filled with the Spirit than speaking in tongues, but tongues are an integral and important part of the manifestation of the Governor's presence in our lives. Speaking in tongues is a flowing stream that should never dry up. It will enrich and build up our spiritual lives. In my experience, speaking in tongues is a critical key in releasing and using other gifts of the Spirit. This, of course, applies to the gift of interpretation of tongues, but also to the other gifts, particularly prophecy, wisdom, and knowledge because they involve language.

Let's briefly look at ten reasons why every kingdom citizen should speak in tongues.

1. A SIGN OF CONNECTION TO THE KINGDOM

Tongues are often the initial supernatural evidence of the indwelling and filling of the Spirit. We see this first in the experience of the followers of Jesus at Pentecost. We also see it in the kingdom service of Paul of Tarsus. The physician Luke wrote, in the book of Acts, "While Apollos was at Corinth, Paul took the road through the interior and arrived at Ephesus. There he found some disciples."

Notice that they were called *disciples*. They were actually followers of John the Baptist, and Paul said to them, in effect, "You are on the right track, but you need to hear about Jesus, the one whom John was referring to, and you need the promise that he provided for you. You need the baptism in the Holy Spirit."

These disciples had said to Paul, "We have never even heard of the Holy Spirit." They are not very different from many people in churches today whose theology has excluded the active working of the Holy Spirit in their lives. They believe in the King and his kingdom, but they are unaware of the full role of the Governor in their lives.

When these disciples heard the gospel of the kingdom, which John had pointed them toward, and which Paul fully explained to them, they were baptized in water in the name of the Lord Jesus. When Paul placed his hands on them and prayed for them, the Holy Spirit came upon them, and they immediately spoke in tongues and prophesied.

An evidence that we are connected to the home country is that we receive heaven-given languages.

2. FOR EDIFICATION

Speaking in tongues builds up, or recharges, our spirits. We are personally strengthened as we interact with the King through the Governor. As Paul wrote, "He who speaks in a tongue edifies himself." Tongues are given to us so that our communication with God can be as it was for Adam—with no interference.

3. TO REMIND US OF THE GOVERNOR'S INDWELLING PRESENCE

Tongues make us aware of the indwelling presence of the Holy Spirit, and when we are conscious of his presence, we are encouraged and comforted. Jesus said,

And I will ask the Father, and he will give you another Counselor to be with you forever—the Spirit of truth. The world cannot accept him, because it neither sees him nor knows him. But you know him, for he lives with you and will be in you.

4. TO KEEP OUR PRAYERS IN LINE WITH THE KING'S WILL

Praying in tongues will keep our prayers in line with God's will and prevent us from praying in selfishness. As I quoted earlier from the writings of Paul,

> In the same way, the Spirit helps us in our weakness. We do not know what we ought to pray for, but the Spirit himself intercedes for us with groans that words cannot express. And he who searches our hearts knows the mind of the Spirit, because the Spirit intercedes for the saints in accordance with God's will.

5. TO STIMULATE FAITH

Praying in tongues stimulates faith. When we know the Spirit is fully communicating our needs, we are enabled to trust God more completely. Having faith also *leads* to praying in tongues as we go to the throne of the King-Father in purpose and confidence. The author of the New Testament book of Jude wrote this about faith and speaking in tongues: "But you, dear friends, build yourselves up in your most holy faith and pray in the Holy Spirit."

6. TO KEEP US FREE FROM WORLDLY CONTAMINATION

Tongues keep us in constant connection with the culture of the kingdom, even as we live in the midst of the culture of the world. We can speak to the King-Father when we are on the job, at home, or anywhere. Our connection with the King through the Governor helps to keep our minds and actions pure. We can also encourage not only ourselves but also others in the ways of the kingdom through heavenly communication. Paul wrote, "Speak to one another with psalms, hymns and spiritual songs. Sing and make music in your heart to the Lord."

7. TO ENABLE US TO PRAY FOR THE UNKNOWN

The Spirit knows things we know nothing about; therefore, through heaven-given language, we can intercede with peace and confidence. Again, "we do not know what we ought to pray for, but the Spirit himself intercedes for us with groans that words cannot express."

8. TO GIVE SPIRITUAL REFRESHING

Tongues are a type of spiritual therapy for anxiety, turmoil, and perplexity. Paul wrote,

> Do not be anxious about anything, but in everything, by prayer and petition, with thanksgiving, present your requests to God. And the peace of God, which transcends all understanding, will guard your hearts and your minds in Christ Jesus.

9. TO HELP US IN GIVING THANKS

Tongues help those who are unlearned in spiritual things—and all of us, in fact—to offer the kind of thanks and praise to the King that he deserves. A combination of praying in human and spiritual language helps our minds and spirits to express our gratitude, in addition to other communication, to the King. Paul wrote, "I will pray with my spirit, but I will also pray with my mind; I will sing with my spirit, but I will also sing with my mind."

10. TO BRING THE TONGUE UNDER SUBJECTION

Last—but not least—speaking in heaven-given languages places our tongues under the control of the Spirit of God, something that is much needed in all of our lives. We read in the New Testament book of James, "But no man can tame the tongue. It is a restless evil, full of deadly poison.... Out of the same mouth come praise and cursing. My brothers, this should not be. Can both fresh water and salt water flow from the same spring?" Only as the tongue is yielded to the Governor can it be controlled to speak words of life in keeping with the King and his kingdom.

TONGUES ARE MEANT FOR THE ENTIRE HUMAN RACE

To conclude this chapter about the manifestation of kingdom culture, I want to emphasize that speaking in tongues does not "belong" to charismatic or Pentecostal Christians. It is meant for the whole world because it is a gift the King-Son came to provide for all the inhabitants of the earth. It is intended for the seven billion people on earth right now. It is meant for all ethnic groups—Chinese, French, Sudanese, Australians, Danes, Mexicans—no one is excluded from God's intentions.

At Pentecost, Peter said, "The promise is for you and your children and for all who are far off—for all whom the Lord our God will call." It is our job as kingdom representatives to help people from all backgrounds enter the kingdom of heaven so they may receive this gift and other gifts from the Governor, which will enable them to live the kingdom life on earth.

REMEMBERING THE PURPOSE OF TONGUES: COMMUNICATION

Tongues are beautiful, but they've sometimes been made into a doctrine, a denomination, even a whole religion. We've lost sight that tongues are heaven-given languages that are a means to an end: providing communication between heaven and earth.

We've been treating tongues as if they are a religious issue when they are really a *governmental* one in terms of the kingdom of God; through tongues, the Governor communicates our requests to the King, and the King's will to us. We can't pray effectively without the Governor, because he knows the mind of the King and how our requests fit with the purposes of the kingdom.

Speaking in tongues is as natural as speaking your own human language, whether that is English, Spanish, French, or Swahili. Paul spoke in tongues frequently. He said, "I will pray with the understanding, and I will pray in the Spirit." As citizens of the kingdom of heaven, we are to do the same.

CHAPTER TWELVE STUDY QUESTIONS

QUESTION FOR REFLECTION

1. Do you ever have difficulty communicating your needs or requests to God? In what ways?

EXPLORING PRINCIPLES AND PURPOSES

2. Which of the four characteristics of all nations is the primary manifestation of its culture?

3. List the six reasons this characteristic is so important to a nation.

4. What kinds of things is a common language able to transmit that are vital to the health and preservation of a nation?

5. What happened in terms of language and communication when humanity rebelled against the King?

6. What were the circumstances that made it necessary for the King to change humanity's one language to many languages, and to hinder their communication with one another?

7. What is one of the first things the Governor gives us after we receive his infilling?

8. List two types of heaven-given language.

9. What does the Governor enable human beings to do through heaven-given languages?

10. What statement did Jesus make that shows us heaven-given languages, or tongues, are part of the evidence of lives that have been reconnected to the heavenly kingdom?

11. The Holy Spirit was poured out at Pentecost in fulfillment of the King's promise. The international crowds who were gathered heard the disciples of Jesus speaking the King's plan of restoration in their own languages. List several facts this event revealed.

12. What are the four vital purposes for speaking in heaven-given languages?

13. What do tongues provide for us when we find it difficult to express our desires and needs to the heavenly government in our earthly language?

14. Many people are uncomfortable with the idea of speaking in tongues and even wonder if tongues are real. This is usually because tongues have been presented to them as something strange or abnormal. What should we realize that will take away this idea of the strangeness of tongues?

15. Why are tongues relevant for us today, as much as they were relevant during the time of the disciples?

16. List two ways tongues are used in communication.

17. What are the differences in how these two types of tongues are used for the benefit of kingdom citizens?

18. Speaking in tongues can be a critical key in _____ and _____ other gifts of the Spirit.

19. Dr. Munroe presents ten reasons why every kingdom citizen should speak in tongues. What are these reasons?

20. How are tongues a governmental issue in terms of the kingdom of God rather than a religious issue?

APPLYING THE PRINCIPLES OF KINGDOM LIVING

THINKING IT OVER

+ What was your perspective of tongues, or heaven-given languages, before reading this book?

+ How has your perspective of tongues changed since reading this chapter and answering the questions in this study?

ACTING ON IT

+ If you have not yet received the gift of speaking in heaven-given languages, ask your heavenly Father to give you this gift through the Governor. Then trust him to give it to you and step out in faith to receive it.

+ If you have already received the gift of tongues, how often have you been exercising it? Have you been making use of this gift to meet various spiritual needs, such as edification, faith, giving thanks, and spiritual refreshing, that are identified in this chapter? Make a point to include more prayer in tongues in your daily prayers.

PRAYING ABOUT IT

+ Dr. Munroe said that tongues are our key to overcoming obstacles in many areas of our lives. He gave the example of how praying to the Father in tongues helped him in his studies so that he went from failing grades to becoming a top student. Think about areas in your life that you are struggling with. Bring these areas before the Father in prayer as you pray in heaven-given languages. The Governor helps us to pray according to the will of the heavenly government. As you pray in tongues, pray in confidence that the Father hears your prayers and is answering them.

Tongues are a direct line to the heavenly King.

THIRTEEN

THE GOVERNOR'S ADMINISTRATION

THE NEED FOR GOVERNMENT IS EVIDENCED IN HUMANITY'S FAILURE TO MANAGE ITSELF.

The primary responsibility of a governor is administration over the territory entrusted to him. Likewise, the heavenly Governor is responsible for governmental administration over the colony of earth. He is present to train kingdom citizens on how to have dominion in the territory, because that's our official function under his leadership.

As we saw in chapter ten, the gifts of the Spirit are the delegation and distribution of powers by the Governor to kingdom citizens, in order to execute government business in the colony. They are for the purpose of *impacting* the earthly environment. When the King-Son was on earth, he healed people, cast out demons, did miracles, and even turned water into wine to help out the host of a wedding. He did *practical* works on earth. He was out solving people's problems through the power of the Governor. And this is the work he continues in our lives today through the Holy Spirit.

AUTHORIZED POWER IS GIVEN AS THE GOVERNOR WILLS

In an earthly kingdom, the governor was given power by the king to appoint various people to governmental posts in the colony. The same is true concerning the heavenly government. Paul, after listing various gifts of the Spirit, wrote, "All these are the work of one and the same Spirit, and he gives them to each one, *just as he determines.*" What gifts, and to whom he delegates them, are his prerogative and responsibility. We need to learn how to use the authority and power of the Governor in the right way so we can deliver his wonderful works to the world and bring about a change of kingdoms on earth.

Paul listed a number of gifts of the Spirit in his first letter to the kingdom citizens living in the city of Corinth:

Now about spiritual gifts, brothers, I do not want you to be igno-rant…. To one there is given through the Spirit the message [or, "word"] of wisdom, to another the message [or, "word"] of knowl-edge by means of the same Spirit, to another faith by the same Spirit, to another gifts of healing by that one Spirit, to another miraculous powers [or, "the working of miracles"], to another prophecy, to another distinguishing between spirits [or, "discern-ing of spirits"], to another speaking in different kinds of tongues, and to still another the interpretation of tongues.

AUTHORIZED POWER IS GIVEN FOR THE SERVICE OF THE HEAVENLY GOVERNMENT

Any authority and power that we receive from the Governor is for the service of the heavenly kingdom; it is not for our private benefit. As the Governor delegates kingdom authority to us, he teaches us, directly and through the Constitution of the kingdom, how to administer his gifts correctly and effectively. He shows us that administration has to do with serving others, not lording it over them. Peter wrote, in his first book, "Each one should use whatever gift he has received *to serve others*, faithfully *administering* God's grace in its various forms." Likewise, Paul affirmed,

There are different kinds of gifts, but the same Spirit. There are different kinds of service [or "administrations"], but the same Lord. There are different kinds of working, but the same God works all of them in all men. Now to each one *the manifestation of the Spirit is given for the common good.*

Unfortunately, there are some disturbing trends today in regard to the use of spiritual gifts. Some people are using their gifts to make money off fellow kingdom citizens. They're "selling" healings by telling people they will become well if they send money to them. Or they're abusing their gifts by using, for example, a gift of prophecy to intimidate others by claiming to have a message from God that condemns rather than restores or builds up.

The purpose of true government is to serve its citizens. Therefore, if the Governor of the heavenly kingdom gives you a gift, you are to use it in service to your fellow kingdom citizens. It is not for making money, boosting your ego, or giving you control over others.

AUTHORIZED POWER IS NOT PERSONAL PROPERTY

In an earthly government, if a governmental employee is given a car or a computer to carry out his duties, this is not his personal property to use in whatever way he chooses. It is to be used only to help fulfill his official responsibilities. The car or computer doesn't belong to him; he has to return it if the government requests it or he leaves his employment. His use of such things is a privilege, not a right.

The same thing is true of spiritual gifts given by the heavenly government. Some kingdom citizens, however, start to believe that the power they have been authorized to use by the Governor actually comes from their own abilities. This leads to the problem we just discussed, that of using this power for their own purposes. This is dangerous for both the person abusing the power and the ones he is supposed to be serving. He fails to fulfill his call, and the ones who are meant to benefit from his service go without the help they could have received.

THE AUTHORIZATION OF POWER ADDRESSES ALL THE NEEDS OF THE COLONY

The Governor, in conjunction with the King-Son, delegates power to kingdom citizens in order to address all the needs of the colony for the greatest impact of the heavenly kingdom on earth. Paul wrote to the kingdom citizens in the city of Ephesus,

> It was [Jesus] who gave some to be apostles, some to be prophets, some to be evangelists, and some to be pastors and teachers, to prepare God's people for works of service, so that the body of Christ may be built up until we all reach unity in the faith and in the knowledge of the Son of God and become mature, attaining to the whole measure of the fullness of Christ.

Here Paul talked about spiritual gifts in terms of specific roles, which are for building up all citizens in the kingdom. Thus, the kingdom shows its presence by its influence on the people and environment of the world. The authorized power given by the Governor to kingdom citizens also equips them to deal with conflict and opposition from the kingdom of darkness, which exists not to benefit, but to destroy, the inhabitants of earth.

MANIFESTING THE AUTHORIZED POWER OF THE GOVERNOR: THE GIFTS OF THE SPIRIT IN KINGDOM TERMS

Let us now explore nine gifts of the Spirit, as listed by Paul in his first letter to the Corinthians. We will look at them in terms of specific administrations of the Governor on earth. There are three categories of gifts listed:

+ Three of them *say* something.

+ Three of them *do* something.

+ Three of them *reveal* something.

The three that "say" are gifts of utterance: prophecy, different kinds of tongues, and the interpretation of tongues. The three that "do" are gifts of power: faith, miraculous powers or the working of miracles, and gifts of healing. The three that "reveal" are gifts of revelation: the message or word of wisdom, the message or word of knowledge, and distinguishing or discerning between spirits.

While there are a variety of gifts, they have a unity of purpose—serving citizens of the kingdom by enabling them to take on the nature of the King and use the power of the kingdom to transform the earth into the image of heaven. We begin with the revelation gifts, which address things such as facts, events, purpose, motivation, destiny, and whether something is human, whether it is of the kingdom of heaven, or whether it is of the kingdom of darkness.

THE AUTHORIZED WORD OF WISDOM

"To one there is given through the Spirit the message of wisdom." The message or word of wisdom is a supernatural revelation by the Holy Spirit concerning the mind and will of God and his divine purposes. It is authorized power from the Governor that gives kingdom citizens the ability to know the best thing to do in difficult or perplexing situations. For example, when you need legal advice, you contact a lawyer, and he gives you legal wisdom that is appropriate to your situation. The word of wisdom is special instructions from the King, through his Governor, about what to say or what to do in a particular instance.

There is natural wisdom that can be gained through a knowledge of the Constitution of the kingdom. For example, in the Old Testament book of Joshua, God encouraged Joshua, Moses' successor, to apply what he learned from the Scriptures in order to have success in life: "Do not let this Book of the Law depart from your mouth; meditate on it day and night, so that you may be careful to do everything written in it. Then you will be prosperous and successful."

A word of supernatural wisdom is different from natural wisdom, however, in that it comes directly from the King to a citizen (or citizens) through the Governor, enabling him to deal judiciously in the affairs of life. Scriptural accounts reveal that this wisdom may come in the form of a vision, a dream, an angel (messenger) from the King, or a word or impression given to a kingdom citizen by the Governor. For example, in the life of Paul...

- The Holy Spirit spoke to kingdom citizens in the city of Antioch, instructing them that they were to set apart Paul and Barnabas for the work of the kingdom to which they were called.

- When Paul was being taken prisoner by ship to Rome, and the ship encountered a violent storm, Paul received a message of hope and encouragement for all who were on board:

   I urge you to keep up your courage, because not one of you will be lost; only the ship will be destroyed. Last night an angel of the God whose I am and whom I serve stood beside me and said, "Do not be afraid, Paul. You must stand trial before Caesar; and God has graciously given you the lives of all who sail with you." So keep up your courage, men, for I have faith in God that it will happen just as he told me. Nevertheless, we must run aground on some island.

Paul's encouragement, which he received from a messenger of the King, showed them how they were to respond to this life-threatening situation.

A word of wisdom may apply to the person who receives it, or it may apply to someone else. In both instances, the kingdom government is teaching its citizens regarding how to best apply governmental policy and purposes in the colony of earth.

THE AUTHORIZED WORD OF KNOWLEDGE

"To another the message of knowledge by means of the same Spirit." While wisdom is about application, knowledge is about having the *information* you need to make the best decisions in executing delegated authority in the colony. It refers to the government providing you with the ability to understand its policies; but especially, it gives you the ability to understand what the King is thinking; it is supernatural revelation by the Governor of certain facts in the mind of the King.

The King has all knowledge, but he doesn't reveal everything to his citizens. The word of knowledge gives them part of what he knows—what they specifically need to know to carry out their assignments. Some human governments give their employees classified information on a "need to know" basis, which is only what they need to know to fulfill their responsibilities. The word of knowledge operates in a similar way.

The word of knowledge may be manifested through an inward revelation, the interpretation of tongues, a word of prophecy, a vision, or an angel. Again, this is not natural knowledge that can be gained from experience or information, or even a profound acquaintance with the Scriptures. It is supernatural, meaning it is something we would not ordinarily be able to know and cannot learn on our own. For example…

+ Jesus demonstrated a word of knowledge when he talked with a woman he had just met and told her she had had five husbands and was currently living with another man. This demonstration of knowledge was for the purpose of gaining her attention and building faith in the King so she and others would understand how to be reconciled to the heavenly government.

+ A prophet named Agabus was given a word of knowledge that a severe famine would afflict the entire Roman world. (In a demonstration of the relationship between the word of knowledge and the word of wisdom, the kingdom citizens took this knowledge and applied it [wisdom], deciding to send relief to kingdom citizens living in Judea.)

+ Peter was given supernatural knowledge that a couple named Ananias and Sapphira were lying about the money they donated to the church.

♦ Through a vision, the disciple John was given knowledge of the inner spiritual conditions of seven assemblies of kingdom citizens in Asia, so that he could give them messages of warning and encouragement from the King.

Through the word of knowledge, therefore, the Governor may communicate a message from the King to his citizens, saying, "This is what is going wrong here," or "This is what's going right in the colony; keep up the good work." He may also reveal important information to a kingdom citizen, so that he can convey to another citizen what he needs to function properly in the kingdom.

THE AUTHORIZED POWER OF FAITH

"To another faith by the same Spirit." The authorized power of faith is a supernatural belief or confidence. It is the government providing its citizens with special ability to believe in its policies so they will take action to carry them out.

Every kingdom citizen has faith. In fact, the author of the book of Hebrews wrote, "Without faith it is impossible to please God, because anyone who comes to him must believe that he exists and that he rewards those who earnestly seek him." The gift of faith, therefore, is not the same as the faith with which we enter the kingdom through belief in the sacrifice of the King-Son on our behalf, and the forgiveness we receive as a result. *That* faith comes through belief in the Constitution of the kingdom. As Paul wrote, "Faith comes from hearing the message, and the message is heard through the word of Christ." Neither is the gift of faith the same thing as the fruit of the Spirit known as "faithfulness." Nor is it the faith by which kingdom believers daily live as they trust the King to carry out his purposes through their lives and to bring them encouragement and peace. Again, such faith can be increased through exposure to and application of the King's Word.

Instead, the gift of faith is a special authorization by the government to a kingdom citizen so that he knows, without a doubt, that a particular outcome will ultimately be manifested for the purposes of the kingdom. Some examples of this kind of faith follow. As you review them, note the close relationship between the gift of faith and the working of miracles. (In this context, one Bible commentator referred to the gift of faith as "wonder-working" faith.)

+ The belief of three Hebrew men, who were governmental officials in the ancient kingdom of Babylon, that God could deliver them even if they were thrown into a blazing furnace.

+ Jesus's confidence that Lazarus, who had been dead for four days, would be raised to life.

+ The unwavering belief of Peter and John that a man who had been crippled from birth would be healed in the name of Jesus.

The gift of faith is therefore the Governor motivating kingdom citizens to trust in the promises and power of the heavenly government. The Governor encourages the citizens to courageously carry out their assignments in the belief that he will take care of everything that needs to be done to accomplish the work.

THE AUTHORIZED POWER OF HEALING

"To another gifts of healing by that one Spirit." Gifts of healing are supernatural cures for disease and disability. No natural means are involved, whether medical science or other forms of the application of human knowledge. In terms of the administration of the heavenly government on earth, healing is the King's commitment to the welfare of his citizens, as well as his program for securing that welfare.

This healing power is mentioned in the plural—*gifts* of healing. The word *healing* is sometimes used in the plural in this context, as well: "*gifts of healings*." The plural usage refers to the ability to heal different kinds of diseases. The book of Matthew records, "Jesus was going about in all Galilee, teaching in their synagogues, and proclaiming the gospel of the kingdom, and healing *every kind of disease* and *every kind of sickness* among the people."

The gifts of healing address a variety of sickness, both mental and physical, that bring us into disharmony with ourselves, other people, or the King-Father. This would include things such as fear, loneliness, and depression. Gifts of healing are for the restoration of the whole person.

We should recognize that all healing ultimately comes from God, whether it is through a doctor's care or the body's natural healing processes. The gifts of healing do not negate doctors. However, we should be aware that supernatural healing, a physician's care, and the body's natural ability to heal are distinct channels of healing. The first comes from another world, the second only *assists* the healing ability that our Creator has placed within our own bodies, and the third is an inbuilt capacity. In addition, there is a distinction between gifts of healing and our receiving healing by exercising faith in Scriptures that state the King's desire to heal us. A person may be healed by applying to himself statements such as this one from the first book of Peter: "He himself bore our sins in his body on the tree, so that we might die to sins and live for righteousness; by his wounds you have been healed." Yet gifts of healing are manifested through a kingdom citizen to whom the Governor gives a special administration of healing; they occur through the activity of a kingdom citizen as empowered by the Governor.

We should also understand that we cannot make gifts of healing, or any of the gifts, operate according to our own wills. They are given only according to the will of the Governor, and we should maintain an open mind to receive whatever gift he may give us.

The following are some examples of healing that go beyond medical help and were administered through the intervention of a person empowered by the Governor:

+ A man's shriveled or withered hand was completely restored; a centurion's servant who was paralyzed and on his deathbed was cured; a man who was born blind was given his sight; a woman who had suffered from a hemorrhage for twelve years—and who had been to many physicians without help—was made completely well. Each was healed by Jesus working in the power of the Spirit.

+ Through Peter's ministry, a man named Aeneas, who was paralyzed and bedridden for eight years, was made totally well.

+ Paul healed a man on Malta who suffered from apparently recurring bouts of fever and dysentery.

It has been said that healing and compassion go hand in hand. Sympathy alone is ineffective. Sympathy means that you feel sorry for the person, empathize with his illness, and want to help him. Compassion, however, is an almost irresistible urge to free a person from the sickness or problem afflicting him. There is true passion in com*passion* that alleviates suffering.

In the administration of the kingdom of heaven on earth, therefore, the gifts of healing are the Governor's authorization of kingdom citizens to free others from being invaded by anything that is abnormal to the kingdom. In this way, the government shows evidence that it is present and can address negative conditions in the colony. In the kingdom of God, healing is executing justice. The Governor confirms the rights of the citizens to live in wholeness.

THE AUTHORIZED POWER OF MIRACLES

"To another miraculous powers." In one sense, all gifts of the Spirit are miracles because they are beyond our natural experience. But miraculous powers or the working of miracles are specific acts that defy human understanding. They "blow the mind." As such, a miracle is a supernatural intervention in the ordinary course of nature, a temporary suspension in the accustomed order of things by an act of the Spirit of God. Some examples of this gift include...

+ Moses' parting of the Red Sea, which allowed the Israelites to escape the pursuing Egyptians on dry ground.

+ The continual flow of a widow's supply of oil and flour during a famine, through the intervention of the prophet Elijah.

+ Jesus's feeding of more than five thousand people by the multiplication of just five small loaves and two fish.

+ Jesus's raising of Lazarus from the dead.

+ Peter's raising of Dorcas from the dead.

+ The temporary blinding of Elymas the sorcerer, who opposed Paul's proclamation of the gospel of the kingdom.

Interestingly, the Greek word for miraculous or miracles, in reference to this gift, is *dunamis*, the same word used for the power that Jesus said would come upon his followers when the Holy Spirit was poured out upon them.[1] Miracles are an "explosion" of kingdom power; they are wonders that bring astonishment to people who witness them.

In the administration of the kingdom of heaven on earth, then, miracles are the government providing for the special needs of people. Whatever the miracle is, whether it is supplying food, raising the dead, or something else, it is provision. Miracles are not entertainment; they are the result of the Governor, through citizens under his authority, performing actions that confirm the presence of the kingdom and its ability to transform the environment of the colony.

THE AUTHORIZED POWER OF PROPHECY

"To another prophecy." Prophecy is a message from the King, supernaturally given, in an earthly language known to the hearer or hearers. It is the heavenly government giving its citizens confirmation about information the government has previously told them.

Paul wrote this concerning the gift of prophecy:

> Pursue love, yet desire earnestly spiritual gifts, but especially that you may prophesy. For one who speaks in a tongue does not speak to men, but to God; for no one understands, but in his spirit he speaks mysteries. But one who prophesies speaks to men for edification and exhortation and consolation [or, "comfort"]. One who speaks in a tongue edifies himself; but one who prophesies edifies the church. Now I wish that you all spoke in tongues, but even more that you would prophesy; and greater is one who prophesies than one who speaks in tongues, unless he interprets, so that the church may receive edifying.

The purpose of prophecy, Paul said, is for edification, exhortation, and consolation or comfort. He indicated that prophecy is the most important gift of all because it edifies kingdom citizens. The word *edification* in the Greek means "'the act of building'...in the sense of...the promotion of spiritual growth."[2] It therefore signifies strengthening or building people up in the ways of the kingdom. The Greek word translated *exhortation* means "'a calling to one's side'; hence, either 'an exhortation, or consolation, comfort."[3] *Comfort* means "'a speaking closely to anyone,' hence denotes 'consolation, comfort,' with a greater degree of tenderness" than exhortation.[4] I think of this word in the sense of calming people down in the face of difficulty and bringing peace to them.

Paul specifically said that the gift of prophecy should be earnestly sought, for the betterment of others. As the prophet Joel said, "Your sons and daughters will prophesy," and "Even on my servants, both men and women, I will pour out my Spirit in those days, and they will prophesy."

Prophecy is obviously a vital gift to kingdom citizens, but it has been too often misused. Here are some guidelines in using this gift:

1. Prophecy is not one-sided. It must be confirmed by giver and receiver.

2. Prophecy usually confirms something already known by the receiver, rather than being the means of giving direction to that person.

3. Prophecy speaks to the intellect and understanding.

4. Edification, exhortation, and comfort may be delivered through a biblical teaching from a leader in an assembly of kingdom citizens.

5. The gift of prophecy should not be rejected. Paul wrote, "Do not quench the Spirit. Do not despise prophecies."

6. Prophecy should be tested rather than automatically accepted. Paul also said, "Test everything. Hold on to the good," and "Two or three prophets should speak, and the others should weigh carefully what is said."

7. Someone who gives a prophecy is not "under the control" of the prophecy. He has a choice whether or not to speak it and can decide when is an appropriate time to speak it. When someone receives a prophecy, he must draw on the qualities or fruit of the Spirit, exercising self-control in regard to its use. As Paul said, "For you can all prophesy in turn so that everyone may be instructed and encouraged," and "The spirits of prophets are subject to the control of prophets. For God is not a God of disorder but of peace."

We should also note that there is a distinction between the gift of prophecy, which all citizens are encouraged to seek, and the office of prophet, which is given by the Spirit to certain kingdom citizens. We can think of the distinction in this way: the gift of prophecy is about *forth*-telling, or declaring the will of the King, while the office of prophet also includes *fore*telling, or the government giving a citizen the ability to receive news before it happens. This may be an announcement of what the King plans to do in the future. A prophet usually has other revelation gifts operating in his life, as well, such as the word of knowledge or wisdom, or the discerning of spirits.

If someone exercises the gift of prophecy, this doesn't necessarily mean he has the office of prophet. In other words, this may not be his regular position or responsibility on behalf of the heavenly government. It just means he has been given special information from the King at that particular time. Some people witness others exercising the office of prophet and decide that they'd like to foretell the future, too. If they try to prophesy in an unauthorized way, this leads to confusion and an abuse of the gift. Each person should function only in the gifts the Governor gives him.

The following are some examples of prophecy:

+ The disciples at Ephesus "spoke in tongues and prophesied" when they received the baptism in the Holy Spirit.

+ Philip the evangelist had four daughters who prophesied.

+ Agabus the prophet predicted the famine in the Roman world as well as Paul's being taken prisoner to face Caesar in Rome.

The authorized power of prophecy, therefore, is the Governor providing a kingdom citizen with information that supports and encourages his fellow citizens in the life of the kingdom. For example, when the Bahamas was still under the kingdom of Great Britain, we would receive various communications from the government, such as, "A storm is coming, but we have a plan in place to address any problems that may arise. If something should happen, here's what the government will do." Similarly, a prophecy from the heavenly kingdom might be, "You're going through a tough time, but we're sending help to address the problems and relieve your distress."

In this way, prophecy is a reminder to kingdom citizens that the heavenly government is still at work on their behalf, no matter what they might be going through. After we have received a prophecy, even if we don't see it immediately manifested, we can know that everything we need is on the way—whether it's deliverance, freedom, peace, or healing.

THE AUTHORIZED POWER OF DISCERNMENT

"To another distinguishing between spirits." Distinguishing between spirits or the discerning of spirits gives a kingdom citizen insight into the supernatural world and its workings. Its revelation is focused on a single class of beings, spirits, and should not be confused with discernment that comes as a result of a word of wisdom. It is not a kind of spiritual mind reading, psychic insight, or mental penetration. Neither is it the discerning of other people's character or faults. It concerns nonhuman spiritual entities. Some believe it only has to do with discerning *evil* spirits; however, it refers to discerning both good spiritual beings, who are part of the heavenly kingdom, and evil spiritual beings, who are part of the kingdom of darkness. Paul wrote, "Satan himself masquerades as an angel of light." We need to be able to tell whether messages or impressions we receive are from the King or his enemy.

One example of the authorized power of discernment is the ability to discern the visible likeness of God.

+ Moses was given this capability, as he recorded in his second book, Exodus:

Then the LORD said, "There is a place near me where you may stand on a rock. When my glory passes by, I will put you in a cleft in the rock and cover you with my hand until I have passed by. Then I will remove my hand and you will see my back; but my face must not be seen."

+ Isaiah the prophet was given this capacity through a vision of the holy King of heaven. He wrote,

In the year that King Uzziah died, I saw the Lord seated on a throne, high and exalted, and the train of his robe filled the temple. Above him were seraphs, each with six wings: with two wings they covered their faces, with two they covered their feet, and with two they were flying. And they were calling to one another: "Holy, holy, holy is the LORD Almighty; the whole earth is full of his glory."

Another example of this gift is the revelation of the source of a supernatural manifestation:

+ Paul discerned that the slave girl who had a spirit of divination, or the ability to predict the future, was under the control of the power of the kingdom of darkness, and he cast the demon out of her.

+ A centurion named Cornelius recognized that the angel who appeared to him in a vision was from God, and he acted on the instructions he was given in that vision, so that he and his family and friends were connected to the heavenly kingdom.

The authorized power of discernment often works in conjunction with the word of wisdom or the word of knowledge. In terms of kingdom administration, this gift is the government giving a kingdom citizen sensitivity to the supernatural environment around him. For example, if you are experiencing difficulty in an area of delegated authority and can't seem to accomplish your assignment, the authorized power of discernment may enable you to see that you are under attack from agents of the kingdom of darkness, and tell you what you need to do to overcome them.

THE AUTHORIZED POWER OF SPECIAL OR DIFFERENT KINDS OF TONGUES

"To another speaking in different kinds of tongues." Different kinds of tongues are supernatural utterances given by the Holy Spirit in languages not necessarily understood by the speaker or hearer. They are either expressions from the Governor to the King on behalf of the citizens, or expressions from the King through the Governor in response to the citizens.

In the previous chapter, we talked about tongues as the initial evidence of a kingdom citizen being filled with the Holy Spirit. The emphasis was on heaven-given languages that every believer may receive. The purpose of speaking in these tongues is for individual communication with the King-Father. It is mainly a devotional experience through which we praise and worship him and offer him requests. While devotional tongues is usually private, and has to do with oneself, the gift of different kinds of tongues is public, and is in regard to others.

We may therefore call the gift of different kinds of tongues the public ministry of tongues, as opposed to the personal expression of tongues. The gift of different kinds of tongues is manifested within a gathering of kingdom citizens. Paul wrote, "Do all have gifts of healing? Do all speak in tongues? Do all interpret?" He was referring to specific and special gifts given by the Governor to whom he wills, for the benefit of all citizens.

Paul gave an example of how this gift is to be used in a gathering of kingdom citizens:

> When you come together, everyone has a hymn, or a word of instruction, a revelation, a tongue or an interpretation. All of these must be done for the strengthening of the church. If anyone speaks in a tongue, two—or at the most three—should speak, one at a time, and someone must interpret. If there is no interpreter, the speaker should keep quiet in the church and speak to himself and God.

When the gift of tongues is in operation in a gathering of kingdom citizens, it is not to be expressed continuously or at exactly the same time as others who are speaking in tongues. It is done in sequence, and it involves only two or three people. Paul wrote that if no one is available to interpret, tongues should not be spoken out loud in the gathering. This is his reasoning: "If you are praising God with your spirit, how can one who finds himself among those who do not understand say 'Amen' to your thanksgiving, since he does not know what you are saying?" Paul also indicated that a person can pray to receive an interpretation of the tongues he is receiving, so that it can be spoken to the assembly. "For this reason anyone who speaks in a tongue should pray that he may interpret what he says."

Apparently, there are times when the King will want us to know exactly what we are praying in tongues, and other times when he will choose not to reveal it to us. When he does not provide means of revealing it, we should not speak it in the assembly.

How might you know if the gift of tongues is working in you? You may feel an intense interest in and compassion for the people around you. Some of the words may start forming in your mind. You might even almost be able to "see" the words in your mind's eye, or "feel" the words coming. You then speak them on the basis of your faith in the government's communication and your yieldedness to the Governor's prompting.

A person who receives an interpretation shouldn't wait for another to speak it (unless someone else is already speaking), but should faithfully deliver the interpretation so as not to cause others to miss a word from the King. Also, when a word is truly from the King, it will build up his citizens, not condemn them or cause them to be discouraged. Like prophecy, special tongues is usually a confirmation, rather than a new direction, regarding something. And a prophecy may sometimes follow tongues.

Again, anyone who exercises this or any other spiritual gift has to subject himself to self-control and the evaluation of the assembly. This is for the purpose of keeping order and peace among all kingdom citizens. We must remember that tongues and other gifts are not given because of who we are or how "spiritual" we are, but because the King loves us and our fellow citizens and desires to communicate with us.

Finally, the gift of special tongues sometimes takes the form of earthly language(s) that those outside the kingdom can understand, and by which they can be drawn to be reconciled with the King. Therefore, tongues are the heavenly government giving a kingdom citizen the ability to communicate its policies, wishes, and intents to both citizens of the kingdom and other inhabitants of the earth.

THE AUTHORIZED POWER OF INTERPRETATION OF TONGUES

"To still another the interpretation of tongues." The power of interpretation of tongues is manifested when the Governor reveals to a kingdom citizen the meaning of an utterance spoken in special tongues, and the person speaks that interpretation to the assembly. I believe the word *interpretation* is important in this context. This is not a word-for-word translation but an interpretation that makes the communication comprehensible in the human language of the citizens.

For example, when we are dealing with human languages, there are some phrases and idioms in one language that cannot be translated into another language on a word-by-word basis and still convey their essential meaning, especially if colloquialisms are involved. This might occur when, for example, we take something spoken in English and interpret it for French-speaking people. For this reason, there may be a difference in length between the original statement and its interpretation. The same thing applies in the interpretation of tongues. An utterance in a heaven-given language may lead to an interpretation of longer or shorter length than the original utterance.

Interpretation of tongues obviously does not operate as an independent gift; it is dependent on the gift of tongues. Its purpose is to render the meaning of tongues intelligible to the hearers so that the whole assembly of kingdom citizens can be instructed, warned, strengthened, or encouraged by it. As Paul wrote, "He who prophesies is greater than one who speaks in tongues, *unless he interprets*, so that the church may be *edified*."

EFFECTIVE SERVICE

All these examples of authorized power are very practical and have to do with effective service on behalf of the heavenly kingdom in the colony of earth. Each gift comes from and is working for the same Spirit. Again, the gifts exist to show evidence of the presence of the government in the colony and to reveal the benevolent nature of the King and his desire to give the best to his citizens. All are given by the same Governor, who delegates them as he chooses. He may cause someone to exercise a gift just one time or he may enable him to continually manifest it. We must be sensitive to the ways in which the Governor is working and not try to force something he isn't doing or quench something he is doing.

RECEIVING THE BAPTISM IN THE HOLY SPIRIT

Authorized power comes through the baptism in the Holy Spirit. All kingdom citizens need this baptism in order to live victoriously on earth and fulfill their calling as ambassadors of the King. As we have seen, receiving the new birth is the first step; being baptized in the Holy Spirit is the second step. Without the baptism, we're not prepared to live on earth and serve the kingdom of heaven as well as we could. Many believers have entered into a relationship with the King but have experienced little of the power of the King, which is necessary for kingdom life to be fully and effectively expressed.

Spiritual power is the privilege of every believer who seeks to be filled to overflowing with the presence of the Governor. We receive the legal right or authority of the King when we receive the new birth. John the disciple wrote, "But as many as received him, to them gave he power to become the sons of God." But Jesus said we would also receive a different kind of power, a power of enablement, an explosive power: "You will receive power when the Holy Spirit comes on you." Again, the Greek word translated power here is *dunamis*, or "miraculous power," from which we get the word *dynamite*.[5]

This enablement is present to some degree in conversion, but its fullness is received with the baptism in the Holy Spirit, and as we continue to walk in the Spirit. We receive the *person* of the Holy Spirit in the new birth, and we receive the *power* of the Holy Spirit in the baptism. We need the person of the Holy Spirit to enter into the kingdom of heaven, but we need the baptism in the Spirit to live victoriously on earth.

First, this power gives us the ability to witness to the nature and purpose of Jesus Christ in reconciling the world to the King-Father. Second, this power is available at all times and in all places. Before the outpouring of the Spirit at Pentecost, Jesus's disciples experienced kingdom power when he commissioned them to heal the sick and cast out demons in the towns of Judea. Yet this power was not a permanent presence in their lives. However, because Jesus has returned to the Father and poured out his Spirit into our lives, this power can now remain within us.

The King-Son has placed his plans for redeeming and healing the world in our hands through the administration of the Governor. Enabling power is imperative for us if we are to fulfill this role. But we must also understand the nature of this power. I know some people who have been baptized in the Holy Spirit without really understanding the gift they have been given. At some point, they need to understand the baptism or its power will never be fully realized in them, or they will abuse it.

I would therefore like to close this chapter with some guidelines for understanding and receiving the baptism in the Holy Spirit:

1. Know that the Holy Spirit, the Governor, is a gift to be received.

2. Put yourself in a position to receive the outpouring of the Spirit. The new birth, or salvation, is a prerequisite. The disciple Peter said, "Repent and be baptized, every one of you, in the name of Jesus Christ for the forgiveness of your sins. And you will receive the gift of the Holy Spirit." (Please reread the end of chapter eight if you have not yet entered in to the new birth.)

3. Ask the King-Father for the outpouring of his Spirit, and do not be afraid that you will receive something false. We can be sure that our King-Father will not give his children a counterfeit when they ask to receive his Holy Spirit.

4. Expect to speak in tongues. The Holy Spirit will give you the words, but you will do the speaking. Some people wait for the Holy Spirit to "take over" their tongues. Yet the whole experience is a cooperative act between the divine and the human. Allow your spirit, not your intellect or previous experience, to lead you.

5. Continue to walk in the Spirit. We remain filled with the Spirit and ready to be used by the King-Father as we daily seek the Governor, yield to him, and obey his directions. Since the Spirit works through the Word of God, we must read the Scriptures continually to understand the mind and heart of the King and to be ready to combine his will with his power for fulfilling it.

The baptism in the Holy Spirit is a release of heavenly power—in and through you. Praying in tongues is an interpersonal experience between you, the Holy Spirit, and the Father. Therefore, as you experience a release of God's power in your life, and as you pray to the Father in a heaven-given language, you may experience emotion. This is not emotion for emotion's sake, but emotion that is related to God's power and truth. Though the experience can be emotional, God expects us to have a proper handle on our emotions. Paul taught, "The spirits of prophets are subject to the control of prophets." In this way, we won't be carried away with our own desires and plans, rather than God's.

May the King bless you as you administer his nature and will on earth through his kingdom power.

CHAPTER THIRTEEN STUDY QUESTIONS

QUESTION FOR REFLECTION

1. Have you ever been given a job or assignment to do, but not the adequate resources with which to do it? How did the job or assignment work out? Compare that experience with one in which you had all the resources you needed. What were the differences in the way you worked, felt, and were effective?

EXPLORING PRINCIPLES AND PURPOSES

2. How can the gifts of the Spirit be defined in a kingdom context?

3. What work did the King-Son do on earth that he continues in our lives today through the Governor?

4. Some spiritual gifts are given to kingdom citizens in terms of specific roles, such as apostles, prophets, evangelists, pastors, and teachers. What is the purpose of these gifts?

5. How is the authorized power of the Governor involved in the heavenly kingdom's confrontation with the kingdom of darkness?

6. In addition to the gifts that are in the form of specific roles, there are nine gifts of the Holy Spirit, which are listed in Paul's first letter to kingdom citizens living in the city of Corinth. These are *specific administrations* of the Governor on earth. What are these nine gifts, listed according to the three categories they come under?

    (1)

    (2)

    (3)

7. What is the authorized word of wisdom?

8. In what forms might we receive a word of supernatural wisdom, based on scriptural examples?

9. How is the authorized word of knowledge different from the authorized word of wisdom?

10. How may a word of knowledge be manifested?

11. What is the authorized power of faith?

12. What is the authorized power of healing?

13. Explain how gifts of healing are for the restoration of the whole person.

14. What is the authorized power of miracles, and how is this gift both similar to and distinct from the other gifts?

15. Summarize the purpose of miracles in terms of the administration of the kingdom of heaven on earth.

16. What is the authorized power of prophecy? What are its three purposes?

17. What is the distinction between the gift of prophecy, which all kingdom citizens are encouraged to seek, and the office or specific role of prophet, which is given by the Governor to certain citizens?

18. What is the authorized power of discernment?

19. With what two gifts does the authorized power of discernment often work in conjunction?

20. What is the authorized power of special or different kinds of tongues?

21. Where is the gift of different kinds of tongues manifested, and to whom is it given?

22. What are some guidelines for the proper exercise of the authorized gift of tongues in an assembly of kingdom citizens?

23. Why does the gift of tongues sometimes take the form of earthly languages?

24. What is the authorized power of interpretation of tongues?

25. All authorized power from the Governor comes through the _____ in the Holy Spirit.

APPLYING THE PRINCIPLES OF KINGDOM LIVING

THINKING IT OVER

+ How have you seen the gifts of the Spirit manifested in your life?

+ How have you seen the gifts of the Spirit manifested in an assembly of believers or on other occasions? What were the benefits to those present? Were there any problems or misuses of gifts? If so, how were these addressed?

+ What new insights about the authorized power of the Governor to kingdom citizens have you gained from this chapter? How might your exercise and experience of the gifts be different now?

ACTING ON IT

+ If you have not yet received the baptism in the Holy Spirit, or feel you do not really understand it, review the section in this chapter on receiving the baptism. Then, be open to receiving the baptism so you may have the power to serve the King in his kingdom.

+ Paul said prophecy is the most important gift because it edifies kingdom citizens. Review the guidelines for prophecy in this chapter so you can be prepared to use and help facilitate this gift in an assembly of kingdom citizens.

PRAYING ABOUT IT

+ Ask your King-Father, in the name of the King-Son, to give you all the authorized gifts of the Governor that are important for fulfilling your role in the kingdom—serving other kingdom believers and reaching out to those who are not yet in the kingdom. As you do, determine to use them faithfully in service to others.

> *"To each one the manifestation of the Spirit is given*
> *for the common good."*
> —1 Corinthians 12:7

FOURTEEN

WHY THE WHOLE WORLD NEEDS THE GOVERNOR

ANY EFFECTIVE AND APPROPRIATE HELP FOR OUR WORLD AND ITS PLIGHT CANNOT COME FROM THE WORLD ITSELF.

As the millennial clock struck, measuring and recording the passage of time on planet earth, ushering us into the uncharted waters of the twenty-first century, everything in our world and generation seemed to begin to unravel. All the secure foundations of our long-established institutions have been shaken to the core.

With the advent of global terrorism; economic uncertainty and insecurity; escalating oil prices and fuel costs; the reemerging threat of nuclear weapons; ethnic, cultural, religious, and racial conflicts; political and diplomatic compromise; moral and social disintegration; and a global upsurge in human fear, the spirit of despair among earth's planet dwellers is becoming a norm.

This fear is compounded by the attempts of humankind, with its limited appreciation for human beings' inherent defects, to address these global conditions through intellectual, religious, scientific, philosophical, and political systems. Perhaps the greatest evidence of humanity's failure in this regard is the seemingly impotent effects of primary human institutions and coalitions, such as the United Nations, the International Monetary Fund, the World Bank, the World Trade Organization, and the Group of Eight.

If one is to be honest, perhaps it may be realistic to conclude that any effective and appropriate help for our world and its plight cannot come from the world itself. We need help from another world. It is my conviction and experience that humankind cannot and will not solve its self-generated problems. Humanity must look to another world for assistance. My conviction of this fact was the foundation for, and became the essence of, this book.

Our natural world needs relevant, practical, and effective help. We need our governing institutions to be governed by a higher, more superior government.

This is why the whole world—each individual in it, as well as the world collectively—needs to acknowledge and experience the return of the Governor. We have seen that the restoration of the heavenly kingdom on earth can come only through the life and power of the King, given to us through the Governor. This kingdom is infinitely higher and more powerful than any government on earth, and yet it is immediately relevant to the world we live in.

Nations are only as good as their communities, and communities are only as good as the families that comprise them. Families are only as good as the individuals of which they consist. Therefore, the quality of a nation is determined by the quality of its people. This is especially true and critical in regard to the leadership of a nation. Often, as the leaders go, so goes the nation. The values, standards, and moral consciences of our leaders frequently determine the decisions and laws of our nations, and they influence the lifestyles and cultures of the people.

It is imperative, therefore, to understand that if the people of our nations, the individuals we appoint as leaders over us, and the institutions of our societies do not have a higher source of reference for their convictions, beliefs, morals, values, and standards, then we will continue to be victims of our own corrupt nature.

This is why the Creator's design for humankind's life on earth requires that human beings be filled with the very Spirit of the Creator himself—the Holy Spirit—the Governor of heaven. In essence, national community and global life on earth was intended to be lived through and by the Holy Spirit, the Governor. The person and role of the Holy Spirit is not a religious issue, but a social, economic, cultural, and political concern. The Holy Spirit is therefore a national and international issue and must be seen and presented as such.

INDIVIDUAL PURPOSE AND FULFILLMENT

As individuals, each of us needs the Governor for true life, purpose, and effectiveness. The breath of the Spirit that originally ignited life in the first human being did so in three distinct ways: (1) in the invisible spirit of man, made in the image of God; (2) in the soul of man—the total human consciousness of mind, will, and emotions; and (3) in the physical body of man, the living vessel housing his spirit and soul. While Adam's soul and body gave him an awareness of his earthly environment, the Spirit of God within him gave his spirit a consciousness of his Creator-King and the ability to communicate directly with the heavenly government.

Human beings must return to this life and wholeness again. We were created to express the nature of God, and we can relate to and reflect his nature only if we actually have his nature within us through his indwelling Spirit.

The meaning of our individual lives—living out our purposes and exercising our full potential—is therefore totally dependent on our receiving the Governor.

A WORLD COMMUNITY OF KINGS AND PRIESTS

While our King communicates with us individually, it is not his intention that the citizens of his kingdom live in isolation. His plan is a *community* of kings and priests who will reign on earth. The Governor is the key to life for *all* of humanity. The world community therefore needs to be led by the Governor if it, also, is to become what it was created to be.

Corporately, the world has rejected the presence and influence of the Governor. This is why we experience wars, natural disasters, and social crises on earth.

The King wants the world to receive the Governor again. He wants the earth to be rid of the pain, sorrow, destruction, and death that are plaguing it. The restoration of the heavenly government reinstates humankind's ability to affect and control circumstances on earth through the Holy Spirit.

When a community of kings and priests works together for the right reasons—honoring and expressing the nature of our King—and acts in genuine unity, we will have powerful potential to influence the earth with the nature of the kingdom. It will enable us to encourage and create social stability, economic development, environmental soundness, educational advancement, physical health and wholeness, scientific innovation, political honesty, governmental justice, and intercultural understanding.

A BENEVOLENT RULER

Who wouldn't want to function under a government that provides for, encourages, and enables the fulfillment of the greatest individual and corporate potential in life? The prophet Isaiah described this heavenly government, under the rule of the King-Son through the Governor:

> Power and peace will be in his kingdom and will continue to grow forever. He will rule as king on David's throne and over David's kingdom. He will make it strong by ruling with justice and goodness from now on and forever. The LORD All-Powerful will do this *because of his strong love for his people.*

Again, this rule is a reality only because of the King's great love for his citizens, and his desire for their highest good in life.

The Scriptures, however, also talk about the very real presence of another, malevolent ruler and his cohorts who seek to control this world:

> The ruler of the kingdom of the air, the spirit who is now at work in those who are disobedient.

> Our struggle is not against flesh and blood, but against the rulers, against the authorities, against the powers of this dark world and against the spiritual forces of evil in the heavenly realms.

> For false Christs and false prophets will appear and perform great signs and miracles to deceive even the elect—if that were possible.

The ruler of this dark world is Lucifer, or Satan, the treasonous former general and worship leader of heaven who has attacked the good of humankind since the very beginning of our existence. He would like to perpetuate the sorrow and darkness of the world so that he can continue to control it. He desires to consolidate the people of the world under his harsh rule so they can never become free.

This is why it was essential that the King-Son came to destroy Satan's power over the world, transferring us from being under the darkness of a corrupt world into the light of the heavenly kingdom. The prophet Isaiah wrote,

> The people living in darkness have seen a great light; on those living in the land of the shadow of death a light has dawned.

While Satan is described in terms of darkness and death, Jesus, the King-Son, is described in the Scriptures in terms of light and life:

[He will] shine on those living in darkness and in the shadow of death, to guide our feet into the path of peace.

He was with God in the beginning. Through him all things were made; without him nothing was made that has been made. In him was life, and that life was the light of men. The light shines in the darkness, but the darkness has not understood it.

Jesus spoke of himself in these terms:

I am the light of the world. Whoever follows me will never walk in darkness, but will have the light of life.

I have come into the world as a light, so that no one who believes in me should stay in darkness.

Jesus told the theologian-apostle Paul,

I am sending you to [the world] to open their eyes and turn them from darkness to light, and from the power of Satan to God, so that they may receive forgiveness of sins and a place among those who are sanctified by faith in me.

Paul taught first-century kingdom believers,

For you were once darkness, but now you are light in the Lord. Live as children of light (for the fruit of the light consists in all goodness, righteousness and truth).

For he has rescued us from the dominion of darkness and brought us into the kingdom of the Son he loves, in whom we have redemption, the forgiveness of sins.

The nations of the world urgently need the light and life of the kingdom, which comes only from the Son-King through the Governor. The presence of the kingdom of heaven on earth, through the Holy Spirit's return, is the message of the Scriptures, and it is the message of Jesus. The story of humanity—and therefore of all of us—is inextricably tied to this kingdom. Exercising kingdom dominion on earth, under the guidance of the Governor, is our collective purpose and calling.

As we yield to the Governor's presence and work in our lives, we will spread the kingdom of God on earth. Change will take place in all areas of life and in people of all national and ethnic backgrounds, East and West; and from all social and economic circumstances. The CEO, the teacher, the artist, the financial analyst, the health care worker, the farmer, the scientist, the economist, the seamstress, the governmental leader, and the homemaker will be transformed according to the heavenly kingdom, so that life, and not confusion, stress, and death, will be the result.

The Spirit gives *life* to the world, in the fullest extent of the word. Whatever comes into being through the influence of the Spirit will eventually bring life to people, and can reach whole countries and influence the world community. For example, if all the judges in a nation are under the guidance of the heavenly Governor, and if their minds are immersed in the philosophy of the kingdom, you will not have to wonder what kind of judgments they will hand down, nor will you have to suffer under unjust laws. A culture influenced by the Spirit will be a culture that preserves and protects life. "The mind controlled by the Spirit is life and peace."

THE COMPLETE TRANSFORMATION OF THE EARTH INTO THE KINGDOM

The world is ultimately moving toward complete transformation into the King's image and nature. This plan will climax in the creation of a new heaven and earth. In effect, heaven and earth will become one, so that there will be no essential distinction between the two, and God himself will live among his people.

The disciple John described the earth's total transformation into the kingdom of heaven's nature, mind-set, and values. In the italicized words in brackets, I describe what I see as the implications for kingdom life:

> Then I saw a new heaven and a new earth, for the first heaven and the first earth had passed away [*the earth is totally aligned with the heavenly kingdom, with no trace of the kingdom of darkness*]....

> I saw the Holy City, the new Jerusalem, coming down out of heaven from God, prepared as a bride beautifully dressed for her

husband [*the citizens of the kingdom are totally pure, set apart, and integrated; they are one with the nature of God and in harmony with themselves*]....

And I heard a loud voice from the throne saying, "Now the dwelling of God is with men, and he will live with them. They will be his people, and God himself will be with them and be their God." [*The Governor continues to dwell within the King's people, and there is nothing to separate the King from his beloved children.*]

He will wipe every tear from their eyes. There will be no more death or mourning or crying or pain, for the old order of things has passed away. He who was seated on the throne said, "I am making everything new!" [*The kingdom of darkness has been completely destroyed, and the kingdom of life and light totally reigns on earth.*]

The creation of a new heaven and earth will be the apex of the plan of the King for the coming of the Governor, which he had in mind from the beginning. The people of earth will be a true world community of kings and priests living out the kingdom life in its fullness.

CITIZENS OF THE KINGDOM

The disciple Peter wrote the following declaration to the kingdom citizens of his day, which applies to us, as well.

But you are a chosen people, a royal priesthood, a holy nation, a people belonging to God, that you may declare the praises of him who called you out of darkness into his wonderful light. Once you were not a people, but now you are the people of God; once you had not received mercy, but now you have received mercy.

The Holy Spirit is the key to the world; he is the most important person on earth because he brings us the presence and power of the kingdom of heaven. May you be reconciled to your Creator-King, receive the Governor into your life, and live as the royal kingdom citizen you were always meant to be!

CHAPTER FOURTEEN STUDY QUESTIONS

QUESTION FOR REFLECTION

1. How effective do you think today's leaders are in addressing the problems and needs in the world? Why?

EXPLORING PRINCIPLES AND PURPOSES

2. Since humanity cannot solve its self-generated problems, what kind of help does our world need?

3. What will be the cause if we continue to be victims of our own corrupt nature?

4. What does the Creator-King's design for humanity's life on earth require?

5. Each of us needs the Governor for true life, purpose, and _____.

6. It is not the King's intention that his kingdom citizens live in isolation. What is his plan?

7. When will we have powerful potential to influence the earth with the nature of the kingdom?

8. What does the heavenly government provide for, encourage, and enable?

9. What is the King's attitude toward his citizens?

10. What does the King's enemy, Lucifer, desire for this world?

11. What did the King-Son do to counteract the power and purposes of Lucifer?

12. What is the message of Jesus and the Scriptures?

13. What is humanity's collective purpose and calling?

14. What will happen as we yield to the Governor's presence and work in our lives?

15. How is the world ultimately moving toward complete transformation into the King's image and nature?

16. Why is the Holy Spirit the most important person on earth?

APPLYING THE PRINCIPLES OF KINGDOM LIVING

THINKING IT OVER

+ What have you learned in this book about the ability of the Holy Spirit, the Governor, to address the fundamental needs and issues of the world?

+ What does it mean for you to be part of a community of "kings and priests" who are to reign on earth under the guidance of the Governor? What are the benefits and responsibilities?

ACTING ON IT

+ Your ability to live out your unique life purpose and exercise your full potential is totally dependent on receiving the Holy Spirit and allowing him to guide and direct you. Make a commitment now to enter the kingdom of heaven and to live according to the purposes of the King under the direction of the Governor.

+ If you are used to thinking of your relationship with the Creator-King as an isolated one, write down some specific ideas of how you can live your life in the heavenly kingdom in conjunction with your fellow-citizens in the realm. As you do, include aspects of kingdom life highlighted in the chapters of this book.

PRAYING ABOUT IT

+ Daily acknowledge your desire to spread the heavenly kingdom on earth by praying, "Father, 'Not my will, but yours be done'" (Luke 22:42).

+ Pray that the King-Father would direct you to those who need to hear the life-giving message of the return of his kingdom. Then trust the Governor to give you the words and actions that will draw others to the Father and into the kingdom.

> *"But seek first his kingdom and his righteousness,*
> *and all these things will be given to you as well."*
> —Matthew 6:33

NOTES

CHAPTER ONE

1. *Thomas Nelson's New Illustrated Bible Dictionary* (Nashville: Thomas Nelson Publishers, 1995, 1986), s.v. "Colony," 287.
2. *Merriam-Webster's 11ᵗʰ Collegiate Dictionary*, s.v. "Colony."
3. Attributed to Harry Thurston Pecks, *Harper's Dictionary of Classical Antiquity*, 1898 <http://en.wikipedia.org/wiki/Apoikia. (June 9, 2006)>

CHAPTER TWO

1. See, for example: <http://helios.gsfc.nasa.gov/qa_sp_gl.html> <http://starchild. gsfc.nasa.gov/docs/StarChild/universe_level2/galaxies.html.> <http://hypertextbook. com/facts/2000/MarissaWagner.shtml/> <http://curious.astro.cornell.edu/question. php?number=31> <http://curious.astro.cornell.edu/question.php?number=40> < http:// curious.astro.cornell.edu/question.php?number=510> (All sites accessed July 28 2006)
2. <http://nasaexplores.nasa.gov/search_nav_9_12.php?id=01-079&gl=912 (November 6, 2006)>
3. See W. E. Vine, Merrill F. Unger, and William White, Jr., eds., *Vine's Complete Expository Dictionary of Old and New Testament Words* (Nashville: Thomas Nelson Publishers, 1996), Old Testament Words, s.v. "Statue," 244.
4. Ibid, Old Testament words, s.v. "Likeness," B. Noun, 137.
5. Attributed to Harry Thurston Pecks, *Harper's Dictionary of Classical Antiquity*, 1898 <http://en.wikipedia.org/wiki/Apoikia. (June 9, 2006)>

CHAPTER FOUR

1. For a broader discussion on the origin and usage of the word *holy* in this context, see W. E. Vine, Merrill F. Unger, and William White, Jr., eds., *Vine's Complete Expository Dictionary of Old and New Testament Words* (Nashville: Thomas Nelson Publishers, 1996), Old Testament Words, s.v. "Holy," A. Adjective, 113–14.
2. See *Strong's Exhaustive Concordance*, #H4467.
3. See *Strong's*, #H3068.

CHAPTER FIVE

1. See the *New American Standard Exhaustive Concordance of the Bible* (NASC), The Lockman Foundation, #G3341. Used by permission.
2. See *Strong's Exhaustive Concordance*, #G3101.
3. See *Strong's* and NASC, #G4680; #G5384; #G5385; #G5386.
4. See *Strong's*, #G3860, and W. E. Vine, Merrill F. Unger, and William White, Jr., eds., *Vine's Complete Expository Dictionary of Old and New Testament Words* (Nashville: Thomas Nelson Publishers, 1996), New Testament Words, s.v. "Yield," No. 5, 691.

CHAPTER SEVEN

1. *Merriam-Webster's 11ᵗʰ Collegiate Dictionary*, s.v. "Receive," "Re-."
2. See *Strong's Exhaustive Concordance*, #G4005.

3. See *Strong's*, #G3187, and the *New American Standard Exhaustive Concordance of the Bible* (*NASC*), The Lockman Foundation, #G3187. Used by permission.

CHAPTER EIGHT

1. See *Strong's Exhaustive Concordance*, #G1411, and the *New American Standard Exhaustive Concordance of the Bible* (*NASC*), The Lockman Foundation, #G1411. Used by permission.
2. See *Strong's*, #G3142.

CHAPTER NINE

1. See *Strong's Exhaustive Concordance*, #G4395, and the *New American Standard Exhaustive Concordance of the Bible* (*NASC*), The Lockman Foundation, #G4395. Used by permission.
2. See *Strong's*, #G1849, and *NASC*, #G1849.
3. See *Strong's*, #G1411, and *NASC*, #G1411.
4. See *Strong's*, #H1870.

CHAPTER TEN

1. See *Strong's Exhaustive Concordance*, #G3875.
2. See *Strong's*, #G1484, and the *New American Standard Exhaustive Concordance of the Bible* (*NASC*), The Lockman Foundation, #G1484. Used by permission.

CHAPTER TWELVE

1. See *Strong's Exhaustive Concordance*, #H894.

CHAPTER THIRTEEN

1. See *Strong's Exhaustive Concordance*, #G1411, and the *New American Standard Exhaustive Concordance of the Bible* (*NASC*), The Lockman Foundation, #G1411. Used by permission.
2. See *Strong's*, #G3619, and W. E. Vine, Merrill F. Unger, and William White, Jr., eds., *Vine's Complete Expository Dictionary of Old and New Testament Words* (Nashville: Thomas Nelson Publishers, 1996), New Testament Words, s.v. "Edification, Edify, Edifying," A. Noun, 194.
3. See *Vine's Complete Expository Dictionary of Old and New Testament Words*, s.v. "Comfort, Comforter, Comfortless," A. Nouns, No. 1, 110; see also *Strong's*, #G3874; and *NASC*, #G3874.
4. See *Vine's Complete Expository Dictionary of Old and New Testament Words* (Nashville: Thomas Nelson Publishers, 1996), New Testament Words, s.v. "Comfort, Comforter, Comfortless," No. 2, 111.
5. See *Strong's*, #G1411, and *NASC*, #G1411.

SCRIPTURE REFERENCES

(ALL EMPHASIS IN THE SCRIPTURE QUOTATIONS IS THE AUTHOR'S.)

INTRODUCTION

p. 9: "Since the creation of the world...." (Romans 1:20)

p. 9: "So we fix our eyes not on what is seen...." (2 Corinthians 4:18)

p. 10: "My kingdom is not of this world...." (John 18:36)

p. 11: "By him all things were created...." (Colossians 1:16)

PROLOGUE

p. 12: "In the beginning was the King's Word...." See John 1:1–5.

p. 12: "In the beginning, the King created...." See Genesis 1:1–2.

CHAPTER ONE: THE POWER OF INFLUENCE

p. 24: "As they stretched him out to flog him...." (Acts 22:25–29)

p. 26: "The time has come...." (Mark 1:15)

CHAPTER TWO: THE ADAMIC ADMINISTRATION

p. 31: "In the beginning God...." (Genesis 1:1)

p. 32: "the blessed and only Ruler...." (1 Timothy 6:15–16)

p. 32: "There's nobody keeping this universe in order." See Psalm 14:1; 53:1.

p. 33: "The universe was formed at God's command...." (Hebrews 11:3)

p. 34: "Let us make man in our image, in our likeness...." (Genesis 1:26–27); ["have dominion"]: (Genesis 1:26 NKJV]

p. 34: "the compassionate and gracious God...." (Exodus 34:6)

p. 35: "The LORD God formed the man...." (Genesis 2:7)

p. 36: "The God who made the world...." (Acts 17:24)

p. 36: "Do you not know that your body is a temple...?" (1 Corinthians 6:19)

p. 36: "Then God blessed them, and God said to them, 'Be fruitful....'" (Genesis 1:28 NKJV)

p. 36: "You are free to eat from any tree...." (Genesis 2:16–17)

p. 38: "For who among men knows the thoughts...." (1 Corinthians 2:11)

p. 38: "The highest heavens belong to the LORD...." (Psalm 115:16)

p. 39: "The LORD God took the man...." (Genesis 2:15)

CHAPTER THREE: DECLARATION OF INDEPENDENCE

p. 44: "Now the serpent...said to the woman...." (Genesis 3:1–7)

p. 45: "After [the Creator-King] drove the man out...." (Genesis 3:24)

p. 46: "You are free to eat...." (Genesis 2:16–17)

p. 48: "realized" (Genesis 3:7) or "knew" (Genesis 3:7 NKJV)

p. 50: "Rule over...all the earth." (Genesis 1:26)

p. 50: "Cursed is the ground...." (Genesis 3:17–19)

p. 50: "Some paths in life seem right...." See Proverbs 14:12.

p. 51: "For all have sinned and fall short...." (Romans 3:23)

p. 52: Jesus describing Lucifer as the "father of lies" and a "murderer." (John 8:44)

p. 52: "The thief comes only to steal...." (John 10:10)

p. 53: "I will put enmity between you and the woman...." (Genesis 3:15)

CHAPTER FOUR: THE PROMISE OF THE GOVERNOR'S RETURN

p. 62: "You will be for me a kingdom of priests...." (Exodus 19:6)

p. 62: "holy unto me" (Leviticus 20:26 KJV)

p. 62: The Creator King describing himself as a "holy" God: See, for example, Leviticus 11:44–45.

p. 63: "Be perfect, just as your [King-Father] is perfect." (Matthew 5:48)

p. 64: The Offspring would "crush the head" of the serpent: See Genesis 3:15.

p. 64: "For to us a child is born...." (Isaiah 9:6)

p. 64: "Sacrifice and offering you did not desire...." (Hebrews 10:5)

p. 65: Account of Noah and the flood: See Genesis 6:5–9:1.

p. 65: "Then God blessed Noah...." (Genesis 9:1)

pp. 65–66: Promise to Abraham regarding having a child who would become a great nation, and its fulfillment. See Genesis 15:1–6; 17:15–21; 18:2–19; 21:1–7.

p. 66: Noah and Abraham's right standing with God. See Genesis 6:8; 15:6; Romans 4:3; Galatians 3:6; Hebrews 11:7–12; James 2:23.

p. 66: Jacob chosen to carry on the lineage of the coming Messiah/name changed to Israel: See Genesis 25:21–26; 28:10–15; 35:10–12.

p. 66: The twelve sons of Jacob/the origin of the tribes of Israel: See Genesis 35:22–26; 49:1–28.

p. 66: Judah chosen to carry on the lineage of the coming Messiah: See Genesis 49:8–12.

p. 66: The twelve tribes in Egypt/preserved through Joseph: See Genesis 37; 39:1–47:12, 27.

p. 66: The twelve tribes becoming slaves in Egypt: See Exodus 1:6–14.

p. 66: Moses called to free the Israelites: See Exodus 1:15–4:31.

p. 67: Moses bringing the plagues in Egypt: See Exodus 6:28–12:36.

p. 67: The parting of the Red Sea: See Exodus 13:17–14:31.

p. 67: "a kingdom of priests and a holy nation" (Exodus 19:6)

p. 67: God telling the Israelites he would make them the greatest nation if they believed and obeyed him: See Exodus 19:3–6; 34:9–11.

pp. 67–68: Israel given instructions for living, or the law: See, for example, Exodus 20:1–23:3; 24:12 31:18; 34:12–27; 35:1–19; 40:1–15; Leviticus 1–7; 11:1–24:9; 25–27.

p. 68: "This is what you are to say to the house of Jacob...." (Exodus 19:3–6)

pp. 68–69: The Israelites meeting with God at the mountain: See Exodus 19:9–20:21.

p. 69: "This is the covenant I will make with the house of Israel...." (Jeremiah 31:33)

p. 69: The Israelites agreeing to obey the law: See Exodus 24:7–8.

p. 69: The parting of the river Jordan: See Joshua 3.

p. 69: The collapse of the walls of Jericho: See Joshua 6:1–20.

p. 69: The sun standing still for an entire day: See Joshua 10:12–14.

p. 70: The appointment of Aaron's family as the priesthood and other Levites as their assistants: See Exodus 28–29; Exodus 32:25–29; Numbers 1:47–53; 3:5–13; 8:5–26.

p. 70: "The law requires that nearly everything be cleansed...." (Hebrews 9:22)

p. 71: The Spirit of God dwelling between the cherubim on the mercy seat: See, for example, Exodus 25:22; Leviticus 16:2–34.

p. 72: The Israelites asking God for an earthly king: See 1 Samuel 8:4–22.

p. 73: "the Lord told [Samuel]: 'Listen to all....'" (1 Samuel 8:7)

p. 73: King David as a man who desired what the heavenly government desires: See 1 Samuel 13:13–14.

p. 73: David's slaying of Goliath: See 1 Samuel 17:4–51.

p. 73: "You come against me with sword...." (1 Samuel 17:45)

p. 73: The Offspring would be a descendant of King David: See 2 Samuel 7:12–16; Isaiah 11:1–10; Matthew 1:1–17.

pp. 73–74: The role of the prophet: See Deuteronomy 18:15–22.

p. 74: Elijah bringing a woman's son back to life: See 1 Kings 17:17–24.

p. 74: Daniel receiving prophecy concerning the future of the Israelite people: See Daniel 10:1–12:13.

p. 74: Daniel being delivered from the lion's den: See Daniel 6:3–23.

p. 74: Mistreatment of the prophets: See, for example, Matthew 5:11–12; Matthew 23:29–37.
pp. 74–75: The Spirit of God leaving the temple: See Ezekiel 8:1–11:23.
p. 75: "For to us a child is born…." (Isaiah 9:6–7)
pp. 75–76: "There was a landowner…." (Matthew 21:33–40, 43)
p. 76: "He will turn the hearts…." (Malachi 4:6)
pp. 74–75: "Afterward, I will pour out my Spirit…." (Joel 2:28–29)
p. 77: "day of the Lord" (Joel 2:11)
p. 77: "See, I will send my messenger…." (Malachi 3:1)
pp. 77–78: "Turn the hearts of the fathers…." (Malachi 4:6)
p. 78: "In those days John the Baptism came…." (Matthew 3:1–3)
p. 78: "I baptize you with water…." (Matthew 3:11)

CHAPTER FIVE: THE REBIRTH OF A KINGDOM

pp. 85–86: "God sent the angel Gabriel…." (Luke 1:26–30)
p. 86: "You will be with child…." (Luke 1:31–35, 37–38)
p. 87: "The life of every creature is its blood." (Leviticus 17:14)
p. 87: "The one who *comes from heaven* is above all…." (John 3:31, 34)
p. 87: "He will baptize you with the Holy Spirit…." (Luke 3:16)
p. 87: "If you love me you will obey…." (John 14:15–20)
p. 88: "The next day John saw Jesus…." (John 1:29–34)
p. 88: "In Christ all the fullness of the Deity…." (Colossians 2:9)
p. 88: "In the beginning was the Word…." (John 1:1)
p. 89: "The time has come…." (Mark 1:15)
p. 89: "day of the Lord" (Joel 2:11)
p. 89: "The earth is the Lord's…." (Psalm 24:1)
p. 89: "The thief comes only to steal…." (John 10:10)
p. 89: "How can one enter a strong man's…." (Matthew 12:29 NKJV)
p. 89: Jesus the "last" or Second Adam: See 1 Corinthians 15:45.
p. 90: "Our Father in heaven, hallowed…." (Matthew 6:9–10)
p. 90: "A kingdom of priests and a holy nation." (Exodus 19:6)
p. 90: "Repent, for the kingdom of heaven is near." (Matthew 4:17)
p. 90: "Jesus went throughout Galilee…." (Matthew 4:23)
p. 91: "But if I drive out demons by the Spirit…." (Matthew 12:28)
p. 91: "The kingdom of heaven is like a king…." (Matthew 18:23)
p. 91: "The kingdom of heaven is like a landowner…." (Matthew 20:1)
p. 91: "The kingdom of God will be…given…." (Matthew 21:43)
p. 91: "The devil took him to a very high mountain…." (Matthew 4:8–11)
p. 92: "baptism of repentance": See, for example, Mark 1:4.
p. 92: "the company of the prophets": See, for example 2 Kings 2:3; 4:1.
p. 93: "You should be the teacher, not me!": See Matthew 3:13–14
p. 94: "After me will come one more powerful…." (Mark 1:7–8)
p. 94: "Let it be so now; it is proper…." (Matthew 3:15)
p. 94: "The next day John was there…." (John 1:35–40)
p. 95: "As soon as Jesus was baptized…." (Matthew 3:16–17)
p. 95: "This is my Son, whom I love. Listen to him!" (Mark 9:7)
p. 95: "Follow me": See, for example, Matthew 4:19.
p. 95: "No one can serve two masters…." (Matthew 6:24)
p. 95: "baptize…with the *Holy Spirit* and with *fire*." (Matthew 3:11)
p. 96: "As a person thinks within himself, so he is." See Proverbs 23:7 (NKJV).
p. 96: "My thoughts are not your thoughts…." (Isaiah 55:8–9)
p. 96: "full of the Holy Spirit,…." (Luke 4:1–2)
p. 96: "Jesus returned to Galilee" (Luke 4:14)
p. 96: "From that time on Jesus began to preach…." (Matthew 4:17)
p. 97: "My teaching is not my own…." (John 7:16)
p. 97: "These words you hear are not my own…." (John 14:24)

p. 97: "My Father is always at his work...." (John 5:17)
p. 97: "I and the Father are one." (John 10:30)
p. 97: "I tell you the truth, the Son can do nothing by himself...." (John 5:19)
p. 97: "Do not believe me unless I do what my Father...." (John 10:37–38)
p. 97: "If God were your Father...." (John 8:42)
p. 97: "I came from the Father...." (John 16:28)
p. 97: Jesus healing the sick: See, for example, Luke 7:2–10.
p. 97: Jesus delivering someone possessed by an agent of Lucifer: See, for example, Mark 5:2–15.
p. 97: Jesus feeding thousands by multiplying small amounts of food: See, for example, Luke 9:11–17.
p. 97: Jesus raising people from the dead: See, for example, Luke 7:11–15.
p. 99: "The reason my Father loves me...." (John 10:17–18)
p. 99: "Do you not know that as many of us as were baptized...." (Romans 6:3–4 NKJV)
p. 99: "I am the good shepherd...." (John 10:14–16)
p. 100: "This is what is written [was predicted by the King's prophet]...." (Luke 24:46)
p. 100: "It is finished." (John 19:30)
p. 100: "Father, the time has come...." (John 17:1–5)
p. 100: "The earth will be filled with the knowledge...." (Habakkuk 2:14)
p. 101: "For the sinful nature desires...." (Galatians 5:17–18)
p. 101: "Not my will, but yours be done." (Luke 22:42)
p. 101: "If you love me...." (John 14:15–16)
p. 101: "Remain in me, and I will remain in you...." (John 15:4–6)
pp. 101–102: "My grace is sufficient for you...." (2 Corinthians 12:9)
p. 102: "When I am weak, then I am strong." (2 Corinthians 12:10)
p. 102: "He lives with you and will be in you." (John 14:17)
p. 102: "I am going to send you what my Father has promised." (Luke 24:49)
p. 103: "He will baptize you with the Holy Spirit and with fire." (Matthew 3:11)
p. 103: "The Spirit of truth...lives *with* you and will be *in* you." (John 14:17)
p. 103: Jesus walking on water: See, for example, Matthew 14:23–33.
p. 103: Jesus causing an extraordinary catch of fish: See Luke 5:3–11.
p. 103: Jesus cleansing a leper: See, for example, Mark 1:40–42.
p. 104: "Everything I'm about to suffer...." and "I'm going to leave you, but don't panic or worry....": See John 14.
p. 104: The curtain in the temple torn from top to bottom: See, for example, Mark 15:37–38.
pp. 104–105: "When the time had fully come...." (Galatians 4:4–7)
p. 105: "When the Counselor comes...." (John 15:26)
p. 105: "I am going to send you what my Father has promised...." (Luke 24:49).
p. 105: "We have no king but Caesar"/Pilate's choice to crucify Jesus: See John 19:12–16.
p. 106: "gave up his spirit" (John 19:30)
p. 106: "And if the Spirit of him who raised Jesus...." (Romans 8:11)

CHAPTER SIX: A KING'S LOVE FOR HIS CITIZENS
p. 111: "For God so loved the world...." (John 3:16)
p. 112: In order to live, one had to die to oneself; in order to be strong in kingdom power, one had to be weak in oneself: See for example, John 11:25–26; Matthew 5:3.
p. 112: "being in the form of God...." (Philippians 2:6–8)
p. 112: "And I will ask the Father...." (John 14:16–20)
p. 113: "For you know the grace of our Lord Jesus...." (2 Corinthians 8:9)
p. 113: "I tell you the truth, the Son can do nothing by himself...." (John 5:19)
p. 113: "Father, glorify me in your presence...." See John 17:5.
p. 113: "Jesus took with him Peter, James and John...." (Matthew 17:1–5)
p. 114: "When the time had fully come...." (Galatians 4:4–5)
p. 114: Jesus submitted himself to the requirements of the law so he could fulfill them: See, for example, Matthew 3:15; 5:17.
p. 114: "I will give them an undivided heart...." (Ezekiel 11:19–20)
p. 114: Jesus asking for a drink of water: See John 4:5–7.

p. 114: Jesus stopping to pick fruit: See Matthew 21:19.
p. 114: "neither slumbers nor sleeps": See Psalm 121:4.
p. 114: Jesus asleep in a boat in the middle of a violent storm: See Luke 8:22–25.
p. 114: Jesus took away the sting of death from humanity: See 1 Corinthians 15:55–57.
p. 114: It pleased the King-Father for the King-Son to suffer and die: See Isaiah 53:10–11.
p. 115: "The wages of sin is death...." (Romans 6:23)
p. 115: "By his power God raised...." (1 Corinthians 6:14)
p. 115: "God made him who had no sin to be sin...." (2 Corinthians 5:21)
p. 115: "For God so loved the world...." (John 3:16)
p. 115: "I am the good shepherd...." (John 10:14–15)
p. 116: "Now I am going to him who sent me...." (John 16:5–7, 16)
p. 117: "My going away....The Governor is *with* you now....": See John 16:7; John 14:17.
p. 117: "If I go to the cross....": See John 12:32.
p. 117: "If you then, though you are evil...." (Matthew 7:11)
p. 117: "Your Father has been pleased to give you the kingdom." (Luke 12:32)

CHAPTER SEVEN: RESTORING THE CONNECTION

p. 121: "He lives with you and will be in you." (John 14:17)
p. 121: "'As the Father has sent me,...." (John 20:21–22)
p. 121: "The LORD God formed the man.... (Genesis 2:7)
p. 122: "In my former book...." (Acts 1:1–3)
p. 123: "Once, having been asked by the Pharisees...." (Luke 17:20–21)
p. 123: "I tell you the truth, some who are standing...." (Mark 9:1)
p. 123: About one hundred twenty disciples present when the Holy Spirit was poured out at Pentecost:
  See Acts 1:15–2:3.
p. 123: "After the Lord Jesus had spoken...." (Mark 16:19)
p. 123: "And I will ask the Father...." (John 14:16–17)
p. 123: "The Counselor, the Holy Spirit...." (John 14:26)
p. 124: "I am going to send you what my Father has promised...." (Luke 24:49)
p. 124: "On one occasion, while he was eating with them...." (Acts 1:4–5, 8)
p. 125: "on high" (Luke 24:49)
p. 125: "When the day of Pentecost came...." (Acts 2:1–4)
p. 125: Disciples of Jesus given the ability to speak in a variety of languages: See Acts 2:5–11.
p. 125: "And these signs will accompany...." (Mark 16:17)
p. 125: "Why are you speaking like this....?" See Acts 2:12–13.
pp. 125–126: "Fellow Jews and all of you...." (Acts 2:14–18, 32–33)
pp. 126–127: "My kingdom is not of this world." (John 18:36)
p. 127: "I tell you the truth, anyone who has faith in me...." (John 14:12)
p. 127: "And I will do whatever you ask in my name...." (John 14:13)

CHAPTER EIGHT: REINSTATING THE GOVERNOR

p. 131: "Whoever drinks the water...." (John 4:14)
p. 132: "Now it is God who makes...." (2 Corinthians 1:21–22)
p. 132: "Now it is God who has made us...." (2 Corinthians 5:5)
p. 132: "And you also were included in Christ...." (Ephesians 1:13–14)
p. 132: "Consequently, you are no longer foreigners...." (Ephesians 2:19)
p. 133: "I tell you the truth, whatever you bind on earth...." (Matthew 18:18–20)
p. 133: "I tell you the truth, no one can enter the kingdom...." (John 3:5–7)
p. 133: "Be imitators of God...." (Ephesians 5:1–2)
p. 134: "You will receive power...." (Acts 1:8)
p. 134: "If anyone is thirsty, let him come...." (John 7:37–38)
p. 134: "By this he meant the Spirit...." (John 7:39)
p. 135: "If I drive out demons by the Spirit of God...." (Matthew 12:28)
p. 135: "When John heard in prison...." (Matthew 11:2–5)

p. 135: "And this gospel of the kingdom...." (Matthew 24:14)

p. 136: "The heavens declare the glory of God...." (Psalm 19:1–4)

p. 136: "Let your light shine before men...." (Matthew 5:16)

p. 137: "Seven sons of Sceva...." (Acts 19:14–17)

p. 137: "Repent and be baptized...." (Acts 2:38)

p. 138: "newness of life" (Romans 6:4 NKJV)

p. 138: "Do not worry, saying, 'What shall we eat?'...." (Matthew 6:31–34)

CHAPTER NINE: RESULTS OF RECONNECTION

p. 142: "I tell you the truth, no one can enter the kingdom...." (John 3:5–6)

p. 143: The government on the King's shoulders/the King's names, such as Wonderful Counselor: See Isaiah 9:6.

p. 143: "And afterward, I will pour out my Spirit...." (Joel 2:28–29)

p. 144: "You are all sons of God through faith...." (Galatians 3:26–29)

p. 145: "Repent and be baptized, every one of you...." (Acts 2:38–39)

p. 145: "The Lord is not slow in keeping his promise...." (2 Peter 3:9)

p. 145: "For it is by grace you have been saved...." (Ephesians 2:8–9)

p. 146: "He is the atoning sacrifice for our sins...." (1 John 2:2)

p. 146: "The kingdom of God is...[a matter of] righteousness...." (Romans 14:17–18)

p. 147: "I have the authority to take your life or to give it to you.": See John 19:10 (NASB).

p. 147: Jesus's ability to call twelve legions of angels: See Matthew 26:51–54.

p. 147: "You would have no authority over me....": See John 19:11 (NASB).

p. 148: "All authority in heaven and on earth...." (Matthew 28:18–20)

p. 148: "You will receive power...." (Acts 1:8)

p. 148: "I did not speak of my own accord...." (John 12:49)

p. 148: "But the Counselor, the Holy Spirit...." (John 14:26)

p. 148: "But when he, the Spirit of truth...." (John 16:13–15)

p. 149: "Now is your time of grief...." (John 16:22–24, 26–28)

p. 149: "I will give you the keys of the kingdom...." (Matthew 16:19)

p. 150: "But in keeping with his promise...." (2 Peter 3:13)

p. 150: "Then I saw a new heaven and a new earth...." (Revelation 21:1–5)

p. 151: "For the sinful nature desires...." (Galatians 5:17)

p. 151: "Live by the Spirit, and you will not gratify...." (Galatians 5:16)

p. 151: "We demolish arguments and every pretension...." (2 Corinthians 10:5)

p. 151: "My thoughts are not your thoughts...." (Isaiah 55:8–9)

p. 152: "If anyone is in Christ, he is a new creation...." (2 Corinthians 5:17)

p. 152: "'This is the covenant I will make....'" (Hebrews 10:16–17)

p. 152: "righteousness, peace and joy in the Holy Spirit" (Romans 14:17)

p. 152: "Let us draw near to God...." (Hebrews 10:22)

p. 152: "Do not conform any longer..." (Romans 12:2)

p. 153: "He who has seen me has seen the Father." (John 14:9)

p. 153: "You, dear children, are from God...." (1 John 4:4)

p. 153: "My friends, do not be afraid of those who kill the body...." (Luke 12:4–8)

p. 153: The King has not given us the spirit of fear: See 2 Timothy 1:7 (NKJV).

p. 154: "For we are God's workmanship...." (Ephesians 2:10)

p. 156: "Let us then approach the throne of grace...." (Hebrews 4:16)

p. 156: "Who among men knows the thoughts of a man...." (1 Corinthians 2:11)

p. 156: Jesus often went off by himself to pray: See, for example, Mark 1:35; Luke 5:16.

p. 156: "When you pray...." See, for example, Matthew 6:5–7.

CHAPTER TEN: THE NATURE OF THE GOVERNOR

p. 166: "But when he, the Spirit of truth, comes...." (John 16:13–14)

p. 167: "A great and powerful wind tore the mountains...." (1 Kings 19:11–13)

p. 167: "being in the form of God...." (Philippians 2:6–7 NKJV)

p. 168: "The Holy Spirit will come upon you...." (Luke 1:35)

p. 168: "I and the Father are one." (John 10:30)

p. 168: "If anyone loves me, he will obey...." (John 14:23)

p. 168: "God is spirit, and his worshipers...." (John 4:24)

p. 168: *another* Counselor" (John 14:16)

p. 168: "When the Counselor comes...." (John 15:26)

pp. 168–169: "I tell you the truth, all the sins...." (Mark 3:28–29)

p. 169: "As the Holy Spirit says: 'Today, if you hear....'" (Hebrews 3:7–8)

p. 169: The Scriptures speak about God as longsuffering: See, for example, Exodus 34:6 NKJV;
Romans 2:4 NKJV.

p. 170: "Do not grieve the Holy Spirit of God...." (Ephesians 4:30)

p. 171: "The Spirit of truth," Jesus said, "...will not speak...." (John 16:13–14)

p. 172: "But the Counselor, the Holy Spirit...." (John 14:26)

p. 172: "And I will ask the Father...." (John 14:16)

p. 172: "In a little while you will see me no more...." (John 16:16)

p. 172: Analogy of a shepherd looking for one lost sheep: See, for example, Luke 15:4–7.

p. 173: "But when he, the Spirit of truth...." (John 16:13)

p. 173: "The Spirit of the LORD will rest on him...." (Isaiah 11:2)

p. 174: "The Spirit of the Lord is on me...." (Luke 4:18–19)

p. 174: "the earth will be filled with the knowledge...." (Habakkuk 2:14)

p. 174: "go and make disciples of all nations...." (Matthew 28:19–20)

p. 175: "For we are God's workmanship...." (Ephesians 2:10)

p. 175: "No eye has seen...." (1 Corinthians 2:9–10)

p. 175: "We have not received the spirit of the world...." (1 Corinthians 2:12)

p. 176: "The man without the Spirit...." (1 Corinthians 2:14)

p. 176: "When he comes, he will convict the world...." (John 16:8–11)

p. 177: "I led them with cords...." (Hosea 11:4)

p. 177: "He will not speak on his own...." (John 16:13)

p. 178: "From the beginning God chose you...." (2 Thessalonians 2:13)

CHAPTER ELEVEN: THE GOVERNOR'S CULTURE

p. 184: "Like a roaring lion...." (Proverbs 28:15–16)

p. 184: "When the righteous increase...." (Proverbs 29:2 NASB)

p. 184: "Nadab son of Jeroboam...." (1 Kings 15:25–26)

p. 184: "provoked the LORD, the God of Israel, to anger." (1 Kings 15:30)

p. 184: Jeroboam causing the people of Israel to worship idols and appointing priests who were not
Levites: See 1 Kings 12:26–33; 13:33–34.

p. 184: "Ahab...did more evil in the eyes of the LORD...." (1 Kings 16:30–33)

p. 184: "The Lord had seen how bitterly...." (2 Kings 14:26)

p. 185: "He did what was right in the eyes of the LORD...." (2 Kings 18:3, 5–7)

p. 185: The Lord delivered the people of Judah from a boastful, vengeful enemy: See
2 Kings 18:13–19:37.

p. 185: "I am the good shepherd...." (John 10:11)

p. 185: "I am the bread of life...." (John 6:35)

p. 185: "Come to me, all you who are weary...." (Matthew 11:28–30)

p. 186: "You know that the rulers of the Gentiles...." (Matthew 20:25–28)

p. 186: "The kingdom of heaven is near." (Matthew 4:17)

p. 186: List of the essential qualities that make up the character of the King: See Galatians 5:22–23.

p. 187: "the fruit of the Spirit." (Galatians 5:22)

p. 187: "Blessed are the meek, for they will inherit the earth." (Matthew 5:5)

p. 188: "By their fruit you will recognize them." (Matthew 7:16, 20)

p. 189: "our citizenship is in heaven." (Philippians 3:20)

p. 189: "Those who belong to Christ Jesus...." (Galatians 5:24–25)

p. 189: "The one who is in you is greater...." (1 John 4:4)

pp. 189–190: "Live by the Spirit, and you will not gratify...." (Galatians 5:16–18)

p. 190: "The acts of the sinful nature...." (Galatians 5:19–21)

p. 190: Internal warning system of our consciences: See Romans 2:14–15.

p. 190: The Governor reminds us of the teachings of the King: See John 14:26.

p. 190: "Not my will, but yours be done." (Luke 22:42)

pp. 190–191: "The Spirit gives life; the flesh counts for nothing...." (John 6:63)

p. 191: "Abba, Father." (Romans 8:15; Galatians 4:6)

p. 191: The King doesn't only *act* in love or demonstrate peace; he *is* love and peace: See 1 John 4:8, 16; Ephesians 2:14.

p. 191: "Be perfect, therefore, as your heavenly Father is perfect." (Matthew 5:48)

p. 191: "Do you not know that your body is a temple...." (1 Corinthians 6:19–20)

p. 192: "Your eye is the lamp of your body...." (Luke 11:34)

p. 192: "My prayer is not that you take them out of the world...." (John 17:15–16, 18)

p. 192: "You were dead in your transgressions and sins...." (Ephesians 2:1–6, 10)

p. 193: "Let your light shine before men...." (Matthew 5:16)

p. 193: "the gifts of the Spirit." See, for example, 1 Corinthians 12:7–11.

p. 194: "Those who accepted [Peter's] message [about the kingdom]...." (Acts 2:41–47)

CHAPTER TWELVE: MANIFESTING KINGDOM CULTURE

p. 204: "Now the whole world had one language...." (Genesis 11:1–2)

p. 204: The entrance to the eastern side of the garden of Eden guarded: See Genesis 3:24.

p. 204: The full incident of the Tower of Babel: See Genesis 11:1–9.

p. 204: "We will build a tower and make a name for ourselves." See Genesis 11:4.

p. 204: "If as one people speaking the same language...." (Genesis 11:6)

p. 205: "Come, let us go down and *confuse*...." (Genesis 11:7)

p. 205: "That is why it was called Babel...." (Genesis 11:9)

p. 206: "You will receive power...." (Acts 1:8)

p. 206: "These signs will accompany those who believe...." (Mark 16:17–18)

p. 207: "When the day of Pentecost came...." (Acts 2:1–11)

p. 208: "God has raised this Jesus to life...." (Acts 2:32–33)

p. 209: "In the same way, the Spirit helps us...." (Romans 8:26–27)

p. 209: "Tongues, then, are a sign...." (1 Corinthians 14:22)

p. 210: "for they heard them speaking in tongues...." (Acts 10:46)

p. 211: "The LORD said, 'If as one people....'" (Genesis 11:6–9)

p. 212: "Undoubtedly there are all sorts of languages...." (1 Corinthians 14:10–11)

p. 213: "For anyone who speaks in a tongue...." (1 Corinthians 14:2)

p. 213: "Paul of Tarsus's statement that we should earnestly desire spiritual gifts: See 1 Corinthians 14:1 (NASB).

p. 214: ""Anyone who speaks in a tongue...." (1 Corinthians 14:2)

p. 214: "Now to each one the manifestation of the Spirit...." (1 Corinthians 12:7–8, 10)

p. 214: "Now you are the body of Christ...." (1 Corinthians 12:27–30)

pp. 214–215: "When you come together...." (1 Corinthians 14:26–27)

p. 215: "For this reason anyone who speaks in a tongue...." (1 Corinthians 14:13)

p. 215: "Therefore, my brothers, be eager to prophesy...." (1 Corinthians 14:39–40)

pp. 215–216: "While Apollos was at Corinth...." (Acts 19:1)

p. 216: "You are on the right track...." See Acts 19:2–4.

p. 216: "We have never even heard of the Holy Spirit." See Acts 19:2.

p. 216: The Ephesus disciples being baptized in water, the Holy Spirit coming on them, and their speaking in tongues and prophesying: See Acts 19:5–6.

p. 216: "He who speaks in a tongue edifies himself." (1 Corinthians 14:4)

p. 216: "And I will ask the Father...." (John 14:16–17)

p. 217: "In the same way, the Spirit helps us...." (Romans 8:26–27)

p. 217: "But you, dear friends, build yourselves up...." (Jude 20)

p. 217: "Speak to one another with psalms...." (Ephesians 5:19)

p. 217: "we do not know what we ought to pray for...." (Romans 8:26)

p. 218: "Do not be anxious about anything...." (Philippians 4:6–7)

p. 218: "I will pray with my spirit...." (1 Corinthians 14:15)

p. 218: "But no man can tame the tongue...." (James 3:8, 10–11)

p. 219: "The promise is for you and your children...." (Acts 2:39)

p. 219: Paul spoke in tongues frequently: See 1 Corinthians 14:18.

p. 219: "I will pray with the understanding...." See 1 Corinthians 14:15 (NKJV).

CHAPTER THIRTEEN: THE GOVERNOR'S ADMINISTRATION

p. 224: "All these are the work of one and the same Spirit...." (1 Corinthians 12:11)

p. 225: "Now about spiritual gifts...." (1 Corinthians 12:1, 8–10); "word of wisdom," "word of knowledge," "the working of miracles," and "discerning of spirits": (NKJV)

p. 225: "Each one should use whatever gift...." (1 Peter 4:10)

p. 225: "There are different kinds of gifts...." (1 Corinthians 12:4–7); "administrations": (KJV)

p. 226: "It was [Jesus] who gave some to be apostles...." (Ephesians 4:11–13)

p. 227: "To one there is given...the message of wisdom." (1 Corinthians 12:8)

p. 228: "Do not let this Book of the Law depart...." (Joshua 1:8)

p. 228: The Holy Spirit giving a word of wisdom setting apart Paul and Barnabas for the work of the kingdom: See Acts 13:1–4.

p. 228: For background on Paul's being taken prisoner by ship to Rome, and the ship encountering a violent storm, see Acts 27:1–21.

p. 228: "I urge you to keep up your courage...." (Acts 27:22–26)

p. 229: "To another the message of knowledge...." (1 Corinthians 12:8)

p. 229: "Jesus demonstrating a word of knowledge regarding the woman who had had five husbands: See John 4:5–42.

p. 229: Agabus receiving a word of knowledge about a severe famine: See Acts 11:27–30.

p. 229: Peter receiving words of knowledge that Ananias and Sapphira were lying about money they donated to the church: See Acts 5:1–11.

p. 230: John being given words of knowledge, through a vision, concerning the spiritual conditions of seven assemblies of kingdom citizens in Asia: See Revelation 1:1–4; 2:1–3:22.

p. 230: "To another faith by the same Spirit." (1 Corinthians 12:9)

p. 230: "Without faith it is impossible to please God...." (Hebrews 11:6)

p. 230: "Faith comes from hearing the message...." (Romans 10:17)

p. 231: The belief of three Hebrew men who trusted God to deliver them even if they were thrown into a blazing furnace: See Daniel 3:1–28.

p. 231: Jesus's confidence that Lazarus would be raised from the dead: See John 11:1–45.

p. 231: The faith of Peter and John that a man crippled from birth would be healed: See Acts 3:1–8.

p. 231: "To another gifts of healing by that one Spirit." (1 Corinthians 12:9)

p. 231: *gifts of healings*: (1 Corinthians 12:9 NKJV)

p. 231: "Jesus was going about in all Galilee...." (Matthew 4:23 NASB)

p. 232: "He himself bore our sins in his body...." (1 Peter 2:24)

p. 232: A man's shriveled hand restored: See Mark 3:1–5; a centurion's paralyzed and dying servant cured: See Matthew 8:5–13 and Luke 7:1–10; a man born blind given his sight: See John 9:1–7; a woman suffering from a hemorrhage for twelve years made completely well: See, for example, Mark 5:24–34.

p. 232: A man named Aeneas, paralyzed and bedridden for eight years, made totally well: See Acts 9:32–35.

p. 232: A man on Malta healed from apparently recurring bouts of fever and dysentery: See Acts 28:7–8 (NASB).

p. 233: "To another miraculous powers." (1 Corinthians 12:10)

p. 233: Moses' parting of the Red Sea: See Exodus 14:5–31.

p. 233: The continual flow of a widow's supply of oil and flour during a famine: See 1 Kings 17:1–16.

p. 233: Jesus's feeding of more than five thousand people with just five small loaves and two fish: See, for example, John 6:5–14.

p. 233: Jesus's raising of Lazarus from the dead: See John 11:38–45.

p. 233: Peter's raising of Dorcas from the dead: See Acts 9:36–42.

p. 233: The temporary blinding of Elymas: See Acts 13:6–12.

p. 234: "To another prophecy." (1 Corinthians 12:10)

p. 234: "Pursue love, yet desire earnestly spiritual gifts...." (1 Corinthians 14:1–5 NASB); "comfort": (NKJV)

p. 235: "Your sons and daughters will prophesy." (Acts 2:17)

p. 235: "Even on my servants, both men and women...." (Acts 2:18)

p. 235: "Do not quench the Spirit...." (1 Thessalonians 5:19–20 NKJV)

p. 235: "Test everything. Hold on to the good." (1 Thessalonians 5:21)

p. 235: "Two or three prophets should speak...." (1 Corinthians 14:29)

p. 235: "For you can all prophesy in turn...." (1 Corinthians 14:31)

p. 235: "The spirits of prophets are subject...." (1 Corinthians 14:32–33)

p. 236: The disciples at Ephesus "spoke in tongues and prophesied." See Acts 19:1–7.

p. 236: Philip the evangelist had four daughters who prophesied. See Acts 21:8–9.

p. 236: Agabus the prophet predicted the famine and Paul's being taken prisoner: See Acts 11:27–28; 21:10–11.

p. 237: "To another distinguishing between spirits." (1 Corinthians 12:10)

p. 237: "Satan himself masquerades as an angel of light." (2 Corinthians 11:14)

p. 237: "Then the LORD said, 'There is a place near me....'" (Exodus 33:21–23)

pp. 237–238: "In the year that King Uzziah died...." (Isaiah 6:1–3)

p. 238: Paul of Tarsus discerning a spirit of divination in a slave girl: See Acts 16:16–18.

p. 238: Cornelius the centurion discerning that the angel who appeared to him in a vision was from God: See Acts 10:1–48.

p. 238: "To another speaking in different kinds of tongues." (1 Corinthians 12:10)

p. 239: "Do all have gifts of healing? Do all speak in tongues....?" (1 Corinthians 12:30)

p. 239: "When you come together, everyone has a hymn...." (1 Corinthians 14:26–28)

p. 239: "If you are praising God with your spirit...." (1 Corinthians 14:16)

p. 239: "For this reason anyone who speaks in a tongue...." (1 Corinthians 14:13)

p. 240: "To still another the interpretation of tongues." (1 Corinthians 12:10)

p. 241: "He who prophesies is greater..., *unless he interprets*...." (1 Corinthians 14:5)

p. 242: "But as many as received him...." (John 1:12 KJV)

p. 242: "You will receive power when the Holy Spirit comes on you." (Acts 1:8)

p. 242: Before Pentecost, Jesus's disciples experiencing kingdom power to heal and cast out demons: See, for example, Luke 9:1–6, 10; 10:1–20.

p. 243: "Repent and be baptized...." (Acts 2:38)

p. 243: "The spirits of prophets are subject to the control of prophets." (1 Corinthians 14:32)

CHAPTER FOURTEEN: WHY THE WHOLE WORLD NEEDS THE GOVERNOR

p. 252: "Power and peace will be in his kingdom...." (Isaiah 9:6–7 NCV)

p. 252: "The ruler of the kingdom of the air...." (Ephesians 2:2)

p. 252: "Our struggle is not against flesh and blood...." (Ephesians 6:12)

p. 252: "For false Christs and false prophets will appear...." (Matthew 24:24)

p. 252: "The people living in darkness...." (Matthew 4:16)

p. 253: "[He will] shine on those living in darkness...." (Luke 1:79)

p. 253: "He was with God in the beginning...." (John 1:2–5)

p. 253: "I am the light of the world...." (John 8:12)

p. 253: "I have come into the world as a light...." (John 12:46)

p. 253: "I am sending you to [the world]...." (Acts 26:17–18)

p. 253: "For you were once darkness...." (Ephesians 5:8–9)

p. 253: "For he has rescued us...." (Colossians 1:13–14)

p. 254: "The mind controlled by the Spirit is life and peace." (Romans 8:6)

pp. 254–255: "Then I saw a new heaven and a new earth....[ff]" (Revelation 21:1–5)

p. 255: "But you are a chosen people...." (1 Peter 2:9–10)

ABOUT THE AUTHOR

Dr. Myles Munroe (1954–2014) was an international motivational speaker, best-selling author, educator, leadership mentor, and consultant for government and business. Traveling extensively throughout the world, Dr. Munroe addressed critical issues affecting the full range of human, social, and spiritual development. He was a popular author of more than forty books, including *The Power of Character in Leadership*, *The Purpose and Power of Authority*, *The Principles and Benefits of Change*, *Becoming a Leader*, *The Purpose and Power of the Holy Spirit*, *The Spirit of Leadership*, *The Principles and Power of Vision*, *Understanding the Purpose and Power of Prayer*, *Understanding the Purpose and Power of Woman*, and *Understanding the Purpose and Power of Men*. Dr. Munroe was founder and president of Bahamas Faith Ministries International (BFMI), a multidimensional organization headquartered in Nassau, Bahamas. He was chief executive officer and chairman of the board of the International Third World Leaders Association, president of the International Leadership Training Institute, and the founder and executive producer of a number of radio and television programs aired worldwide.

Dr. Munroe earned B.A. and M.A. degrees from Oral Roberts University and the University of Tulsa, and was awarded a number of honorary doctoral degrees. He also served as an adjunct professor of the Graduate School of Theology at Oral Roberts University.

The parents of two adult children, Charisa and Chairo (Myles Jr.), Dr. Munroe and his wife, Ruth, traveled as a team and were involved in teaching seminars together. Both were leaders who ministered with sensitive hearts and international vision. In November 2014, they were tragically killed in an airplane crash en route to an annual leadership conference sponsored by Bahamas Faith Ministries International. A statement from Dr. Munroe in his book *The Power of Character in Leadership* summarizes his own legacy: "Remember that character ensures the longevity of leadership, and men and women of principle will leave important legacies and be remembered by future generations."